# When Languages Die

# When Languages Die

## The Extinction of the World's Languages and the Erosion of Human Knowledge

**K. David Harrison**

OXFORD
UNIVERSITY PRESS

Oxford University Press, Inc., publishes works that further
Oxford University's objective of excellence
in research, scholarship, and education.

Oxford New York
Auckland Cape Town Dar es Salaam Hong Kong Karachi
Kuala Lumpur Madrid Melbourne Mexico City Nairobi
New Delhi Shanghai Taipei Toronto

With offices in
Argentina Austria Brazil Chile Czech Republic France Greece
Guatemala Hungary Italy Japan Poland Portugal Singapore
South Korea Switzerland Thailand Turkey Ukraine Vietnam



Published by Oxford University Press, Inc.
198 Madison Avenue, New York, New York 10016

www.oup.com

First issued as an Oxford University Press paperback, 2008

Oxford is a registered trademark of Oxford University Press



Library of Congress Cataloging-in-Publication Data
Harrison, K. David
When languages die : the extinction of the world's languages
and the erosion of human knowledge / K. David Harrison.
p. cm.
Includes bibliographical references and index.
ISBN 978-0-19-518192-0; 978-0-19-537206-9 (pbk.)
1. Language obsolescence. I. Title
P40.5.L33H37 2007
417'.7—dc22 2006045308

9

Printed in the United States of America
on acid-free paper

*For my parents,*

*Catherine Hart and*

*David M. Harrison*

# Preface

> The entire world needs a diversity of ethnolinguistic entities for its own salvation, for its greater creativity, for the more certain solution of human problems, for the constant rehumanization of humanity in the face of materialism, for fostering greater esthetic, intellectual, and emotional capacities for humanity as a whole, indeed, for arriving at a higher state of human functioning.
>
> —Joshua A. Fishman (1982)

When ideas go extinct, we all grow poorer. The voices of the last speakers of many languages are now fading away, never to be heard again. Linguists like me, too few in number, rush to record these tongues, while a few native communities struggle to revive them. Some of these last voices will be preserved in archives, in print, or as digital recordings. Those last speakers who have generously shared their knowledge with others may see their ideas persist a bit longer, perhaps published in books like this one. Most ideas live on only in memory, and with the extinction of languages vanish forever.

Why we should care about this? Isn't it simply the natural order of things? Empires come and go, languages ebb and flow. Is any individual's knowledge really so special? Can't it be re-created later? What exactly is lost when a language, the most massive, complex constellation of ideas we know, ceases to be spoken?

This book is my attempt to explain why language death matters. On a personal level, I have formed close personal friendships with the last speakers of many languages, and with their children and grandchildren. I have spent countless hours interviewing them, in settings ranging from medieval Lithuanian towns to nomads' camps in Mongolia, from remote

Siberian villages to bazaars in India. I have listened attentively as last speakers expressed their dismay and sadness at the impending loss of their language. I came to share their sadness, and I wrote this book as my own small contribution to their cause. I also came to believe that only a very different kind of world order, one that truly values and fosters diversity of thought and sustainability of traditional ways of life, can improve things. Most likely, the disappearance of languages will continue unchecked and will even speed up. What will be the consequences for us in this twenty-first century and beyond?

The extinction of ideas we now face has no parallel in human history. Since most of the world's languages remain undescribed by scientists, we do not even know what it is that we stand to lose. This book explores only a tiny fraction of the vast knowledge that will soon be lost, an accretion of many centuries of human thinking about time, seasons, sea creatures, reindeer, flowers, mathematics, landscapes, myths, music, infinity, cyclicity, the unknown, and the everyday. By demonstrating the beauty, complexity, and underlying logic of these knowledge systems, I hope to motivate more people—speakers, language-lovers, and scientists alike—to work harder to ensure their survival.

# Acknowledgments

Recognizing that nothing is achieved alone, I thank the many people and organizations who helped make this book—and the years of research behind it—possible. Robert E. Hart provided tireless research and a creative energy that has infused much of this book. My talented students at Swarthmore College read early drafts. For helpful feedback, I thank reviewers Dr. Suzanne Romaine and Dr. Leanne Hinton. Dr. Gregory Anderson collaborated with me on numerous field expeditions and scholarly projects. To make their inspiring documentary film "The Linguists", Seth Kramer and Daniel Miller of Ironbound films accompanied me and Greg Anderson to Siberia in 2003, and in 2007 they came (along with Jeremy Newberger) to India and Bolivia.

Generous funding for my research over the years has come from the Wenner-Gren Foundation for Anthropological Research, IREX, Volkswagen Stiftung, Hans Rausing Endangered Languages Project, Swarthmore College, National Science Foundation, Mellon Foundation, Living Tongues Institute for Endangered Languages, and National Geographic Society Mission Programs.

Numerous individuals who may be counted among the last speakers of their languages inspired this book by generously sharing with me their wisdom, vision, stories, and worldviews. I humbly thank friends in Russia, Tuva, the Philippines, Lithuania, Mongolia, India, Bolivia, the United States, Australia and Canada who have enlightened me about language and cultural survival.

## Contents

# When Languages Die

## Endangered and extinct tongues mentioned in this book

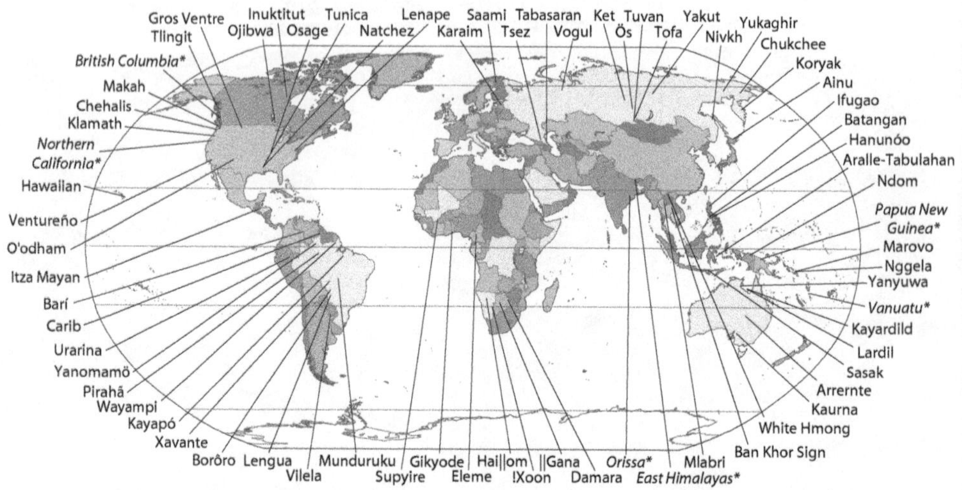


*Hotspots of language diversity

| Northern California: | British Columbia: | East Himalayas: | Orissa: | Papua New Guinea: | Vanuatu: |
|---|---|---|---|---|---|
| Pomo, Yuki, Yurok, Wiyot | Bella Coola, Carrier, Halkomelem, Squamish | Bantawa, Lepcha, Sherpa, Thulung, Yakkha | Ho, Sora, Parengi, Remo | Aiome, Yagwoia, Baruga, Bukiyip, Huli Kalam, Kaluli, Kewa, Kobon, Loboda, Ndom Rotokas, Vanimo, Wampar, Yupno | Araki, Aneityum, Lolovoli, Sie |

The 101 languages mapped here comprise less than 1.5% of the total languages in the world. Locations are approximate.

# 1 A World of Many (Fewer) Voices

You've come too late to learn our language, you should have come earlier. Nowadays we are a numbered people.
—Marta Kongarayeva (born 1930), Tofa speaker

The last speakers of probably half of the world's languages are alive today.[1] As they grow old and die, their voices will fall silent. Their children and grandchildren—by overwhelming majority—will either choose not to learn or will be deprived of the opportunity to learn the ancestral language. Most of the world's languages have never been written down anywhere or scientifically described. We do not even know what exactly we stand to lose—for science, for humanity, for posterity—when languages die. An immense edifice of human knowledge, painstakingly assembled over millennia by countless minds, is eroding, vanishing into oblivion.

In the year 2001, as the second millennium came to a close, at least 6,912 distinct human languages were spoken worldwide.[2] Many linguists now predict that by the end of our current twenty-first century—the year 2101—only about half of these languages may still be spoken. How do we know this? It follows from unrelenting demographic facts and the passage of time. The problem also has a very human face, and in this book we will take a closer look at the lives, experiences, and opinions of last speakers.

In 2005, fully 204 languages had speaker communities numbering fewer than 10 people, a dire scenario. An additional 344 languages had between 10 and 99 speakers. As their speakers grow old and die, these languages too will descend into the fewer-than-10–speakers demographic. The 548 languages with fewer than 99 speakers make up nearly one-tenth of the world's languages, and all are faced with almost certain disappearance. Only in the unlikeliest of scenarios can we expect any of these languages to be transmitted to younger generation speakers or to gain new speakers. Even larger languages, such as Navajo with nearly 150,000 speakers, may find themselves in jeopardy, suggesting that population size alone is no guarantee of security.[3]

What does it feel like to speak a language with 10 or fewer speakers? For people like Vasya Gabov of Siberia, who at age 54 is the youngest fluent speaker of his native Ös language, it means to feel isolated and to rarely have an opportunity to speak one's native tongue. It means to be nearly invisible, surrounded by speakers of another, dominant language who do

**Figure 1.1**
Yuri and Anna Baydashev and I in Central Siberia in 2003. The Baydashevs are the last known household where a married couple speaks to each other in Ös, a language with less than 30 speakers remaining. By 2005, Yuri had suffered a significant hearing loss, limiting his ability to communicate. Photograph by Gregory Anderson, July 2003

not even acknowledge yours. Speakers in this situation tend to forget words, idioms, and grammatical rules due to lack of practice. When asked to speak, for example, by visiting linguists hoping to document the language, they struggle to find words. Ös is now spoken by fewer than 30 individuals, and it is the daily, household language of just a single family. All other speakers reside in households where Russian serves as the medium of most conversations. In this situation, one shared by speakers of thousands of small languages worldwide, it becomes hard to be heard, hard not to forget, hard not to become invisible.

At the current pace, we stand to lose a language about every 10 days for the foreseeable future. Ös will surely be among them. Given life expectancy figures in Russia, we could predict Ös to be gone by the year 2015. All across the world, the loss is accelerating. You do not need to go to Amazonia or Siberia to observe language death; it is going on all around us. As I write this book, I am sitting in my office on the campus of Swarthmore College, near Philadelphia, just 500 yards from the banks of the Crum Creek. 'The Crum' as locals call it, was once home to the Okehocking Lenape Indian tribe. Their language, Lenape, was once spoken by dozens of tribes or bands inhabiting the Delaware valley, New Jersey, and Pennsylvania. The tribe was later forcibly relocated to Oklahoma, where Lenape reportedly still had 5 speakers left in 1996. At that time, the question "*ktalënixsi hàch?*"—"Do you speak Lenape?" was one that might still be asked and answered "*e-e*"—"Yes."[4] But by 2004 not a single speaker remained among the tribe's 10,500 registered members.[5] Languages in our own backyard and in remote corners of the globe vanish apace.

## Crowded Out

Languages do not literally 'die' or go 'extinct', since they are not living organisms. Rather, they are crowded out by bigger languages. Small tongues get abandoned by their speakers, who stop using them in favor of a more dominant, more prestigious, or more widely known tongue. We lack an appropriate technical term to describe people abandoning complex systems of knowledge like languages. So we rely on metaphors, calling it 'language death', 'language shift', 'threatened languages', 'extinction', 'last words', or 'vanishing voices'.[6] Some prefer to say that languages like Tunica, once spoken by native Americans in Alabama, or Wampanoag,

**Figure 1.2**
On the left, Mr. Sukhra Dangada Madji, a young speaker of Remo, a Munda language of India with just a few thousand speakers remaining in a few rural villages. On the right, Ms. Mitula Sira, a young member of the Parengi tribe, who, like her entire generation, does not speak the language of her parents and grandparents, but instead speaks Oriya, the regionally dominant language. Photographs by Mark Eglinton, 2005, courtesy of Living Tongues Institute for Endangered Languages

once spoken by the Mashpee Wampanoag people of Cape Cod, are merely 'sleeping' or 'dormant' and may be 'awakened', 'retrieved', or 'revived' in some hoped-for future.[7]

Extending the biological metaphor, language disappearance only superficially resembles species extinction. Animal species are complex, have evolved over long periods of time, possess unique traits, and have adapted to a specific ecological niche. An extinct dodo bird can be stuffed by taxidermists and displayed in a museum after all its kind are dead and gone. But a stuffed dodo is no substitute for a thriving dodo population. Languages, too, have adapted over time to serve the needs of a particular population in their environment. They have been shaped by people to serve as repositories for cultural knowledge, efficiently packaged and readily transmittable across generations. Like dodo birds in museums, languages may be preserved in dictionaries and books after they are no longer spoken. But a grammar book or dictionary is but a dim reflection of the richness of a spoken tongue in its native social setting.

The accelerating extinction of languages on a global scale has no precedent in human history. And while it is not exactly equivalent to biological extinction of endangered species, it is happening much faster, making species extinction rates look trivial by comparison. Scientists' best estimates show that since the year 1600 the planet lost a full 484 animal species, while 654 plant species were recorded as having gone extinct.[8] Of course, these are underestimates. But even so, they make up less than 7 percent of the total number of identified plant and animal species. Compared to this, the estimated 40 percent of languages that are endangered is a staggering figure. Languages are far more threatened than birds (11% threatened, endangered, or extinct), mammals (18%), fish (5%), or plants (8%).[9]

Language disappearance is an erosion or extinction of ideas, of ways of knowing, and ways of talking about the world and human experience. Linguist Ken Hale, who worked on many endangered languages up until his death in 2001, told a reporter: "When you lose a language, you lose a culture, intellectual wealth, a work of art. It's like dropping a bomb on a museum, the Louvre." Even Hale's metaphor does not go far enough. We simply do not know what we stand to lose with the loss of a single language. This book attempts to answer the question "When a language dies, what is lost?"

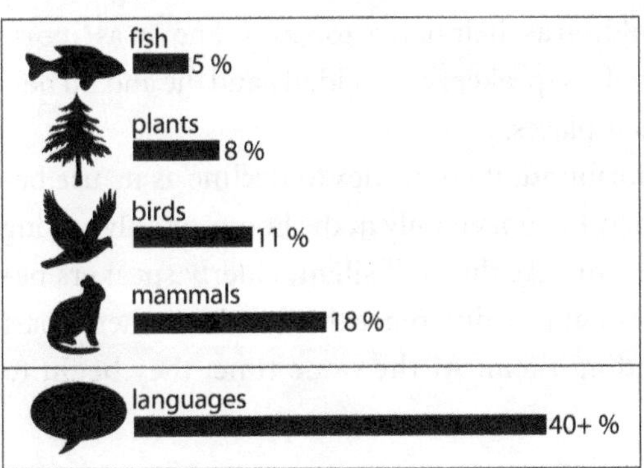


**Figure 1.3**
Known levels of endangerment in animal and plant groups, and for comparison in human languages (based on data in Sutherland 2003).

## Why Speak Tofa?

But first let us ask "How are languages lost?" Looking around the globe, we see populations of people shifting *en masse* from speaking the language of their parents to speaking something else. As people exchange an ancestral tongue for the dominant language of their countries, they become culturally assimilated, linguistically homogenized. There are several recognized stages to the process.

Language death typically begins with political or social discrimination against a language or its speakers. This may take the form of official state policies to suppress speech, or it may be benign neglect. Constantine Mukhaev, one of the last speakers of the Tofa language of Siberia, recalls being punished for speaking his native tongue instead of Russian in school. "When I was a child they sent us to the village school. Lessons were in Russian only, and I couldn't understand anything. The teacher . . . used to beat me when I couldn't answer in Russian. In the mornings, he would test his stick to see if it was supple enough to hit us with."[10]

Faced with such pressures, young speakers like Constantine may abandon their ancestral language. When they grow up, they may fail (or refuse) to transmit it to their children. Many factors can interrupt successful language transmission, but it is rarely the result of free will. The decision tends to be made by the very youngest speakers, 6- and 7-year-olds, under duress or social pressure, and these children then influence the speech behavior of adults in the community.[11] These youngest speakers—acting as tiny social barometers—are acutely sensitive to the disfavored status of their elders' language and may choose to speak the more dominant tongue. Once this happens, the decision tends to be irreversible. A language no longer being learned by children as their native tongue is known as 'moribund'. Its days are numbered, as speakers grow elderly and die and no new speakers appear to take their places.

Once a language is moribund, it continues to decline as its use becomes more restricted. It may be spoken only in the home, or only among elders, or at ceremonial events. As they fall silent, elderly speakers become invisible, lacking any linguistic difference that would set them apart from the people surrounding them. At the same time, they begin to forget.

## Science and Sentiment

Scientists try to avoid being sentimental about what they study. But in working with speakers of disappearing languages, it is hard not to take seriously their own feelings of sadness, regret, even anger at the fate of their language. Svetlana D., one of the last speakers of Tofa, told me in 2001: "The other day my daughter asked me, 'Mom, why didn't you teach us Tofa?' . . . I don't know why. Such a beautiful, difficult language! Now it is all forgotten."

Not all last speakers show such emotions: some are resigned to fate; others think of language shift as progress and do not want their children to speak an obscure and politically inferior tongue.[12] A younger member of the Tofa community told me: "It's useless to try to understand what the old people are saying." Due to attitudes both inside and outside the community, last speakers often share a sense of isolation and invisibility. Language ceases to be language when it is not used for human conversation.

Language loss is an issue that affected communities feel deeply about. Having completed twelve years of fieldwork among endangered language communities, I write with a sense of deep empathy for the plight of last speakers and their soon to be lost knowledge. However, the disappearance of languages is both a social and a scientific reality.

On the social front, many individuals and communities have mounted energetic efforts to preserve, transmit, reclaim, revive, and revitalize languages, knowing that languages only thrive in communities of speakers. Much has been written about these efforts, for example in a book entitled *How to Keep Your Language Alive* by Leanne Hinton and in *The Green Book of Language Revitalization in Practice.*[13] Such projects must be supported and expanded.

The goal of this book is to pursue hard scientific questions, while keeping the human factor in view. On the scientific front, our knowledge is still quite imperfect as to how and why language death occurs, or how individual decisions made by children ripple through societies to create a tidal wave of change. We also lack a clear understanding of what exactly is being lost—is it unique, irreplaceable knowledge, or merely common sense knowledge uniquely packaged? Could such knowledge ever be adequately captured in books and video recordings in the absence of any speakers? Once vanished, can such knowledge be re-created, will it re-emerge spontaneously after a while, or is it forever unrecoverable? This book is an attempt to shed light on these complex questions from a scientific perspective. Linguists and anthropologists have set out to see what science may learn from these knowledge systems while they are still functioning and available for study. Scientists seek to document human knowledge in order to gain a better understanding of our place in the universe. The fact that bodies of knowledge are rapidly passing into forgetfulness makes that task urgent, but it is really no different than other scientific pursuits, for example, the rush to document animal species before they pass into extinction.[14]

While science may also serve the needs of the speech community, this is not scientists' primary goal. Despite the best of intentions, outsiders cannot 'save' or 'rescue' languages or reverse the trend. No one but speakers themselves can preserve languages, since there is no such thing as a living human language without speakers (this includes sign languages, as discussed in chapter 7). Often even speakers' best efforts cannot bring a language back from the brink. What scientists can do is to capture an accurate record in the form of recordings and analyses. These may prove useful to future scientists, future societies, children of heritage-language speakers, and, perhaps even new generations of speakers.

Dire predictions call for a reduction of the world's languages by half in the twenty-first century. Others are more optimistic, citing the resilience of some small languages and modest achievements in revitalizing others. No matter what, several thousand languages may already be at a point where no efforts can arrest the downward trend. If that is the case, then in the interest of science and humanity we must document what we can while we still can.

## Hotspots of Language Diversity

The natural state of human beings—harking back to our hunter-gatherer past—was to live in small bands. This is an ideal situation for language diversity because as each group goes off on its own its speech is free to change rapidly within the group. If one group splits into two, the pace of language change is rapid enough that within just eight or ten generations they may have difficulty communicating. Within two to three centuries, mutual comprehensibility can be lost—where one language was, now there are two.

We often find the greatest diversity in parts of the globe where populations are small and sparsely distributed. For example, the 65 inhabited islands of Vanuatu (together about the size of the state of Connecticut) support 109 distinct tongues in a population of just 205,000 people. That is one entire language for every 1,880 speakers.

The vast deserts of Chad, inhabited by many nomadic groups, support 132 tongues in a population of 9.8 million. These languages enjoy much larger speaker bases, an average of 74,000 each. Like islands, this enormous and sparsely populated desert land, with just over 12 persons per square mile, appears also to encourage linguistic diversity.[15]

Even in America, we see great diversity in Alaska, immense and sparsely populated, with just 1 person per average square mile. Alaska's native population of 86,000 commands 21 languages—most spoken nowhere else on earth.[16] Alaska now has a majority English-speaking population of 640,000 people. Small islands of languages are being submerged in a rising sea of English.

Unlike Alaska, Chad, and Vanuatu, the countries of Western Europe have very little linguistic diversity. They are home to a single large family of related tongues, all belonging to the Indo-European family that stretches from Ireland across Eurasia to India. The sole exception in Western Europe is Basque, spoken in Spain and France, which is an 'isolate' language having no known relatives. Tiny Vanuatu has more languages, with comparable diversity, than all of Western Europe.

The map in figure 1.4 depicts countries of Asia, Oceania, and the Americas sized according to their numbers of indigenous languages. Although it is hard to define exactly what the term 'indigenous' means, people who have inhabited a particular land since before recorded history and have a strong ecological engagement with that land may be considered indigenous. There is clearly a link between language diversity and the presence of indigenous people.

Indigenous cultures and languages are among the most threatened globally. The distribution of linguistic diversity is related to the distribution of indigenous peoples across the globe. Both distributions are highly skewed. As figure 1.4 shows, Papua New Guinea and Indonesia's Irian Jaya loom immensely large as the home to the greatest numbers of indigenous peoples and languages. Nepal, Vanuatu, and Australia, with relatively small populations, also look large on this map because they are so linguistically diverse. The main islands of Japan, with more than a

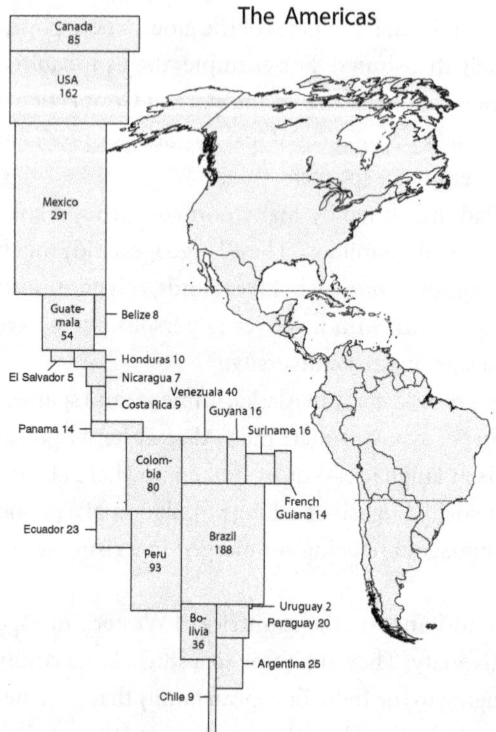
The Americas
Canada 85
USA 162
Mexico 291
Guate-mala 54
Belize 8
Honduras 10
El Salvador 5
Nicaragua 7
Venezuala 40
Costa Rica 9
Guyana 16
Panama 14
Suriname 16
Colom-bia 80
French Guiana 14
Ecuador 23
Brazil 188
Peru 93
Uruguay 2
Bo-livia 36
Paraguay 20
Argentina 25
Chile 9

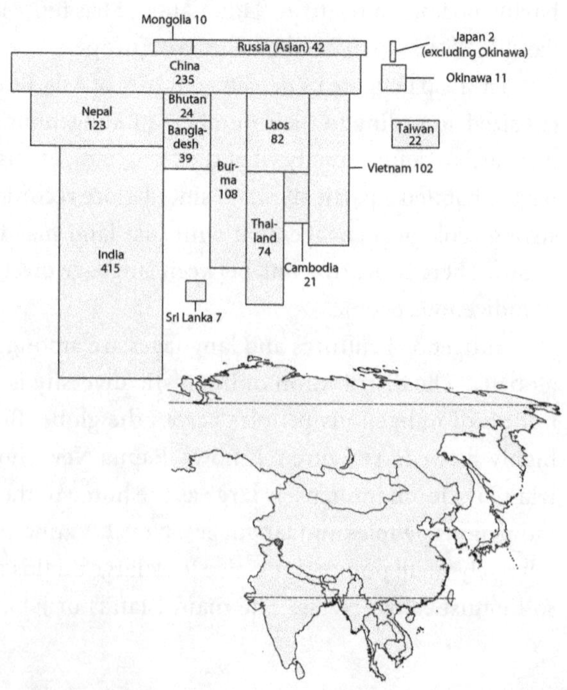
Continental Asia
Mongolia 10
Russia (Asian) 42
Japan 2 (excluding Okinawa)
China 235
Okinawa 11
Bhutan 24
Nepal 123
Laos 82
Taiwan 22
Bangla-desh 39
Bur-ma 108
Vietnam 102
Thai-land 74
India 415
Cambodia 21
Sri Lanka 7

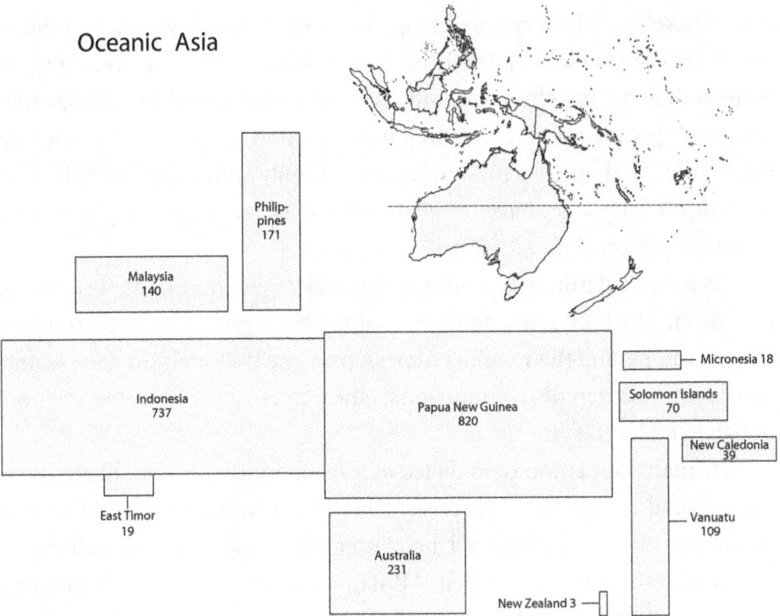


**Figure 1.4** ***(facing and above)***
Selected countries of Asia and the Americas sized by number of indigenous languages. Data from Gordon 2005.

hundred million speakers, appear minuscule because they have almost no diversity with only two thriving indigenous languages—Japanese and Japanese Sign Language—and nearly extinct Ainu.

## Unequal Speaker Bases

The world's 6.34 billion people speak, at latest count, 6,912 languages.[17] If speakers were divided evenly among languages, each tongue would have 917,000 speakers. But languages are surprisingly unequal in their demographic distribution. The top 10 biggest languages have hundreds of millions of speakers each, accounting for just over 50 percent of humans. If we expand this set to include the top 83 languages, we have covered nearly 80 percent of the world's population.

The smallest half of the world's languages—consisting of more than 3,500 languages—are spoken by a mere 0.2 percent of the global population. These include very small languages like Tofa (30 speakers in Siberia), Vilela (2 speakers in Argentina), and Makah (extinct in Washington State as of 2002, but there are some speakers with partial knowledge of it and some people are now learning it as a second language). The median number of speakers for a human language is only about 5,000 people. Half the world's languages have fewer than 5,000 speakers, placing them in a potentially precarious situation.

As people in minority communities seek to advance in their societies, they often feel they must do so by assimilating, giving up ancestral languages and having their children speak only the national tongues. As unequal as the current distribution looks, these pyramids will look even more imbalanced by the year 2020.

Human population is predicted to level off in this century, likely averting a global overpopulation crisis. This is attributed to the fact that as people become more urbanized, no matter what their economic well-being, they tend to have fewer children.[18] But ongoing global migration to urban centers spells more trouble for small languages. In crowded urban spaces, small languages usually lose the conditions they need for survival. There are cases where a small language can co-exist in a stable balance with a big one over a long period of time, but these are rare.[19] Urbanization is growing worldwide, and it will be the death of language diversity.

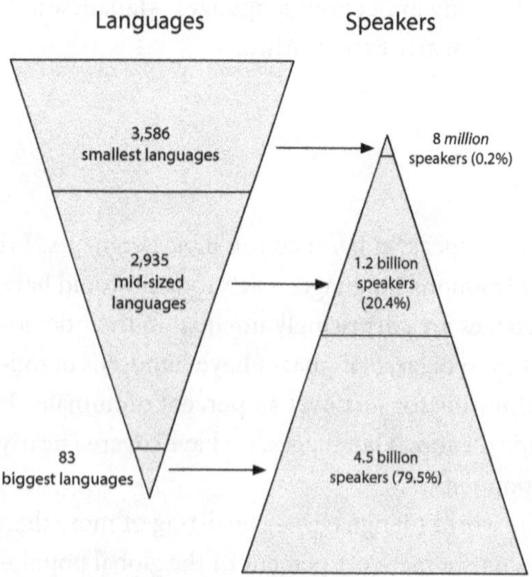


**Figure 1.5**
The unequal proportion between the number of languages and how many speakers those languages have.

## The Eroding Human Knowledge Base

What exactly do we stand to lose when languages vanish? It has become a cliché to talk about a cure for cancer that may be found in the Amazon rainforest, perhaps from a medicinal plant known only to local shamans.[20] But pharmaceutical companies have spared no efforts to get at this knowledge, and in many cases have exploited it to develop useful drugs. An estimated $85 billion in profits per year is made by pharmaceutical companies on medicines derived from plants first known to indigenous peoples for their healing properties.[21]

By credible estimates, an astonishing 87 percent of the world's living plant and animal species have not yet been identified, named, described, or classified by modern science.[22] This number excludes tiny microbes, leaving only organisms large enough to have been observed by the naked eye. It behooves us to look to indigenous cultures to fill in our vast knowledge gap about the natural world. But can they retain their knowledge in the face of global linguistic homogenization?

The human knowledge base extends far beyond uses for medicinal plants. Knowledge systems we explore in this book include fish, reindeer, moon phases, wind patterns, and rice plants. Societies that rely on nature for survival have developed technologies to cultivate, domesticate, and exploit such resources. The fact that we now have modern farming, laboratories, calendars, and libraries does not render traditional knowledge obsolete. If anything, our need for traditional knowledge becomes ever more acute as we strain the planet's carrying capacity.

Much—if not most—of what humankind knows about the natural world lies completely outside of science textbooks, libraries, and databases, existing only in unwritten languages in people's memories. It is only one generation away from extinction and always in jeopardy of not being passed on. This immense knowledge base remains largely unexplored and uncatalogued. We can only hope to access it if the people who possess and nurture it can be encouraged to continue to do so.

If people feel their knowledge is worth keeping, they will do so. If they are told, or come to believe, that it is useless in the modern world, they may well abandon it. Traditional knowledge is not always easily transferred from small, endangered languages to large global ones. How can that be true if any idea is expressible in any language? Couldn't Solomon islanders talk about fish schooling behavior in English just as easily as in Marovo?[23] Do

**Figure 1.6**
An elder of the Ifugao people of the Philippines observes the rice harvest with her son (August 2001). Traditional rice knowledge and cultivation techniques are under threat as new technologies encroach. Photograph by K. David Harrison

the native Seri people of Mexico really need any tongue other than Spanish to describe sea-turtle hibernation and mating cycles?[24] I argue that when small communities abandon their languages and switch to English or Spanish, there is also massive disruption of the transfer of traditional knowledge across generations. This arises in part from the way knowledge is packaged in a particular language.

Consider Western !Xoon, a small language of Namibia (the exclamation mark is a click sound). In !Xoon, clouds are called 'rain houses'.[25] By learning the word for cloud, a !Xoon-speaking child automatically gets (for free) the extra information that clouds contain and are the source of rain. An English child, learning the word 'cloud', or a French child learning '*nuage*' gets no information about rain and has to learn on her own, by observation or by instruction, that rain comes from clouds.

We can find examples like these from more complex systems, like the reindeer classification of native Siberians discussed in the next chapter. I will argue that the disappearance of languages will cause a massive erosion of the human knowledge base precisely because systems like reindeer classification will vanish. When it does, so will important, long-cultivated knowledge that has guided human–environment interaction for millennia. We stand to lose the accumulated wisdom and observations of generations of people about the natural world, plants, animals, weather, soil, and so on. The loss will be incalculable, the knowledge mostly unrecoverable.

## Cultural Heritage

Another answer to "What is lost?" is our human cultural heritage. Where would we be without the traditional wisdom found in oral history, poetry, epic tales, creation stories, jokes, riddles, wise sayings, and lullabies? These genres—the product of human ingenuity, wordplay, and creativity—may be found in all languages. But as I show in chapter 5, the vast majority of human languages have never been written down. Their verbal arts thus exist only in memory and are especially vulnerable to forgetting as languages go extinct.

There is nothing so sacred in a culture that it cannot be forgotten. The Tofa people of Siberia no longer remember the creation myth they once believed. The tale involved a duck and went something like this:

*In the very beginning there were no people, there was nothing at all.*
*There was only the first duck, she was flying along.*
*Having settled down for the night, the duck laid an egg.*
*Then, her egg broke.*
*The liquid of her egg poured out and formed a lake.*
*And the egg shell became earth.*
*And that is how the earth was created.*

Tofa has fewer than 30 elderly speakers, and their creation myth is already lost to memory. In three field expeditions among the Tofa and dozens of interviews with elderly last speakers, I was unable to find a single one who could recite the duck creation story. A few acknowledged that there had been such a story, but none could recount it to their grandchildren.

We may be indifferent to the passing of the Tofa duck story, but all mythical traditions are attempts to make sense of the universe. Each one provides a small piece to the puzzle of how humans understand life, the

**Figure 1.7**
Constantine Mukhaev (born 1948), with his mother Anna Mukhaeva (born 1916), are among the last 30 speakers of Tofa. Here, Constantine tells a traditional Tofa fable about a lost bird. Photographs by K. David Harrison, June 2001

universe, and the sacred. Without the Tofa creation duck, we are surely missing a piece of that puzzle.[26]

## Human Cognition

Languages reveal the limits and possibilities of human cognition—how the mind works. A third answer to the question "What is lost?" has to do with our scientific understanding of the human mind. Every normal human being is capable of language, yet everybody speaks differently and has different things to say. Underneath this Babel lie deep similarities in the way human brains process speech and information. A primary goal of linguistics, as a scientific field, is to uncover universal properties of all human languages. When we discover them, linguists believe, we have learned something about the building blocks and very architecture of human thought.

But to advance their science, linguists need data that can only come from speakers of languages. If linguists had only major world languages to study, say Japanese, Hindi, and Spanish, we would be severely handicapped in understanding human cognition. Linguists sorely need the oddest, quirkiest, and most unusual languages and words to test our theoretical models. Many times linguists' assumptions have been challenged (if not flatly contradicted) by the discovery of odd structures in languages not previously documented.

Urarina, a language spoken by fewer than 3,000 people in the Amazon jungle of Peru, has unusual word order. An Urarina sentence containing three elements in the following order:

Kinkajou's bag + steal + spider monkey

is understood to mean "The spider monkey steals the kinkajou's bag." Urarina places the direct object first, the verb second, and the subject last.[27] Other word order patterns are much more common. English uses subject-verb-object (S-V-O), but this is not the only possibility. Turkish and German put the verb last, using subject-object-verb (S-O-V) order. Welsh is V-S-O, putting verb first, subject second and object last (read + I + book = "I read the book").

But the Urarina O-V-S word order is vanishingly rare among the world's languages. Were it not for Urarina and a few other Amazonian languages, scientists might not even suspect it were possible. They would be free to hypothesize—falsely—that O-V-S word order was cognitively impossible, that the human brain could not process it. Small languages hold in store many more surprises for science, some of which are discussed in chapter 7. Each new grammar pattern we find sheds light on how the human brain creates language. The loss of even one language may forever close the door to a full understanding of human cognitive capacity.

## Our Greatest Conservation Challenge

We have seen at least three compelling reasons to safeguard and document vanishing languages. First is the fact that our human knowledge base is rapidly eroding. Most of what humans have learned over the millennia about how to thrive on this planet is encapsulated in threatened languages. If we let them slip away, we may compromise our very ability to survive as our ballooning human population strains earth's ecosystems. A second reason is our rich patrimony of human cultural heritage, including myth and belief systems, wisdom, poetry, songs, and epic tales. Allowing our own history to be erased, we condemn ourselves to a cultural amnesia that may undermine our sense of purpose and our ability to live in peace with diverse peoples. A third reason is the great puzzle of human cognition, and our ability to understand how the mind organizes and processes information. Much of the human mind is still a black box. We cannot discern its inner workings—and we can often only know its thoughts by what comes out of it in the form of speech. Obscure languages hold at least some of the keys to unlocking the mind. For all these reasons, and with the possibility of dire consequences for failure, documenting endangered languages while they may still be heard, and revitalizing tongues that still may be viable, must be viewed as the greatest conservation challenge of our generation.

## Speaking for Themselves

Science is about trying to understand humankind and our place in the universe. Since language is unique to humans, linguistic science attempts to understand our uniquely human capacity. In analyzing cognitive systems, it is easy to become very abstract, technical, and detached. But the real story of endangered languages revolves around speakers, and what they have to say for themselves. We should take care, in the course of a scientific discussion of language extinction, not to lose sight of real people, their experiences, attitudes, and opinions.

To highlight native perspectives on language extinction, I will present throughout this book the views of speakers of endangered languages with whom I have worked. In six short case studies, we will meet the nomadic Monchak people of Mongolia and the Tofa, reindeer herders of south Siberia. Later we encounter the Ös, fishermen of central Siberia, then the Ifugao, rice cultivators of the Philippines, the Karaim, a minority Turkic people of Lithuania, and finally the Munda tribal people of Northeast India. This is not a balanced selection, but it represents communities and individuals with whom I have worked closely. Each person has a story to tell, in a tongue understood by fewer and fewer people each passing year.

One such individual, Mr. Vasya Gabov, whose story is told in chapter 5, told me how he had been made to feel ashamed as a child in the first grade for being native, dark-skinned, and for speaking his own native Ös tongue. The shame he felt on the playground made him decide not to pass

Ös on to his own four children. But in 2003, now one of the last remaining speakers, he asserted: "I will never throw away my language. I still speak it!"

Marta Kongaraev, a member of the tiny Tofa nation, commented to me how oppressive government policies had wiped out her language: "they wrongly banned our language—that's why the young people don't know it now. It's not their fault, it's the fault of those fools in the government."

Marta's sentiments were echoed by her brother-in-law Spartak Kongaraev, who recalled a time when native dress and speech were banned and Tofa people were forced to assimilate to majority Soviet (Russian) culture: "In the 1950s there was an official order not to speak Tofa too much, only Russian. Now there are many people who have forgotten it; they can't speak, they can't even sing. I still know how to sing, I haven't forgotten it yet." Many small indigenous groups like the Tofa, the Ös, and others express dismay, even anger, at the way their language and culture has been eradicated. Tales like these reflect the history of colonialism and oppression of small groups by larger ones all across the globe and throughout modern history.

The massive language die-off we now face is one of the greatest results of colonialism—the grand project to govern, control, and proselytize non-European peoples. But the die-off is also the result of natural demographic factors. As our world shrinks and we become overcrowded, people migrate of their own free will to cities to enhance their livelihoods. In crowded conditions like those of Bangkok, Mexico City, or New York, global homogenization of language seems all but inevitable.

Among the many of last speakers of a dozen endangered languages I have interviewed in places like Russia, Mongolia, Lithuania, the Philippines, and New York City, only a few were shy or reticent. The vast majority, I found, were delighted that someone showed an interest. And they were more than happy to share songs, stories, traditional knowledge, even jokes. Their wisdom and resilience moved me deeply, both as a human being and as a scientist. With this book, I feel that I have a unique opportunity to share some of their stories with others whom they will never meet. The purpose of this book is to explore scientific questions. But at its heart lies much that I have learned from talking with last speakers and from listening to their wisdom.

# An Extinction of (Ideas about) Species

2

*Nomina si pereunt, perit et cognitio rerum.*
If the names are lost, our knowledge dies as well.
—Johan Christian Fabricius (1745–1808), Danish naturalist

"You don't have to take your genius to the grave," proclaimed a slogan I saw recently on a billboard. The ad urged people to take up careers in teaching in order to pass on their knowledge. In the case of book knowledge, your mother's recipe for apple pie, or your grandfather's fly-fishing technique, this may in fact be true. People can and do pass on valuable knowledge all the time. Writing helps; it is said to make language 'sticky'. Sticky knowledge persists and can be passed on, both across a longer time frame (after the original thinker is long dead) and to a wider audience.

For many endangered languages that have never been put down in writing, entire domains of knowledge are likely to be lost when the language ceases to be spoken. If you speak an unwritten language, one that your children or grandchildren have abandoned in favor of another tongue, you may indeed take your unsticky genius with you to the grave. Much of this genius is the product of adaptation over time to a way of life and ecological niche. Collectively—counting the thousands of languages that lack widespread use of writing and are now endangered—this genius may reflect the greatest accumulation of knowledge of the natural world humans possess, rivaling, if not surpassing, the knowledge now recorded in scientific databases and libraries. This comparison may strike some as unfair. Library and book knowledge is catalogued, indexed, orderly, and it can be searched (or Googled). Traditional knowledge seems much more diffuse, folksy, messy, and prone to being forgotten. But we must not underestimate it.

We do not really have a grip on how much or what kind of knowledge is out there, uncatalogued and unrecorded, existing only in memory. Much of this knowledge—arrayed in a vast web of interconnected facts, a folksonomy—concerns animal and plant species, many still undocumented by modern science. The sobering fact that both animal species and human languages are going extinct in tandem portends an impending loss of human knowledge on a scale not seen before.

Speakers of endangered languages know they will take a great deal of their genius to the grave. Marta Kongaraeva is one of the elderly and last remaining speakers of Tofa, a Siberian language that will be discussed throughout this book. Marta, a lifelong hunter and reindeer herder, remarked to me in 2001: "Soon I'll go berry picking" (a euphemism for dying). "And when I go," Marta continued, "I'll take our language with me."[1] Marta's adult children can understand, but not actively speak, Tofa, while her grandchildren, now in their twenties, know a scant three or four words of their grandmother's mother tongue.

In switching over to speaking exclusively Russian, Marta's children and grandchildren have shut themselves off from much of the knowledge of nature, plants, animals, weather, and geography that their grandmother would have been able to pass on to them. This knowledge is not easily expressed in Marta's less than fluent Russian. We might even go a step further and say that the knowledge Marta possesses *cannot* be expressed in an intact or efficient way in the Russian language. Russian lacks unique words for Tofa concepts like 'smelling of reindeer milk' or 'a 3-year-old male uncastrated rideable reindeer'.

But the basic *ideas* can be expressed in any language (for example, I just expressed them in English). So the claim that such knowledge cannot or perhaps more importantly will not be transferred when people shift from speaking one language to another thus requires more evidence.

In this chapter, I will present evidence from specialized knowledge domains—plants and animals—unique to the environments where speakers of endangered languages live. What these languages do, I argue, is much more than simply naming the menagerie, calling 'lion' and 'tiger' by their names. They afford strategies of packaging information, organizing it into hierarchies, and embedding it within names. The longer a particular people have inhabited and made use of an ecological niche and practiced a particular lifeway, the more likely they will have applied their linguistic genius to describing that ecosystem.

Newcomers to an ecological niche, speaking a language that has not yet developed specialized terms for its plants and animals, can quickly invent or borrow names as needed. But much of this is done by metaphorical extension, and it often obscures or overlooks important connections that people previously living there would have forged over time. Anybody can make up new names for newly encountered creatures (or imaginary ones, like Dr. Seuss's 'sneetches' or A. A. Milne's 'huffalump'). But discerning the subtle connections, similarities, and behavioral traits linking animals, plants, and humans demands careful observation over generations.

Naming showcases human creativity and shows a flair for dramatic metaphor. The Gila Pima people of Arizona (speaking a dialect of O'odham, which has 11,819 speakers in all) coined fanciful names for new plants they encountered: an edible banana species was dubbed 'it looks like an erection'; the sow thistle got called 'mule deer's eyelashes'; a plum tree was named 'dog's testicles' and a date tree 'great horned owl snot'.[2]

Some knowledge of the natural world can be passed on by elder to youngster through instruction. As a child growing up in the city, I spent summers at my grandparents' farm in Michigan. I learned a great deal about nature there, much of it from spoken explanations. 'Sumac', the bright crimson flowering plant, is poisonous, my grandmother taught me, while 'sassafras', a two- or three-fingered leaf, can be munched on. Poison ivy was to be recognized by learning a ditty: "shiny leaves three, stay away from me." Of course, the very name 'poison ivy' contains some useful information about toxicity. The names 'sumac' and 'sassafras' by contrast, tell you nothing about edibility or toxicity; you must be taught these additional facts or learn by experience.

Similarly, if you hear the term 'cow bird' or 'clown fish' you know that the animal in question is a type of bird or a type of fish, rather than a type of cow or clown. But for 'kite' or 'carp' you must learn its qualities from observation or teaching. For efficient communication, the packaging of information is crucial. Names for animals, and the way these names fit into organizational structures, can transmit (or omit) a great deal of information. Each naming system packages information in different ways.

Naming reflects use and culture. Any time people domesticate, cultivate, or rely on a plant or animal species their precision in naming it grows elaborately. Farmers in rural Ethiopia, where sorghum was first domesticated, control an immense repertoire of names for distinct landraces (subspecies) of sorghum that they breed. Different landraces have different notable features, ranging from texture, taste, color, oiliness, to ease of pulverizing, grain shape, and so on. Clusterings of different traits identify specific landraces and are grouped under a label. This label reflects the genetic endowment of the sorghum in question. As sorghum continues to evolve under careful selection and cross-fertilization by Ethiopian farmers, the naming system evolves to reflect new sorghum varieties.[3] Such examples may be found all around the globe, in all climes. From the dry plains of Ethiopia to the wet rice terraces of the Philippines to the mountain forests of Siberia, humans play the naming game. It is one of the best technologies we have for managing the resources that sustain us.

## Reindeer Names

In the remote Sayan Mountains of southern Siberia, the Tofa people, traditional reindeer herders, still practice some elements of their traditional lifeways. Reindeer were once the mainstay of Tofa life, providing fur for boots, milk for children, and transportation for hunters. The reindeer are now reduced to a single, community-owned herd of 400 head. They fall prey to wolves, suffer diseases from inbreeding, and each year some of their number revert to living in the wild.

The youngest (and probably last) of the Tofa reindeer herders is 19-year-old Dmitry A., whom I met on a crisp cold day in November 2001. He was saddling up four reindeer to set out, solo, on a 10-hour ride to join his father and uncle at the winter grazing site. I asked Dmitry many questions about the reindeer herding life, the health of his herds, his daily chores, and his names for deer. Interviewing Dmitry in Russian (because he speaks no Tofa), I learned that he spends up to six weeks at a time, on a rotating basis, living far out in the forests watching over the Tofa people's dwindling collective herd.

Dmitry, born in 1981 and living with reindeer since childhood, is an experienced herder. But he may be hindered in his vocation by a dearth of words for reindeer. Sometime later I also interviewed Dmitry's father and uncle, reindeer herders and still fluent speakers of Tofa. My goal was to document traditional animal naming among the Tofa with a view towards understanding different strategies of information packaging. These two older men still had at their command a large vocabulary of special terms to accurately and quickly describe any given reindeer in terms of its age, sex, rideability, fertility, and tameness.

This complex system allows herders to efficiently single out any reindeer and refer to it by a unique label representing a combination of qualities. We cannot demonstrate that Dmitry is less skilled at reindeer herding because he lacks these words. But on a purely practical level, he cannot group together all these qualities under a single label even if he wishes to do so. As a monolingual Russian speaker—belonging to the generation whose parents abandoned the Tofa language—Dmitry expresses the concept '5-year-old male castrated rideable reindeer' (the most useful kind for riding) only with an entire Russian sentence, just as we must in English. His father and uncle, still Tofa speakers, can encapsulate all this meaning simply by saying *chary*. What has been lost in the translation? Efficiency of information packaging. If language serves human adaptation and survival, then such efficiencies are not merely coincidence or ornament. As unique adaptations of a particular people, to a particular place and lifestyle, they must count for something. Taken cumulatively across the span of history, they have surely contributed to human survival. We abandon them at our own risk.

Whatever small edge reindeer naming may have given Dmitry in herding has now been forfeited. Rather than learning Tofa from his father, he inherited a disdain for the language, reflecting its low status and history of outright oppression. When I asked Dmitry if he spoke his father's language, he retorted: "I don't speak Tofa at all, not a single word. What for?" A very different attitude was expressed by Tofa people belonging to the generation of Dmitry's parents, now in their fifties, the ones who were shamed into abandoning their ancestral tongue. Mr. Spartak K., born in 1930, recalls how the Tofa people were discriminated against and pressured to Russianize themselves: "In the 1950s, old people were told not to come to the village shop wearing the traditional fur clothes. 'Dress Russian, then come!' they were told. We were also told not to be heard speaking Tofa around the village. In this way, we eventually stopped speaking our own language."[4]

Just across the Sayan Mountains from where Dmitry lives, less than 100 miles to the south, another group of native Siberians, the Todzhu

**Figures 2.1 and 2.2**
Dmitry A., a Tofa reindeer herder, speaks Russian and does not know the traditional Tofa reindeer classification system; Ezir S., a Todzhu reindeer herder, speaks Todzhu and retains the reindeer classification system. Photographs by K. David Harrison (above) and Brian Donahoe (right)

people, continue to eke out a living by herding reindeer and hunting, camping in tents year-round. The Todzhu look similar to the Tofa, speak a language that is mutually comprehensible, and share many cultural practices. One crucial difference is that they have not abandoned their ancestral language, Todzhu, in favor of Russian. Todzhu children who grow up herding reindeer learn the reindeer classification system in all its complexity. By learning the labels, they also acquire for free a great deal of extra information about how reindeer are best classified, utilized, and domesticated.

During my travels in Siberia and Mongolia, I had the opportunity to interview people of varying ages who are still actively engaged in reindeer herding. For a 9-year-old Todzhu speaker like Ezir S. (pictured in fig. 2.2), labels for reindeer are second nature. Ezir can immediately pick out from among a large herd a single *döngür* (defined as a 'male domesticated reindeer from second fall to third fall; first mating season; may be castrated or not, but even if not, will probably not be allowed to mate') or a *myndyzhak* ('a female domesticated reindeer in her first autumn of mating') by referring to them with precise labels.[5]

As societies become larger and inhabit a greater range of environments, and as people become urbanized and detached from nature, languages and people shed specialized knowledge pertaining to the environment. English once made fine distinctions in animal names: a castrated goat or sheep was a 'wether', young female sheep 'theaves' (or 'chilvers' or 'tegs'), and young sheep that are older than lambs 'hoggetts'. As we have less to do with animals, naming systems fall into disuse—even new terms like 'baby horse' are making inroads to refer to a foal or colt.[6]

## What Color Is Your Yak?

For Tuvan nomads, who live in Siberia just to the south of the Tofa and Todzhu people, and spend their entire lives breaking, milking, riding, and pasturing horses, the term 'baby horse' evokes chuckles. On the one hand, it is like saying 'baby person', which is redundant. On the other hand, Tuvans still keep a large repertoire of specialized words denoting the age, sex, fertility, and color or pattern of a horse (or yak, sheep, camel, or goat), not just the fact that it is a baby. An additional set of terms classifies horses by their gait or racing ability.[7] Learning extra labels for animals imposes a slight burden on memory, but as an information packaging technology, it affords Tuvans great efficiency in breeding and herding livestock.

Beneath the Tuvan age/sex naming system lies another system of even more powerful descriptive detail. Tuvans use special names for colors, body patterns, and head marking of horses, cows, and yaks. The color and pattern naming system is a strict hierarchy, determined by cultural aesthetics (which yak, horse, or cow colors and patterns Tuvans regard as more desirable, beautiful, or rare) so that if an animal possesses more special features, you may omit mention of the less special ones. If an animal has

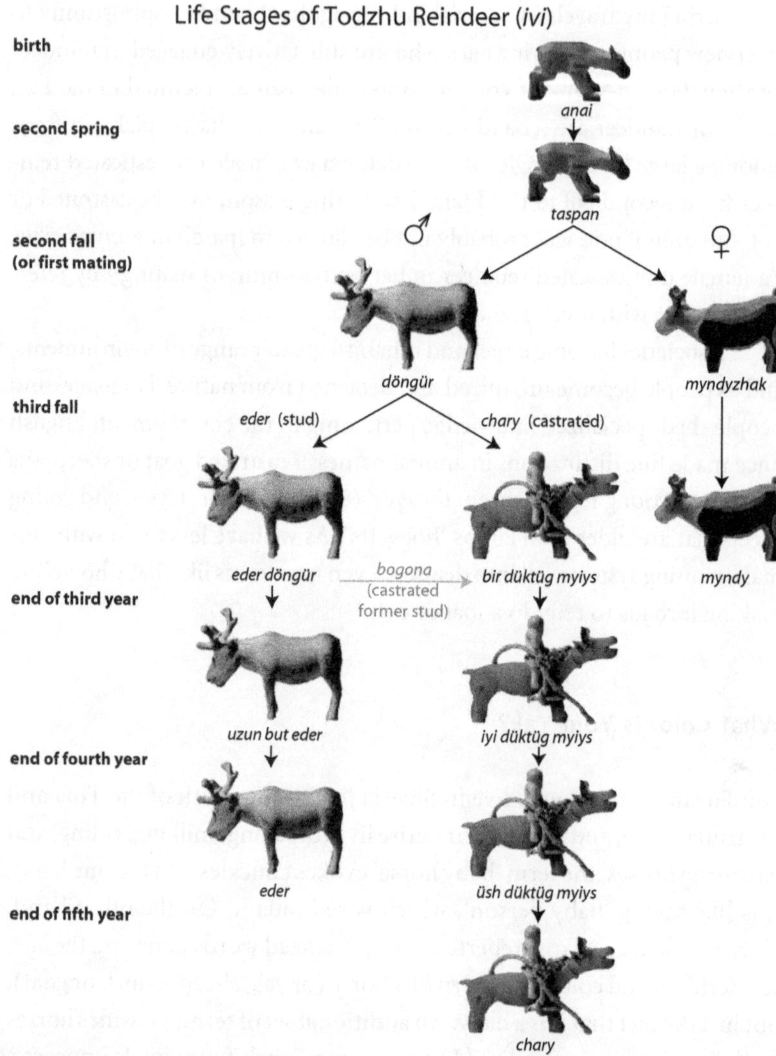


**Figure 2.3**
Life Stages of Todzhu Reindeer (*ivi*). Many similarly complex systems of reindeer classification have been documented, for example among the the Saami of Finland who classify their reindeer according to age and sex, and to a lesser extent fertility and use. Koryak and Chukchee reindeer carvings courtesy of the American Museum of Natural History

only a common feature, such as body color (which all animals possess) you must mention it. If a horse or yak possesses one of several recognized body patterns (e.g., star-spotted), then it will simply be called 'star-spotted' and its color need not be mentioned. A horse or yak possessing the highest feature, a spot on the forehead, will be named by that characteristic alone (see figs. 2.4, 2.5).

Tuvan nomads prefer horses, yaks, and goats of certain colors and patterns. As experienced breeders, they practice genetic modification by selecting preferred outward traits. They do so not by understanding DNA, but by observing how external traits interact and combine, and knowing which are recessive and which dominant. To maximize desired traits, they control breeding among animals. For example, for a good chance of getting a calf with the highly prized 'star-spotted' pattern, you should mate a solid colored bull yak with a spotted yak cow.[8]

In this same way Gregor Mendel (1822–1884), the father of genetic sciences, experimented with cross-pollination of pea plants and discovered which traits would be passed on, and which would be dominant or recessive in a particular combination.[9] Mendel did all this without actually seeing or understanding genes themselves. Humans have been practicing folk genetic engineering as long as they have domesticated plants and animals. Tuvans, like most animal breeding cultures, have not had the luxury of setting their genetic knowledge down in books. Instead, they recruit language—and folk taxonomies, or so-called folksonomies—to encode, store, and transmit this knowledge.[10]

## Naming the Animals

Naming plants and animals is a universal human activity, but each culture develops its own habits. Name choice can reveal how a culture imagines the proper place of creatures in the animal kingdom. For example, Tuvan nomads living in South Siberia have distinct words for 'worm', 'snake', and 'fish'. Their immediate neighbors to the north, the reindeer-herding Tofa people, have the same creatures in their environment, but have no word for snake.[11] They metaphorically name snakes as either 'long worms', 'mountain fish', or 'ground fish'. While the worm/snake analogy may seem obvious, we might easily have overlooked the similarity between fish and snakes. Tofa makes this connection explicit (see Fig. 2.7).

most special

**Head spot**

**Head patterns**

1. dark body with white striped head
2. dark body with white head (and possibly tail)

**Body patterns**

3. star-spotted
4. many small stripes
5. stripe along body
6. big spotted
7. stripe around body

**Body colors**

8. blue
9. white
10. brown, red
11. black
12. grey
13. yellow, etc.

least special

**Figure 2.4**
A hierarchy of Yak colors and patterns.

**Figure 2.5**
Yaks with body patterns 2, 3, 11, 5, and 7. Courtesy of Kelly Richardson

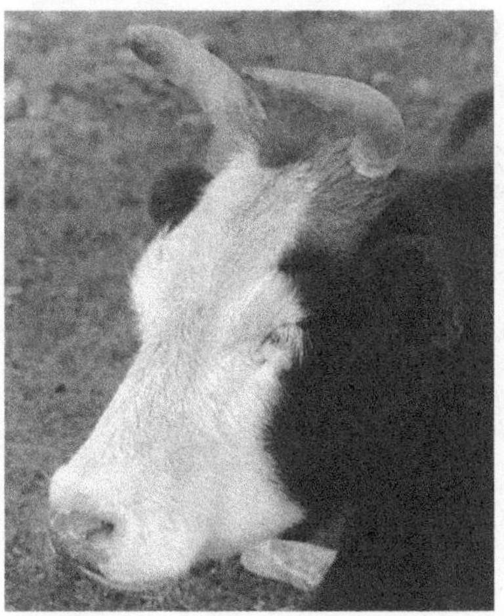

**Figure 2.6**
A Tuvan cow with white-striped head and one with a prized forehead spot. Courtesy of Kelly Richardson

This does not mean that Tofa people have an unsophisticated view that snakes are a kind of worm or fish, or that worms, snakes, and fish form a continuum of life forms or can interbreed. But their language calls attention to subtle similarities, grouping together snakes and worms under one label, and snakes and fish elsewhere. Metaphorical naming does not automatically establish classes, but it points to a conceptual process. We would not want to say, for example, that the English term 'clown fish' sets up an abstract class that includes circus clowns and a fish. But it does provide a handy label for a fish that resembles (to some) a clown. Metaphor makes our naming system open-ended, flexible, and responsive to observed similarities. In case we fail to notice certain similarities, pre-existing labels (like 'earth fish' for snake) bring them anew to our attention.

But the names a language bestows upon animals go beyond mere labels, to include a great deal of information about the proper place of that animal in the world. The Chehalis people of Washington state (no speakers left as of 2005) used to tell a creation story about how their god, Honné, named and assigned behaviors to all animals, including the salmon:

> Honné traveled on up the river and . . . picked up the salmon which had lain on the gravel. He built a fire from drift wood, fixed the salmon and cooked it. After it was cooked and he had

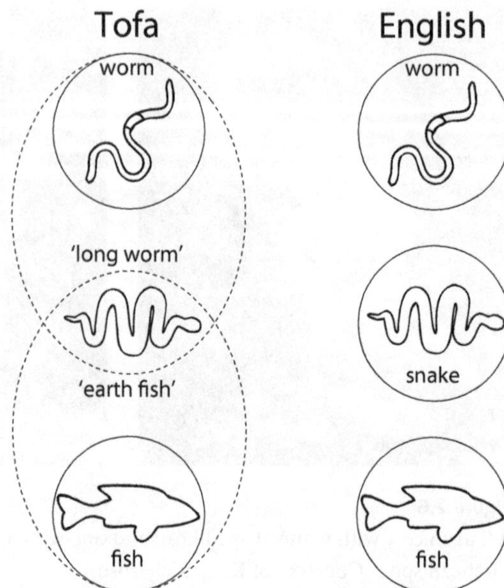


**Figure 2.7**
Naming based on metaphorical extension in Tofa vs. English.

eaten all he wanted, he took the backbone of the fish and said 'Your name will be Twahtwat, the black salmon.'

The backbone said 'What time of year will I come up the river?'

Honné answered, 'You will come up in the fall. You will not stay long but will work fast while you are here for the other salmon will have come ahead of you. When you finish you will go back to the ocean and then you will be young again.' Black salmon went in the river and Honné traveled on.

He went further up the river and cooked the salmon which he carried with him. He ate it and then took the backbone and said to it, 'You will be Squawahee, steelhead salmon. You will always go further up the river than any of the other salmon, and you will have a longer life than the other fishes.'

The fish asked, 'What time of the year will I come up the river?' Honné told him that he would come up in the fall of the year and stay all winter and that he would spawn in the spring of the year. When the pheasant began to drum then it would be time for steelhead to spawn.[12]

Naming the animals is the easy part: as the myth recounts, it was not only names that animals needed but also information about habitat and behavior. Beyond mere naming, what has intellectually engaged mankind for millennia has been classifying, grouping, and describing plant and animal life, behavior, and usefulness to humans. Scientists refer to this practice as taxonomy: naming individuals and groups, sorting things into groups, discovering relations among them.

## Naming as Science

Taxonomy as a branch of science took a great leap forward in eighteenth-century Europe and has remained a prime directive of the natural sciences ever since. The Swedish naturalist Karl Linné (1707–78, often known by the Latinized version of his name 'Carolus Linnaeus') introduced the now standard binomial (two-name) system for classifying plants and animals. Linnaeus's system, though now outmoded in some ways, fundamentally influenced the science of classification during an age when European explorers sailed the world and brought home thousands of exotic specimens to be classified and displayed in European herbariums and museums. These naturalists were unconcerned about the very unnatural existence of plants and animals dried, stuffed, ripped from the complex web of their natural environments and put on display in glass cases. Even less interesting to colonial Europeans was the fact that there already existed vast bodies of knowledge containing animals and plants they proudly 'discovered' and 'named' (often after themselves). Vlaming's Unicorn Fish, renamed for its Dutch discoverer, already had an arguably more useful name to the Solomon Islands' Nggela people, who had dubbed it 'large underwater ripple fish' (after patterns in the water made by its prominent dorsal fin) long before Vlaming's time.[13]

When Captain James Cook undertook his third major voyage in 1776–80, he sailed with a naturalist, botanist, and sketch artist who collected and drew animals and plants unfamiliar to Europeans.[14] Naming strategies used by early explorers and naturalists were impromptu, often relying on culturally specific metaphor and analogy. A fish with a single stripe resembled a British sergeant's uniform and became 'sergeant fish'. A fish with a dark-colored face spotted by Captain Cook's crew off Hawai'i received the exotic name 'moorish idol'. Of course, Hawaiians knew the habits and habitat of this 'moorish idol' fish quite well and had long before named it *kihikihi*, a word meaning both 'crescent shaped' and 'to sail in a zig-zag fashion'.[15]

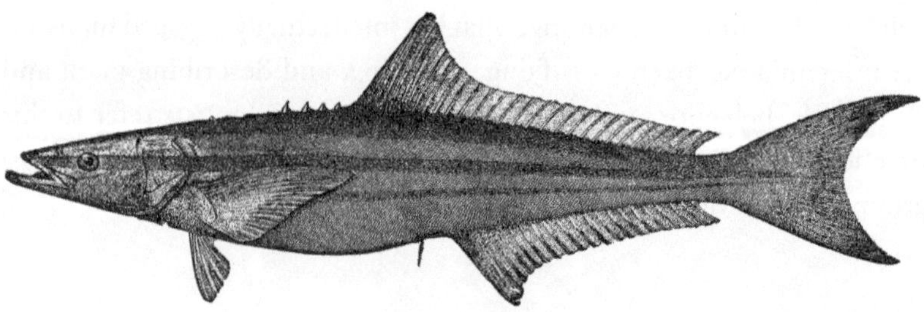

**Figure 2.8**
Sergeantfish—named by Europeans for its stripes.

But the Europeans were uninterested in Hawaiian marine science. They 'discovered' this fish, sketched it, named it, and classified it, all without consulting the unscientific natives.

Like the *kihikihi*, few species would have gone unnoticed, unnamed, or unappreciated for potential uses in their habitat. But that knowledge might as well have been on the moon, as the gulf separating 'rational' European science from folk taxonomies was immense. To this day, that gap has scarcely been noticed, and not yet bridged. Writing in the journal Nature in 2002, a prominent biologist blithely asserts that "taxonomy, the classification of living things, has its origins in ancient Greece."[16] One effort to bridge the gap is the Universal Biological Indexer and Organizer (uBio), available on the Internet, which maps some folk names to scientific ones. It lists the term *kihikihi* and links it to the species *Zanclus cornutus*, so named by Linnaeus in 1758. While uBio, with over 5 million scientific names, is a promising start, it so far has only half a million 'vernacular' names, drawn primarily from major world languages, not indigenous tongues.[17] We are still largely in the position of pressing our noses to a glass case in a museum to observe an isolated specimen, imposing our notion of order on the world, while remaining blissfully ignorant of entire systems of knowledge arrayed all around us.

We should not put folk taxonomies on a pedestal or imagine them to be always deeper or more precise than other bodies of scientific knowledge. But we should expect such systems—because they spring from rational human minds and because they represent the accretion over many centuries of close observations of nature—to contain knowledge worthy of attention and respect. If we dismiss or downplay such systems, we repeat the arrogant mistakes of colonial era naturalists. Folk taxonomies now

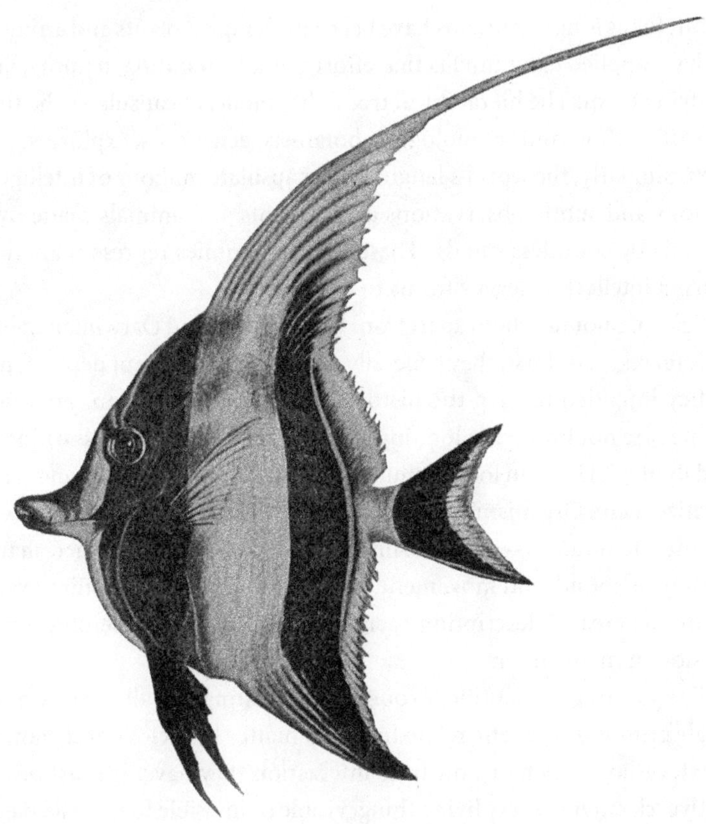

**Figure 2.9**
Moorish Idol—first named *kihikihi* by native Hawaiians.

face rapid abandonment as speakers shift to speaking dominant global languages. This unacknowledged bioinformatics crisis merits urgent scientific attention now.

Linnaeus' binomial naming system, which we have inherited, allows for a neat ordering into at least two levels of structure: species and genus. Charles Darwin's theory of evolution built upon this foundation by positing hierarchal relations further up the tree, such that all living species could in theory be traced back to ancestor species, and grouped according to this common ancestry. All living things thus not only belonged to a species and genus but had a series of higher associations, some yet to be established or controversial. Establishing all these links is an ongoing endeavor, and it will ultimately rest upon both genetic and fossil evidence.

But for as long as humans have been surviving off plants and animals, they have applied great intellectual effort to understanding, naming, and classifying them. The hierarchical tree of life model encapsulates the tireless work of thousands of biologists, botanists, geneticists, explorers, and others. Similarly, the world's languages encapsulate millions of intelligent decisions and subtle observations about plants and animals made over millennia by countless minds. These folk taxonomies represent an awe-inspiring intellectual legacy for us to examine.

Folk taxonomies stand apart from the Linnaean and Darwinian model in several respects. First, they generally make no claims about descent, nor are they intended to map the history of a species' evolution. Folk taxonomies are not limited to looking solely at genetic relatedness or interbreedability.[18] They can look at multiple different dimensions at once, and prioritize them. Organisms may be classified according to social factors—usefulness to humans—or environmental factors like habitat, diet, shape, appearance, sound, and movement. Folk taxonomies may sacrifice exactness in one area of description (genetics), but they gain usefulness and precision in many others.

The goal of the scientific taxonomy is to distinguish all organisms by a single criterion—genetic relatedness, no matter how close or distant in habitat, or how much or how little interaction they have. It must be exhaustive, classifying every living thing, visible or invisible to the naked eye, even tiny archaea living in deep-sea environments completely inaccessible to humans. Finally, it must place all these entities in a giant tree of life.[19] Folk taxonomies, by contrast, are strictly local, not global, and not intended to be exhaustive. No folk taxonomy devised by New Guineans needs to include Greenlandic polar bears.

Because folk taxonomies are local at heart, people do not always make the best possible classification on their first encounter with a new life form. Astute observation and classification may require time, generations even. The Kaurna people, aboriginal Australians living near Adelaide, upon first encountering horses in the early 1800s dubbed them 'European kangaroos'. They combined *pindi*, their word for white men, with *nanto* 'male kangaroo'. In fact, *pindi* was also a metaphor. The Kaurna called pale-skinned Europeans *pindi* meaning 'grave' because they took them to be spirits of the dead returned from the grave. So horse was 'white man's kangaroo' or literally 'grave kangaroo'. Across the cultural divide, Captain James Cook was similarly befuddled when he first encountered kangaroos. He noted in his journal that they bore "no sort of resemblance to any European animal" and compared them in turn to a hare, a greyhound, and a deer.[20]

Folk taxonomies may limit themselves by what is relevant to human survival in a given ecosystem. For example, most people share a popular notion that living things may be divided into plants and animals. But if we consider the actual relationship on the genetic taxonomy, we find that genetically, it is more like a four-way split (see Fig. 2.10)—unless we want to call mushrooms animals.[21]

Such information, albeit crucial to biological science and the project of building genetic taxonomies, has scant practical use outside of the lab. We can carry on with our plant vs. animal distinction (for example, while grocery shopping) and be none the worse for not knowing where slime molds fit in. The Lardil people (with only 2 speakers remaining in the year 2000) do not recognize plant versus animal as a basic distinction. Instead, they adopted what was for them a more practical scheme. To their general term *werne* meaning 'organisms', they add a modifier *wambalmen*, 'land', or *melamen*, 'sea'. They thus divide all living things into those living in the sea vs. those living on land, regardless of whether they are what we would call plants or animals.[22]

Divisions by function, so alien to the scientific classification, are not the exception but the norm in human classification strategies. The ||Gana people (800 speakers—the double vertical line denotes a click sound) of Botswana have no generic word for living things, nor do they recognize a plant versus animal distinction. Instead, they split plants and animals into three broad categories: 'eat-things' (*kx'ooxo*), 'bite-things' (*paaxo*), and 'useless things' (*goõwahaxo*). So-called 'eat-things' are edible to humans, while 'bite-things' are harmful, and 'useless things' neither edible nor harmful. However, these categories are not static—for example, if a gazelle gores a hunter with its horns, its category changes from *kx'ooxo* to *paaxo*.

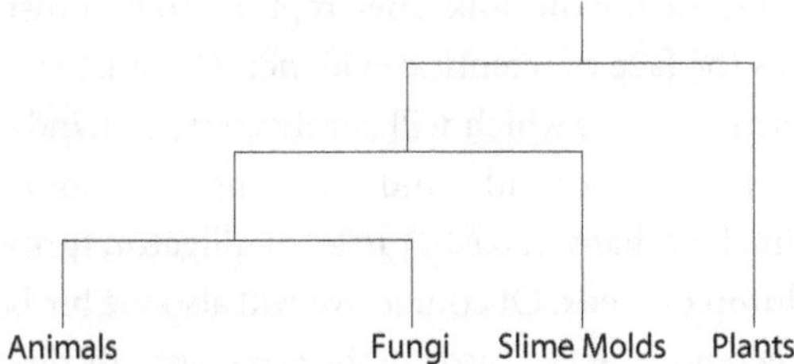


**Figure 2.10**
A tree diagram based on actual genetic relationships differs from our folk conceptions of 'plant' vs. 'animal'.

Folk taxonomies—when they differ from the genetic classification—shed light on human perception of the natural world and survival strategies. And they have an entirely different purpose and rationale from the scientific taxonomy. The former is not to be viewed as a lesser version of the latter, fit to be discarded once we have mapped the human and fruit fly genomes. Folk taxonomies encapsulate generations of subtle and sophisticated observations about how the pieces of the animal and plant kingdom fit together, how they relate to each other and to humans. They differ in which criteria they use to classify organisms, almost always choosing multiple ones over single ones. Criteria may include appearance, behavior, habitat, impact on humans, or some combination of these, as does the Tofa reindeer system. The choice is guided by the standard of usefulness.

Folk taxonomies aid survival. They arise from humans' keen ability to notice and correlate multiple characteristics and interacting patterns, and deploy this information for practical use. They typically contain a great deal of hidden, or implicit, information as well as explicit facts about the plant and animal kingdoms. In the following sections, we will focus on this hidden, or implicit, knowledge. We will ask whether such knowledge may be too specialized or too fragile to be easily transferred when speakers of, say Lardil or Hawaiian (1,000 mother tongue speakers in 1995), shift over to speaking the dominant world language, English.

Folk taxonomies are not merely quaint relics of small cultures. Speakers of major world languages use them as well. English speakers use a term 'reptile', which most people understand to mean something close to the *Oxford English Dictionary* definition: "Those animals which creep or crawl; specifically in modern use, that class of vertebrate animals which includes the snakes, lizards, crocodiles, turtles and tortoises."[23] Though clear and useful, this definition is scientifically false. When we look at the actual genetic tree, we see that, genetically, there can be no grouping of 'reptiles' (meaning crocodiles, snakes, and turtles) that does not also include birds. But birds do not fit within our folk label 'reptile'. So we must abandon our folk concept in the face of scientific evidence. Or must we? We might also keep our term 'reptile', which will surely come in handy when we are canoeing in the Florida everglades and expecting to see some feared but unidentified animal, perhaps a snake, turtle, or alligator, lurking around the very next clump of reeds. Of course, we will also see birds in the Everglades, but we need not react to birds in the same way. By dis-

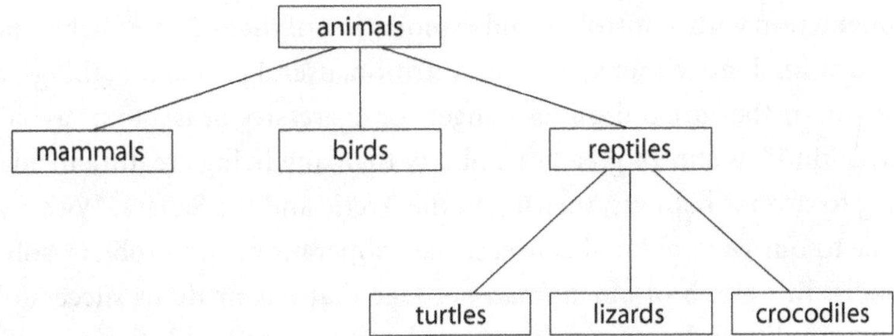


**Figure 2.11**
In the English folk taxonomy, birds, reptiles, and mammals are three of the main subgroups of the animals group, and turtles, lizards, snakes, and crocodiles are members of reptiles.

tinguishing birds from snakes, alligators, and turtles as a class, our folk taxonomy provides us with information that although scientifically suspect, is practically useful.

We have seen from the above example that folk taxonomies may be considered inaccurate when strictly compared to scientific (genetic) ones. But the comparison itself is unfair and perhaps unscientific. Folk classification has a broader and much different mandate: it must provide ways to sensibly organize the plants and animals in a way that facilitates human

**Figure 2.12**
According to genetic classification, mammals and reptiles are two subgroups of animals, but birds are just a minor subgroup of one branch of the reptiles. In any genetic classification, if we group turtles, lizards and snakes, and crocodiles together as reptiles, we must include birds with them.

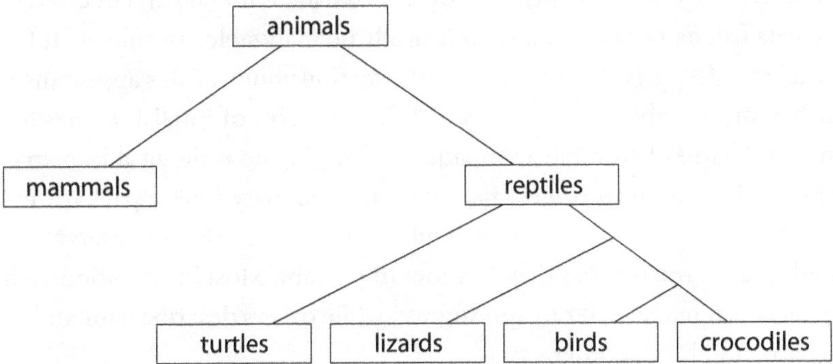

interaction with, control of, and exploitation of them. In this light, plants and animals are either sources of nutrition, useful for making things, and so on, or they are poisonous dangers or aggressive beasts to be avoided. Mankind has shown greater flexibility than any living creature in adapting to diverse habitats, thriving in the Arctic and the Sahara. We survive due to our general intelligence, social cooperation, and problem-solving skills. But much of our human heritage that has made us successful as foragers lies in linguistically encoded and transmitted knowledge. Folk taxonomies contain much of this knowledge, and they do so in ways that are subtle and complex, and not always obvious.

## The Name Game

The West Nggela people (10,000 speakers) of the Solomon Islands live off the sea and possess an intimate knowledge of the habits of sea creatures. Marine biologists have recorded over 350 unique Nggela folk names for fish, many more than the number of scientific names for those fish. Just as we saw with sorghum plants and domestic reindeer, finer categorization occurs for fish the Nggela use as food, while those of lesser economic importance get lumped together.[24]

Names for fish can be divided into opaque and descriptive terms. For example, the English name 'cod' is opaque because it cannot be analyzed or broken down into meaningful parts, and you simply have to learn that this word refers to a given fish species. The English fish name 'bullhead', on the other hand, is more transparent—it contains descriptive meaning. One-word names are usually opaque, seldom descriptive. Two-word names for animals tend to combine one opaque and one descriptive label, such as 'rock cod' or 'clown fish'. Only 30 percent of West Nggela fish names are opaque, or lexically unanalyzable, meaning that for speakers of Nggela they convey no information about a fish's appearance, behavior, or habitat. By contrast, a full 55 percent of English names for native Thames River fish are opaque, packaging no ecological information.[25] Returning to Nggela fish names, a majority (70%) package information, providing us with a window on how the Nggela observe fish and what characteristics they consider important. Most information-rich Nggela fish names refer to appearance, while others describe habitat, behavior, and human interaction.

**Table 2.1**
**West Nggela names for fish often refer to how a fish is used, while their English names more often refer to appearance**

| *West Nggela name* | *Explanation* | *English name* |
|---|---|---|
| *Mala bulua*<br>*Mala* = 'position, rank'<br>*bula* = 'to light with a lamp or torch' | Named for technique used to catch the fish. Reef is illuminated at low tide and fish are taken from the surface. | Doublebar goatfish |
| *Roso taranggua*<br>*Roso* = 'young coconut with soft meat'<br>*taranggau* = 'Nggela name for a fish-eating bird of prey' | "The name refers to the soft flesh of these fishes, which may also be the favorite prey item for the taranggau" | Golden spot hogfish |

*Note*: Quotes from Foale 1998.

## Trout or Salmon?

The Halkomelem Musqueam people (there were no fluent Halkomelem speakers left in the Musqueam band as of 2002, and just a few non-fluent speakers) live in Canada's British Columbia province and have traditionally been fishermen and hunter-gatherers. They trapped salmon with specialized nets, trawls, and weirs constructed for that purpose, and smoked meat for later consumption. Musqueam has a rich vocabulary for describing local flora and fauna, in particular plants or animals that provided nutrients or medicine.[26] Larry Grant, an elder of the Musqueam band who still speaks his language, has collected many words used to group and name fish. The Musqueam group together several fish that in English folk classification are considered distinct, known as either 'trout' or 'salmon'. Fish we call 'steelhead trout' and 'cutthroat trout' are considered by the Musqueam to belong together with salmon.[27]

A genetic study of these so-called trout completed in 2003 fully vindicated the Musqueam grouping.[28] It turns out these two 'trout' genetically should be grouped with the pacific salmon—the genus *Oncorhyncus*. The English grouping, by contrast, fits poorly to the genetic facts: we consider as trout fish that genetically are members of *Oncorhyncus*, *Salmo*, and

*Salvelinus*, and as 'salmon' fish that belong genetically with *Oncorhyncus* and *Salmo*. While we do not know the history of how these fish came to be called trout in English, we are not the only ones who lumped them together with trout. Nearby indigenous groups, the Tlingit and the Klallam people, who live in the same area and also fish, also distinguished 'steelhead' and 'cutthroat' trout from salmon. The point here is not that any one of these groupings is wrong or inadequate. But after centuries of observing animals and their behavior, it is possible for at least some folk taxonomies to achieve genetically 'correct' groupings that are also useful to them in interacting with the animals. Geneticists need not assume that any folk taxonomy gets its genetic facts right, but they ought at least to consider the possibility.

Since there is nothing obvious in the Musqueam names themselves that show these two fish belong with salmon, I asked elder Larry Grant how a Musqueam person would come by such knowledge. He replied that

**Figure 2.13**
The Musqueam Halkomelem group called *sce:ɬtən* (left) matches up precisely with the scientific genus *Oncorhyncus* (center). The English groups called 'trout' and 'salmon' (right) break the genus up into two groups. The data here have been simplified: *sce:ɬtən* has seven members, all of whom are of the genus *Oncorhyncus*, and of course there are many other fish we refer to as trout and salmon.

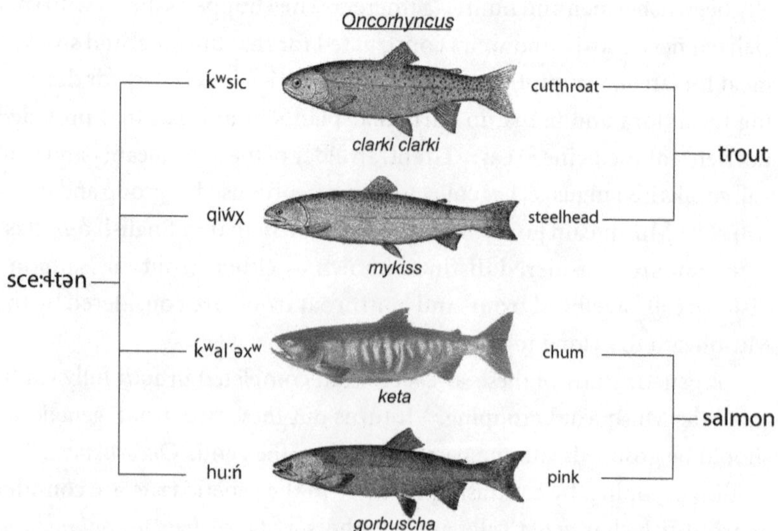

this was part of the general world knowledge that is passed on within the community, and that any Musqueam who knew much about fish should know this. What a Musqueam child has to learn is simply one label, and the fact that its meaning contains all the fish I have mentioned.

## Toucan Chief and Followers

The Wayampi language (1,180 speakers) is spoken in the southern region of French Guiana and just across the border in the Brazilian Amazon.[29] The Wayampi people practice fairly traditional hunting-gathering lifeways in the tropical rainforest. They interact with rainforest birds on a daily basis, using their feathers for decorations, eating their meat, listening to their calls, and in some cases competing with birds for edible fruits. Wayampi bird and animal classification is based on a principle of prototyping—each grouping of birds centers around a model species, known as the 'chief' and considered to be the most perfect representative of the group. Each chief has a number of 'follower' species. The distance between the chief and members of its kingdom depends on similarities in appearance (wing shape, beak shape, feather color, silhouette as seen from a distance, etc.) and behavior (type of call, waking hours, foods eaten, mating habits, etc.).

Relations defined by a family based on prototypes—like that used by the Wayampi—are very different from those based on a tree of common descent. The chief is the concrete expression of key aesthetic and behavioral characteristics of a category. Take, for example, the Wayampi folk family governed by the chief *tukanane*, which we call the White Throated Toucan. While this prototype system can be represented as a hierarchical tree (fig. 2.14[a]) with the chief at the center in position 1, it is perhaps better visualized with the chief at the center and the followers arrayed around him in orbits (fig. 2.14[b]).

Knowledge of this structure is embedded in individual bird names, which reflect the central importance of the chief: the name for the chief can appear as part of the names for each follower (as in 2, 3, 5, and 6). Additionally, the chief's name is used in one form to label the sub-group of toucans most similar to itself (Tukã), and in another form to identify the entire family (Tukãpewar). Besides suggesting relatedness to a chief, many Wayampi bird names include an onomatopoeic representation of that bird's identifying call or song (not unlike our 'chickadee' or 'cuckoo').

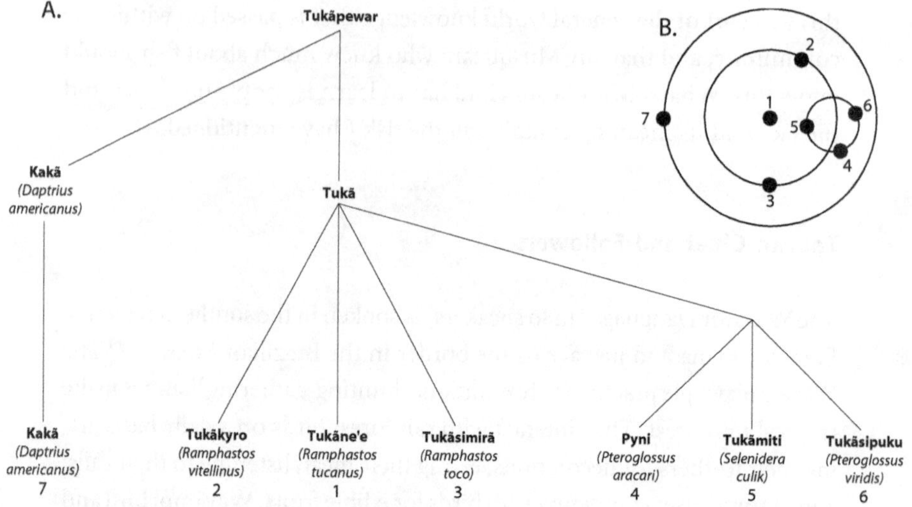


**Figure 2.14**
(a) The Tukãpewar grouping used by Wayampi speakers, which splits into Kakã and Tukã subgroups. The Tukã branch splits once more at an unnamed lower level. In total, Tukãpewar has seven Ethno-species. (b) A representation of how the Wayampi view the Tukãpewar Family, based on a prototypical or "chief" member (1) and the differing inter-relationships of its "followers" (1–6). Graphic by Arpiar Saunders and Robbie Hart

The similarity of a "follower" member to its chief is judged by morphological, ecological, and behavioral criteria. The meaningfulness and priority of these judgments are specific to Wayampi culture. The Linnaean system, by contrast, classifies organisms only by shared descent, and only biological history—not cultural interpretation—matters for membership. Is it surprising that radically different approaches to classification can produce similar groupings? Not exactly: organisms that are historically related may share appearance, habitat, and behavior; they are variants of a common theme. Genetic analysis affords us the most precise tracing of historical and evolutionary relatedness. But without modern tools, genes are invisible, seen only indirectly via the traits they bestow on organisms. Unsurprisingly, those characteristics most important for an organism to procreate are the very same characteristics the Wayampi use to classify: morphology, ecology, and behavior. Through their classification system, the Wayampi gain indirect but accurate access to an organism's genome.

**Figure 2.15**
Members 1, 2, 3, 4, and 7 of the Tukãpewar group. Bird images reprinted by permission from Sick, Helmut, *Birds in Brazil.* © 1993 Princeton University Press

What drives Wayampi classification is keen interest not in genetic history, but in subsistence. In determining the grouping relationship of 'followers' under a 'chief', the Wayampi impose their own political, cultural, and economic views to classify birds. If they choose, for example, an economically important food type, then only birds associated with that food will be linked to the taxonomy. This is the case for the Kakã (7), a falcon, which we might never think of grouping with toucans. While most members of *Falconidae* are carnivores, it is the Kakã's unusual diet that gets it classified with toucans: these birds eat mainly fruit.

A linguist who has studied Wayampi folk knowledge remarks: "Ecological knowledge about the bird species contributes necessary adaptation to daily life . . . Competition between indigenous (human) and bird populations for wild fruits may influence the classification system."[30] Why is eating the same fruit such a big deal for the Wayampi? After all, there are many ecological factors that could be used to judge similarity: loudness and timing of calls, trees where the birds nest, number and density in the forest, and so on. But in the case of the Tukãpewar family, diet trumps all. The reason may be that the Wayampi themselves are competing for the same food.[31] All fruit-eating birds are divided by the Wayampi into two classes: those that can eat the *açai* (*Euterpe oleracea*, a palm fruit) and those that cannot. This division is functional, allowing the young Wayampi to learn the birds with which they must compete just by learning the members of a category.

## Emergence and the Keen Observer

Human environmental knowledge is built upon a vast accretion of observations about animal appearance and behavior. Complex patterns of animal collectives—bird flocking, termite mound building, bee swarming, and fish schooling—have been keenly observed for a very long time by humans. In English we have words for animal groups: a 'pride' of lions, a 'pod' of whales, a 'parade' of elephants; and we have words for group behaviors: 'swarm', 'flock', 'school', 'colony'.

Social animals engage in complex collective behaviors—flocking, schooling, swarming, even synchronized clapping by an audience (yes, we are social animals too)—that appear tightly coordinated but have no leader. Such emergent behaviors have come to the attention of scientists working in complexity theory and the study of self-organizing systems. What are the rules participants in such leaderless groups follow, scientists ask, and how do these give rise to the patterns we observe? For geese flying in a V-formation, the simplest explanation is not that the geese have a master plan or a leader. Each goose adopts simple behaviors: fly forward, stay close to another goose, avoid collision, and minimize air drag. These give rise to the elegant flying V shape, an emergent property.

Termite mounds with their tunnels and arches similarly arise with no blueprint or architect's control. Each individual termite engages in very

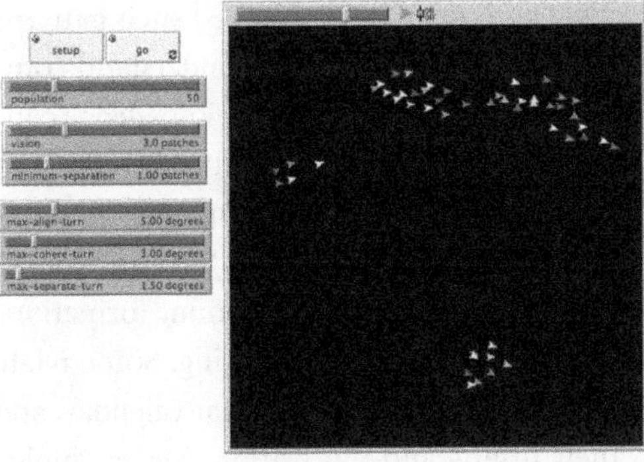


**Figure 2.16**
A simulation (NetLogo) in which artificial agents mimic the flocking behavior such as that of fish or birds by following a set of simple behavioral parameters. Courtesy of NetLogo

simple behaviors: pick up a grain of dirt, deposit it near other grains, secrete pheromones, and so on. The massive edifice that arises out of these simple routines is a truly emergent structure because no single termite carries a master design in its tiny brain. Recently, complexity theorists have begun to build artificial models—called simulations—of patterns like bird flocking and termite mound building that emerge from the sum of very simple individual behaviors.[32] Simulations attempt to mimic complex collective behaviors of animals by endowing a population of artificial agents with very simple desires and behaviors. Designers of simulations hope that these small local behaviors will produce unexpected global patterns of surprising complexity, and provide insights into complex, collective systems and behaviors in nature.

Fish, for example, exhibit many different types of self-organizing behavior—they swim in schools that seem to have common purpose and direction, turning and moving in unison without colliding, they hunt, flee predators, and spawn as groups. Who is directing the traffic? If we take a fish's eye view, there is no 'school' or directed group activity at all. There is merely a set of simple individual behaviors evolved under pressures of predation.[33] A fish that swims off alone gets eaten, while a fish that keeps bumping into schoolmates wastes energy. Schooling benefits the individual (he does not fall prey) and the school (it uses energy efficiently, reduces drag, can spawn and maintain its population). But the 'school' itself as an entity is nonexistent: we project this notion from the outside to help us understand fish behavior. Fish neither know they are in formation nor intentionally swim together. The apparent water ballet is unplanned, completely unlike the behavior of Olympic synchronized swimmers.

Languages spoken by people who have long observed such patterns may shed light on these animal behaviors and help us understand complex organization. This is simply one more area where the knowledge contained in endangered languages can illuminate the natural world and contribute to science. The Marovo people of the Solomon Islands are especially keen observers of fish and have many names for different types of fish aggregations, or schooling behaviors.[34] Distinct swimming formations may aid strategies for hunting, predator evasion, spawning. Some relate to tides or moon phases and can be predicted by the lunar calendar, and others remain a mystery in their timing and motivation. Marine biologists also take a great interest in fish behaviors and have technical terms for describing aggregations. But the Marovo people, whose interest in fish is not merely scientific but also nutritional, have a richer set of terms than do biologists.[35]

When predatory fish patrol for food, say the Marovo, they form *chapa* schools. As soon as these fish spot prey (smaller baitfish), they form an *umoro* school, which they use to drive the smaller fish to the surface, where they will be eaten by their pursuers and by birds. When schools of mullet migrate to spawning grounds, they form long narrow *rovana* schools. When those mullet arrive at their spawning grounds, they change from *rovana* to *bobili* schools, defined as 'non-feeding schools in which the fish mill slowly in a tightly packed circle'. Among the more impressive types of aggregations named by the Marovo are *ukuka* 'the behavior of groups of fish when individuals drift, circle, and float as if drunk'; *udumu*, a large school of fish so dense as to seem a single object; and *sakoto*, 'quiet, almost motionless resting of schools of certain fish, looking, say fishermen, like a gathering of mourners'.

Just as the Marovo are unequalled observers of fish, the Kayapó of Brazil (4,000 speakers) may be among the world's most astute observers of social insects: bees, wasps, and ants. They distinguish 85 folk species of wasps, grouped into 9 solitary and 3 social families. They also name 56 folk species of bees, broken into 15 families depending on flight patterns, aggressive behavior, sound, habitat, geometry of nest structure, shape, color, markings, smell (!) of the bee, quality and quantity of honey, edibility of larvae, quality of wax, and other criteria. They also observe termites, though with considerably less interest because they provide no food or useful products.

The 56 Kayapó folk species of bees correspond to 66 genetic species (11 were new to science at the time they were documented on the Kayapó territory). This means that from the point of view of a genetic taxonomy, the Kayapó system is less precise, because it fits 66 species into 56 categories. But the richness of their classification is obvious, and has real world consequences. The Kayapó aggressively harvest honey, reportedly enjoy eating it in great quantities, and use the wax for various purposes. They hunt honey by running quickly behind a bee to locate its colony. And they have trained their sense of smell to pick up the odor trails of bee swarms, which they call *mehn-nhy-pry* (*mehn* means 'bee', *nhy* denotes the class of social insects, and *pry* means 'odor trail') following them 'as though they were trails of game'.[36]

## Lost Words, Lost Knowledge

Knowledge is fragile and may be lost in translation. This is particularly true for cultures without writing, which must take great care to pass on their traditional wisdom. A single word may reflect generations of close observation of the natural world.[37] Like the Kayapó, the Wayampi of the Amazon prize their specialized ecological knowledge. As linguist Allen Jensen notes: "Those Wayampi who are considered wise by their peers are knowledgeable not only in the ways of nature but also in the cultural reasoning behind that information," How would a Wayampi youth, desiring to become wise, acquire this cultural reasoning? The Wayampi use the occasion of festivals to transmit a wealth of traditional environmental knowledge through song. For example, Jensen notes

> the *japu* festival, [is] directed toward the Crested Oropendola. This bird is the chief of the *japu*. In the lyric of this festival, *japuwy* means 'the japu and his domain'. . . . In this festival several of the *japu* domain are identified by name. They are also identified as 'subordinates' or 'servants'.

During this festival, birds are not only identified as to their respective chief and follower roles but also by behavioral traits, for example, how they group, when they migrate, what their nests look like, what they eat, what eats them, and the sound of their song:

> in the *japu* festival . . . we are told that the *japu* fly together in groups or families, en route to their feeding grounds . . . late in

> the afternoon [they] return to their nests . . . in the Kurmuri tree . . . the female enters the nest to stay with the eggs or with the young . . . the male . . . stays outside the nest singing . . . "*se'ageko-geko.*" In this same festival, three of the *japu*'s principal food staples are mentioned . . . we also learn that the *japu*'s principal predators are two raptorial birds.

Wayampi calendric cycles are also linked to birds, and this information may be transmitted during festivals. The *tarutaru* bird's song announces the beginning of dry season, and he is said to stop towards the latter part of the same season. Festival participants re-enact, through music and dance, the specific connections between birdsong, growing cycles, and the dry season:

> when the *tarutaru* sees the cluster of stars called *sirike* or *sirika* (the Pleiades), in the early morning hours, he starts singing. Later in the dry season, when sweet potatoes start sprouting in the gardens, and the Pleiades is seen in the early evening rather than the early morning, the *tarutaru* stops singing.[38]

Knowledge may be passed along in a many different traditional settings such as storytelling. Like the Chehalis naming myth we discussed before, the Wayampi festival is actually a kind of science lesson, enabling those who hear it to relate specific habitats and behaviors of the animals discussed. The Chehalis myth parallels to the Wayampi toucan classification, as the Chehalis people seem also to group species into chiefs and followers:

> Honné sat down by a slough and gazed for a long time in the clear water. After a while he noticed a fish swimming in the water . . . Honné said, "Oh yes I know you. I had forgotten. You will be the chief of the fish. Your name is *Klahwhi*, dog salmon. This is as far as you will go up the river. You will come up the river quickly and go back quickly. Your life will be short." And Honné gave the fish a striped blanket, which was made of cedar bark and dyed with alder. That is the coat of colors which the fish still wears.[39]

Knowledge transfer by myth equipped young Chehalis speakers to identify fish by color, size, habitat, and spawning behavior. By learning the fish myth and taxonomy they could make efficient use of river resources. With the language all but gone, and the lifestyle radically changed, most indigenous knowledge about the habits of creatures in America's northwestern coastal forests will have already vanished. Because knowledge transfer relies on oral transmission, its effectiveness is tied to language endangerment. In many (or perhaps most) cases where people shift to speaking a dominant language, they leave behind vast domains of knowledge, myth, and song.

Languages package and structure knowledge in particular ways. You cannot merely substitute labels or names from another language and hold onto all of the implicit, hidden knowledge that resides in a taxonomy or naming system.[40] Still, each language and speech community is unique, and language shift takes places at different speeds and under very different conditions. Can we then predict what proportion of traditional knowledge in a given situation will successfully be transferred, and how much will be lost?

Some scientists have tried to do just that. The Barí language (1,500–2,500 speakers) of Venezuela was studied by linguists who posed the question of how much knowledge of the plant world was being lost and how much retained. The Barí live in intimate relations with the rainforest and have learned to use many of its plants for food, material goods, medicine, and construction of houses. One scientist found that the loss of Barí traditional knowledge corresponded with diminishing use of forest resources and a shift from the traditional hunter-gatherer lifestyle, along with a shift to speaking Spanish. His conservative estimate of the rate of knowledge loss should be a wake-up call to all: "Using data on knowledge of forest trees by 20 Barí collaborators over nearly 17,000 naming events, I estimate that the real loss of ethnobotanical knowledge from one generation to the next may be on the order of 40 to 60 percent. This process has occurred over the 30 years since they were contacted."[41]

Breaking this down by social group, the scientist found a direct correlation between level of knowledge of traditional Barí ethnobotany and daily engagement with the living forest (see table 2.2).

This is a dire scenario: Barí people who have limited engagement with the forest have lost up to 45 percent of traditional plant names. Similar trajectories of knowledge erosion may be observed among indigenous peoples all around the world as they undergo cultural shift away from traditional lifeways and languages. The Rofaifo people, hunter-gatherers of Papua New Guinea, are rapidly losing their fine-grained system for classi-

**Table 2.2**
**Use of the forest corresponds to retention of traditional taxonomic knowledge among Barí speakers of Venezuela**

| *Type of subsistence pattern related to use of the forest* | *Approximate % of elicited terms that agree with accepted local taxon names* |
|---|---|
| 1. Little hunting and forest use | 55 |
| 2. Moderate use, hunting and gathering of forest products | 70 |
| 3. Frequent use, hunting and gathering of forest products | 85 |
| 4. Heavy use and daily hunting | 95 |

fying marsupials, cassowaries, and other forest creatures essential to their livelihood.[42] The Saami, reindeer herders of Norway, once had complex taxonomies for reindeer, sea mammals, and wolves, classifying them by age and sex. The rich Saami vocabulary for naming these animals was documented as far back as 1756. By the 1970s, only the reindeer taxonomy was remembered, and only by some speakers.[43]

Some researchers offer hope for the persistence and resilience of very basic forms of traditional knowledge. A study by anthropologist Scott Atran tested residents of Michigan on their knowledge of local mammals: raccoons, bats, deer, cows, and so on. He concluded that elements of folk classification persist even when people have been schooled in modern scientific classification. For example, Michigan students were no better at producing scientifically accurate taxonomies of local wildlife than their less formally educated counterparts in the Itza Mayan community in Mexico. As we saw above, it turns out that categories like 'bird' and 'reptile' remain a powerful conceptual tool by which we organize our world, even when educated about the scientific inadequacy of such labels. Far removed from nature, we cling to folk-ecological ideas adopted by our distant ancestors for survival. Atran concludes that "even when people become largely ignorant of local ecological relationships, as they do in our urban Western culture, they continue to cling to life forms such as *tree* as unforgettable parts of their lives and the evolutionary history of our species."[44]

Though folk knowledge may persist in modern cultures, it should be clear from the examples here that we are also losing traditional knowledge at an alarming rate. This loss is accompanied by a severe reduction in number of species and range of habitats. Perhaps future technologies hold enough promise that humanity will be able to survive on our overcrowded planet without making use of this accumulated ecological knowledge, and so we should not mourn its passing. Perhaps we will grow plants in greenhouses and breed animals in laboratories and feed ourselves via genetic engineering. Perhaps there are no new medicines to be found in the rainforests. All such arguments appeal to ignorance: we do not know what we stand to lose as languages and technologies vanish because much or even most of it remains undocumented. So, it is a gamble to think that we will never avail ourselves of it in the future. Do we really want to place so much faith in future science and pay so little heed to our inherited science?

My Siberian hunter friend, Sergei Kongaraev of the Tofa people (see fig. 3.3), with a moderate knowledge of his parents' language, expressed great respect for the knowledge his parents (illiterate hunter-gatherers) passed on to him. He clearly understands the value and necessity of that knowledge. Sergei has seen a world that his parents, riding through Siberian forests on reindeer-back, never even dreamt of. He has traveled to Moscow, viewed the stars through telescopes, ridden on airplanes across many time zones, and had artillery training while serving in the Soviet army. Sergei's two grown children live two time zones away in a modern city, Irkutsk, where they attend college, use the Internet, watch television game shows, and practice their English. When Sergei is at home in his ancestral village, where his mother, Marta, still lives, he practices the old ways, riding reindeer and hunting fox, squirrels, and deer in the pristine Siberian forests. He feels strongly he is not alone in the forest: he can sense, he told me, the presence of animals and spirits on which his ancestors relied for their very lives. He depends on them too, when he goes out hunting, and on the knowledge of how to appease them, hunt them, and live off their meat and fur: "Of course I still keep the old customs. When I am out in the forest I offer tea and food to the fire god for success in hunting. And I make offerings to the spirits of animals I hunt. My father taught me, he explained it all to me in the Tofa language. How could I not do it? And how could I forget my native tongue?"[45]

## Vanishing Herds and Reindeer Words

*Döngür.* It is a powerful word. It means 'male domesticated reindeer in its third year and first mating season, but not ready for mating', and it allows a tribe of nomadic reindeer herders in Siberia to identify and describe with a single word what would otherwise require a full sentence. But these people, the Tofa, are giving up their ancestral tongue in favor of Russian—the dominant, national language that does not have even a remote equivalent to the word *döngür.* And the Tofa are just one of hundreds of small communities whose language is endangered. When working with such groups, it is hard to keep from wondering not only how knowledge is encoded in language, but what exactly will be lost when these small languages vanish.

Many prominent linguists, including Noam Chomsky and Steven Pinker, have analyzed language as a cognitive domain consisting mainly

A reindeer herder in South Siberia leads his herd out on a hunting expedition. Courtesy of Brian Donahoe

of words and mental rules. An English speaker, for example, has in her mental dictionary the word 'hat', which is simply an arbitrary string of sounds she has learned to associate with an object you wear on your head. She also has a rule of morphology that tells her the plural is 'hats' and a rule of syntax that says when there is an adjective, put it first—'red hat', not 'hat red'. And she has certain cognitive structures, mostly not learned and thought to be genetic. The innate knowledge that nouns and adjectives are different types of things and that one modifies the other, for example, allows her to understand that red describes a type of hat, but hat does not describe a type of red. This cognitive view, while not incorrect, bypasses much of the knowledge that language actually contains.

Languages abound in 'cultural knowledge', which is neither genetic nor explicitly taught, but comes to us in an information package—rich and hierarchical in its structure. Any English-speaking child may know the word 'uncle', but what does he store in his head as its meaning? An uncle may be a mother's brother, or a mother's sister's husband, or perhaps just his parents' adult male friend. An English-speaking child has no explicit linguistic information to indicate these are distinct positions in the kinship tree. Why not? We could speculate that since it was not culturally crucial in our societies to distinguish these positions, our language did not do so. While our mind readily grasps the various types of 'uncle', English provides no ready-made, unique labels to distinguish them. Conversely, in cultures like Tofa with more socially important kinship relations, there exists no general word for 'uncle'. Five different types of uncles would have five completely different labels. By simply learning these labels, the child implicitly learns that these are distinct kinship roles.

Kinship systems are just the tip of the iceberg, but they reveal a common strategy of naming and classifying things. By simply knowing the word *döngür*, the young Tofa reindeer herder has, at the tip of his tongue, the ability to pick out from the herd and identify a specific kind of reindeer. Tofa reindeer herders who have switched to speaking Russian can still talk about and herd reindeer, but they lack the labels to do so as efficiently. Knowledge that their ancestors accumulated over centuries, knowledge that is very specifically adapted to the narrow ecological niche of reindeer herding in south Siberian mountain forests, has essentially been lost.

At its core, all human cognition may be fundamentally the same no matter what tongue a person speaks. This has been the prevailing view in cognitive linguistics for at least thirty years. But some people are beginning to recognize that languages can package knowledge in radically different ways, thus facilitating different ways of conceptualizing, naming, and discussing the world. In the case of the young Tofa reindeer herder who no longer speaks his ancestral tongue, the human knowledge base—as manifested in very specific ways of describing the world of reindeer—has been impoverished. Arcane bits of knowledge get washed away under the pressures of globalization.

Does this erosion of knowledge matter? While this may seem like a minor loss in the face of modernity and progress, we cannot even fathom what the long-term effects will be. Klaus Toepfer, Director of the United Nations Environment Program (UNEP) warns: "Indigenous peoples not only have a right to preserve their way of life. But they also hold vital knowledge on the animals and plants with which they live. Enshrined in their cultures and customs are also secrets of how to manage habitats and the land in environmentally friendly, sustainable ways."[1] If we hold any hope of understanding and fostering eco-diversity on earth, we must learn to value knowledge such as that possessed by Tofa reindeer herders while it still exists.

For more on the Tofa people and reindeer herding, see chapter 2. For more on endangered languages and human cognition, see chapter 7.

## Languages featured in Chapter 3

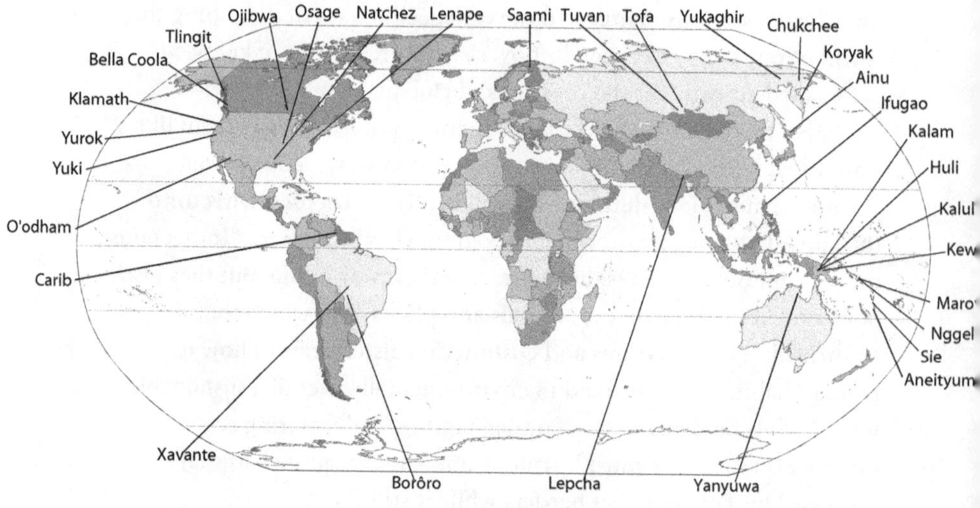

# 3 Many Moons Ago Traditional Calendars and Time-Reckoning

Time is an invention
—Slogan seen on a t-shirt

[N]atural objects like the sun, the moon, and the stars, trees and plants, animals, birds and insects, act as our infallible calendars, time-keepers, direction indicators, and guides. They tell us when to sow our seeds, when to harvest the crops, and what things to look for, and at what times, in forests and rivers.
—A. R. Foning in *Lepcha—My Vanishing Tribe*

World time-keeping is dominated by the 60-second minute, 60-minute hour, 24-hour day, 7-day week, 12-month-365-day year. We take this for granted, but it was not always so. Across a vast span of human prehistory, people reckoned time quite differently. Early humans noticed patterns everywhere—in the sky, the life cycles of plants and animals, the stars, the tides, and the weather—and used all of these patterns to keep track of time.

Until about 12,000 years ago, all humans survived as hunter-gatherers.[1] Survival required close attention to natural cycles. Humans were thus highly motivated to mentally organize these patterns, make sense of them, and use them to anticipate future events. In this way calendars of varying sophistication emerged in different human societies. Most such calendars have now vanished or are in the very process of being forgotten under pressure from the dominant world models of time-keeping.

Traces of earlier time-reckoning techniques may still be found in many small and endangered languages. Frank Analok of Canada's northernmost province, Nunavut, explains how his people, the Inuit, used to delineate months without calendars:

> We did not have calendars back then. [The Inuit] used the moon only. . . . They used the moon as a way to tell seasons long ago. When the moon would come during the spring thaw, when there is water, the caribou are calving and the birds are nesting. That is how it was used. . . . The moon would go away again during the month of June. When it returns you know when the birds are moulting . . . which is during the month of July. The moon was the only way the Inuit knew the time of the year.[2]

Human time-reckoning may have surprisingly early origins. A key discovery was made by Alexander Marshack, when he decoded notches on an eagle bone dug up in France and dating back some 30,000 years. Marshack showed the notches to be a meticulous and accurate record of lunar cycles. He concluded that ice-age man not only cared about time—a full 25,000 years before the emergence of writing and nearly 20,000 years before agriculture—but kept detailed records of its cycles using highly developed "imaging and abstracting capacities."[3] Marshack's claim was an astonishing and radical proposal at the time (in the 1960s). Scholars had until then underestimated the intellectual life of hunter-gatherers in the Upper Paleolithic period (approximately 40,000 B.C.E. to 10,000 B.C.E.), thinking that even though biologically they were just like us, early humans were too busy with hunting, simple tool-making, and basic survival to care much about units of time and intellectual or aesthetic pastimes. But with a brain as large as our own, a keen ability to recognize patterns, and knowledge of the intricacies of language, why would Paleolithic humans fail to notice and record the passage of time? It is now widely accepted that humankind has kept calendars for at least 30,000 years. The calendar thus counts among the earliest purely intellectual creations of humankind attested in the archeological record, albeit scantily.

Beyond archeology, we are fortunate to have a wealth of linguistic evidence about the ancient time-reckoning habits of humankind, which we will explore in this chapter. Across human history, time-reckoning has differed radically from modern methods we are so used to. Since the sun, moon, and planets as viewed from earth have changed little over 40,000 years, how could timekeeping have been so different? One important difference was due to the fact that the exact (and complex) mathematical relations among the lunar and solar years had not yet been calculated, and so timekeeping was far more flexible than it is today.

For prehistoric man, the moon stood at the pinnacle of a system based as much on nearby nature as the distant cosmos, and intrinsically tied to local environmental rhythms. The moon was not some abstract heavenly body, illuminating mankind from above. It was closely bound to earth, linked to the rhythms of plants, animals, foodstuffs, and essential life activities.

This kind of lunar-environmental timekeeping was not mechanized, and therefore less accurate, at least in a modern sense. It offered no fixed point to count to or from, except today, and no uniform units. It was less suited to a linear timeline view of history and to writing histories in which one might want to refer to specific dates in the distant past, say June 13, 1247. It would have been unusable as a standard method of timekeeping across an empire. It would also have been less suited to the kinds of proclamations my nephew is fond of making, such as "I'm six and a quarter years old now."

Despite this inherent imprecision, early timekeeping was ingenious, complex, and ideally suited to human survival. Pre-modern timekeeping adapted to the environmental challenges faced by particular peoples. We have always been moon, bird, and flower watchers; keen noticers of correlations among many natural cycles. Not only did the cycles help us track the passage of time, they were also the very reason timekeeping existed. For hunter-gatherers, the timing of goose migration or acorn harvest could mean life or death. The need to observe these natural rhythms, in combination with man's cognitive predilection to notice patterns, gave us our first calendars.

Today, in our twenty-first century, ancient methods of time-reckoning have all but vanished from major world languages and human consciousness. As people switch over to the world standard 7-day week and 365-day calendar year, old methods of timekeeping linked to local vegetative and animal cycles are rapidly fading from memory. Large world languages lack the notion of a flexible lunar month linked to ecological cycles, and the notion of a mobile week centered around today.[4]

Environmental calendars survive now only in fragmentary, remembered form in a minority of languages. They can point us to an understanding of the rhythms of life that have been crucial to human survival

**Table 3.1**
**Some differences in modern and traditional timekeeping**

| *Modern time-keeping* | *Traditional time-reckoning* |
| --- | --- |
| 1 **hour** = 60 minutes = 60 seconds | Hour-like units based on physical processes, e.g. the time it takes a kettle of water to boil. Also, references to changes in the position of the sun in the sky. |
| 1 **day** = 24-hour period (terrestrial rotation) | 1 **day** = often one night or dark/ sleeptime hours |
| 1 **week** = fixed, sequential 7-day unit | 1 **week** = A mobile unit of 4 to 9 days, centered around today |
| 1 **month** = calendar month of fixed length (approximately 1/12 of the solar year) | 1 **month** = approximately one full lunar cycle |
| 1 **year** = 12 solar, fixed-length months | 1 **year** = aproximately 13 lunar months, of flexible length and often linked to environmental cycles. |
| **human age** counted in years / months | **human age** counted in sequential life stages |

prior to calendars and recorded history. But they are on the wane and have come under great pressure as worldwide calendar systems spread and languages die.[5]

Much of the knowledge encoded in traditional calendars will soon be lost to memory. Already forgotten are the eco-calendars of the Tofa, reindeer herders of Siberia; the Osage, once buffalo hunters of Missouri; and the Sie, fishermen seafarers of Vanuatu. Time-keeping methods that predate the modern world calendar we use today provide important clues about how our ancestors conceptualized time, managed natural resources, adapted to their environmental niche, and viewed the cosmos.

In this chapter, we will look at a range of languages that still retain some use of the traditional lunar month, mobile week, and ecological cycle. We will consider the adaptability and effectiveness of these calendars, and the mindset that underlay them. We also look at the likelihood that they will disappear in the near future as languages vanish. And we will try to answer the question of what exactly will be lost as the languages and the systems they contain are abandoned, and why the loss matters both to science and to humanity.

## A Calendar Dilemma

As a 9-year-old child, I suffered from a calendar dilemma. About once a week, I would ask my mother, "What day is it today?" My mother, wisely wanting me to be self-reliant and information-savvy, always replied, "Go look at the calendar." Dutifully, I would go stand in front of our wall-calendar and gaze at it for awhile. All I was able to glean from it was the month and the year. Since I already knew that I did not know what day of the week it was, nor what the date was, it proved impossible for me to extract that information from the calendar. I tried, but probably failed, to explain to my mother this glaring catch-22. You cannot tell what day it is by looking at a calendar unless you *already* know what day it is, or some equivalent information—that this is the second Tuesday of the month or that yesterday was the 15th or a comparable set of facts.

My mother persisted in her belief that the calendar was a useful device for telling what day it was and continued sending me off to gaze at the calendar each time I inquired. She is surely not alone in this belief, so central an institution is the calendar to our society. Yet many people do live and function quite well not only without calendars but with a radically different concept of how passing time should be divided, marked, and kept track of. The calendar is a modern invention, but its foundation, the lunar cycle (and to a lesser extent the solar year), has always been obvious and noticed by humankind.

We now think of the lunar calendar as a quaint relic of the past. You can still purchase lunar calendars, almanacs, or 365-day calendars that track moon phases, but these are not widely used. But for most of human history the lunar cycle was our primary time-keeping device. The moon has now declined in importance to the point that most people in industrialized societies live in blissful ignorance of its phases, and indeed, seem taken by surprise if they happen to gaze up at the sky and observe a full moon. How did we become so estranged from the moon, the body that dominated human time-reckoning for most of our evolutionary history?

The moon, in fact, was the source of my second calendar dilemma, which occurred when I was living among nomadic Tuvan yak-herders in the snow-capped Altai Mountains of Inner Asia. After living some time at the camps, I woke one morning to realize that I had lost count of how many days I had spent there and had no idea what day it was. Between stints of throwing dried yak dung onto the fire (my job at the camp), I asked my host family what day it was. The question, correctly posed in Tuvan, is "today is how many?" And the answer in Tuvan nomadic culture has nothing to do with days of the week or the calendar month. Instead, you will be answered strictly with lunar phases.[6]

Since Tuvans express time-related numbers as future tense verbs, if the moon was in the 13th day of its cycle, the answer would be 'it's fourteening'. I noticed that if I posed this question in the daytime, I would get a quick answer only about half the time. If I asked it in the night or evening, while outdoors or while the moon was visible through the roof hole of the yurts the nomads live in, my Tuvan friends would always glance up for a split second at the moon then unhesitatingly respond with a number. So astonished was I at their ability to do this that I would ask multiple family members, even the young children, each day, "how many is today?"

My hosts began to joke that their American guest was obsessed with the moon, and wondered at my odd inability to extract calendar information from its most obvious source. For my part, I felt like that same befuddled 9-year-old I had once been, gazing up at a cryptic object and wondering: "How the heck can this thing tell me what day today is unless I already know what day it is?"

In contrast to their disregard for weekdays,[7] I discovered Tuvan nomadic herders to be so keenly attuned to moon phases that they no longer even needed to keep mental track of days of the month. At first, I assumed that looking up at the moon only gave the yak herders part of the information they needed. For example, I figured they would need to keep track in their heads of approximately what day it was in order to tell the miniscule difference between the 13th day after new moon and the 14th day. I figured the progression of the shadow across the moon's surface was fairly subtle, something like 12 degrees each night.

What I failed to factor in was that because of the moon's spheroid shape, we view its middle straight on but its sides at a steep angle. So, rather than moving across the moon's face at a steady rate, the earth's shadow progresses a *different* number of degrees each night. Further complicating the task, people may look at the moon at different times each night. Understanding the dynamic changes in the moon's shape and tracking these changes becomes a daunting task.

It would be an understatement to say that Tuvan nomads know how to read the moon. All activities in Tuvan nomadic life regulate themselves on the lunar schedule, from moving the yaks to new pastures, to planning weddings, to shearing the goats. It is no coincidence that Tuvans, like almost every other culture we deal with in this chapter, have only a single word that means both 'moon' and 'month'.

What they really know is how to track a shifting shadow that moves along at a non-constant velocity. This shadow defines different sized slices each day, which Tuvans link to a specific numbered day. The complexity of this task is illustrated in figure 3.1, which traces the uneven rate of change in the moon's appearance over one month. For example, on the 9th of December 2005, you would easily notice that the shadow had significantly receded, moving 11 percent from its position the previous night. But on the 16th of the month, you would have to notice a nearly invisible change in the shadow of less than 1 percent from midnight the previous night. I can imagine a bewildered Tuvan child asking, his mother, as I used to ask mine, "what day is it?" and being told: "Go look at the moon."

Of course, the Tuvans are not the only ones to use moon phases to mark dates with precision. The Xavante people of Mato Grosso, Brazil, are reportedly able to set exact dates for meetings by 'indicating a certain number of moons and the phase of the moon in which they wish to meet'.[8] We have become lazy in our reliance on wall calendars; our predecessors had the far more difficult task of recognizing subtly shifting moon patterns and keeping mental calendars.

Many cultures pay close attention to moon shape but refer to the phases metaphorically rather than mathematically.[9] The Ifugao people who cultivate rice high in the mountains of the Philippines call the very thinnest waxing of the new moon 'thread moon'. The next stage they know as

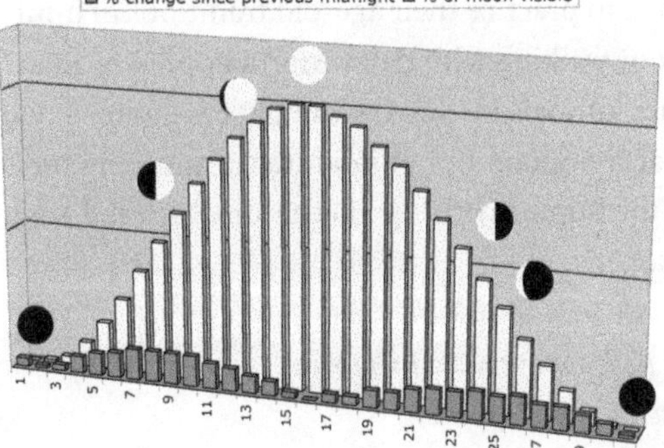


**Figure 3.1**
Dynamic change in the moon's shape from midnight to midnight in December 2005; rate of change in moon phase as a function of moon phase. Graphic based on US Naval Observatory data

'knife moon' because it resembles the curved blade of a knife used for harvesting rice. Later phases are called 'half moon', 'swollen half moon', and 'two-thirds moon'. This system seems to lack the numeric precision we have seen elsewhere, but as the Ifugao maintain a complex calendar based on nature cycles, the moon is only one of many elements they track.

The Carib people of Surinam viewed the lit portion of the moon as a bonfire, and the dark portion as a game animal roasting on a spit over the fire. They thought of the waning moon as having been out hunting each day for successively larger game, appearing as 'rat' when the lighted portion was largest, then waning in size as it caught a porcupine, peccary, wild pig, and anteater. When the lit portion of the moon was at its most slender and the shadow at its largest, they called it 'tapir moon' after the largest game animal they knew.[10] The Carib also relied on moon phases to determine planting and fishing and crop planting times: they planted crops only when the moon was waxing.

After living with Tuvan yak herders I thought I knew a fair amount about lunar calendars. But in 2000, when I began visiting another Siberian tribe—the Tofa people, who are reindeer herders and hunter-gatherers—I understood the moon was not the whole story. In June 2001, I found myself out taking a stroll through a tiny Siberian village with my Tofa friend Aunt Marta (fig. 3.2). Born in 1930, Marta is one of the last fluent speakers of the Tofa language. Although not able to read or write, she possesses immense knowledge of everything having to do with reindeer, hunting, wild plants, and the life cycles of the Siberian forest. The Tofa were traditionally herders of domesticated reindeer and hunter-gathers who lived in birch bark teepees and migrated with their reindeer herds.

Decades of Soviet domination settled the Tofa people in three tiny villages. While watching their reindeer herds dwindle perilously close to extinction, the Tofa continue to practice their age-old traditions of hunting and gathering. I went out walking with Aunt Marta hoping to interview her about things (plants, animals, streams) we might encounter along the way. As we walked, Marta pointed out animal tracks and sang me a little song, a celebration of the hunter-gatherer lifeway of which she was a lifelong and expert practitioner:

*I'll take a shortcut and pick some cedar nuts to eat,*
*take a shortcut and catch a wood grouse,*
*take another shortcut and catch a quail . . .*

Further along a path we met Marta's son and daughter-in-law, equipped with shovels and pails as they set off for a day's trek into the mountain forests. I asked what they planned to collect. "*Saranki*" the answer came, which I knew to be a tiny purple lily-like flower. The Tofa gather the flower's edible underground bulb—which tastes a bit like a mild onion—and consume it year-round to ward off colds, winter malaise, and other illnesses. The edible lily bulb is a common but important plant to many northern indigenous cultures, stretching halfway around the globe from the Saami reindeer herders of Finland to the Koryak people on Russia's Kamchatka peninsula north of Japan to the Bella Coola people of British Columbia. Native Siberians prize *saranki* roots, and even name months or seasons of the year after it. "You know, we used to call June 'edible lily bulb' month," Marta explained, "but now we call it ee-YOON (June) just like the Russians do."[11]

Intrigued at the idea of naming an entire month after a tiny oniony bulb, I asked Aunt Marta if other months had similar names in Tofa. She admitted she had forgotten most of them, and while other Tofa elders I spoke to claimed awareness of the old month-naming system, none could produce it intact from memory. Fortunately, some years prior to our meeting, Marta's daughter had gotten the Tofa ecological lunar calendar down on paper. The impetus for this was a good-natured disagreement Marta had had with a cousin from another Tofa village about how the old people named months. An experienced hunter and forest-trekker, Marta insisted October was 'rounding up male reindeer' month, while her cousin knew it as 'migrate to autumn campsite' month. It turned out that they were both right, and the two villages, only four days' journey apart on reindeer, had different ecological calendars. Aunt Marta, herself not able to write, asked her daughter to write the calendars down on paper. This tattered sheet of paper, which she gave to me, was the last repository of something that for even the knowledgeable Tofa elders had already faded from memory. A mere generation or two ago, this calendar would have been an important mechanism linking the Tofa to nature, to an endless cycle of hunting, lily-bulb gathering, birch bark collecting, rope-braiding, and the long dark days of winter. Important activities that defined their year, their life, and their livelihood were spelled out plainly in their calendar.

In Tofa, as in Tuvan, the words for 'moon' and 'month' are the same. The first Tofa calendar from Gutara village, only partially remembered by

**Table 3.2**
**Tofa hunting and gathering calendars, as remembered by Tofa elders**

| *Month* | *Tofa 'hunting' calendar* | *Tofa 'gathering' calendar* |
|---|---|---|
| January | great white month | empty month |
| February | small white month | big log month |
| March | hunting with dogs month | tree bud month |
| April | tree bud month | good birch bark collecting month |
| May | hunting in the taiga month | digging *saranki* root month |
| June | (forgotten) | bad birch bark collecting month |
| July | hay cutting month | hay cutting month |
| August | (forgotten) | collecting *saranki* month |
| September | preparing skins month | preparing skins month |
| October | rounding up male deer month | move Autumn capsite month |
| November | sable hunting month | hunting month |
| December | cold month | braiding (rope making) month |

*Note:* Although this would have been a 13-month lunar cycle, common to all Siberian peoples, it was now remembered only as a 12-month cycle due to influence from the Russian calendar.

*Source:* K. David Harrison, unpublished field notes, 2000. Marta Kongaraeva, consultant.

elders and shown in the left column of table 3.2, showcases hunting activities. Five of ten named months refer to hunting, including the October round-up of male reindeer, which is preparatory to riding them out to hunt.

The calendar from Aunt Marta's home village emphasizes gathering activities, with two months devoted to *saranki* collecting and two to gathering birch bark (used to make buckets and containers), and one to collecting logs for firewood. The two calendars agree on July for 'hay cutting' and September for 'preparing skins', but differ on whether March or April is 'tree bud month'.

Ecological calendars once regulated the lives of all Siberian hunter-gatherers. They were highly local: from one village to the next people would adopt different month names, changeable over time. Although the Tofa people have probably never numbered more than 500 in their history, they were nomadic reindeer herders dispersed over a large territory. So it is not surprising that earlier visitors to the Tofa noted different calendar systems (see table 3.3), especially when they tried to fit the system into our rigid 12 months.[12]

Tofa month names—in all four versions of the calendar—reflect perfectly the yearly cycle of important subsistence activities and natural

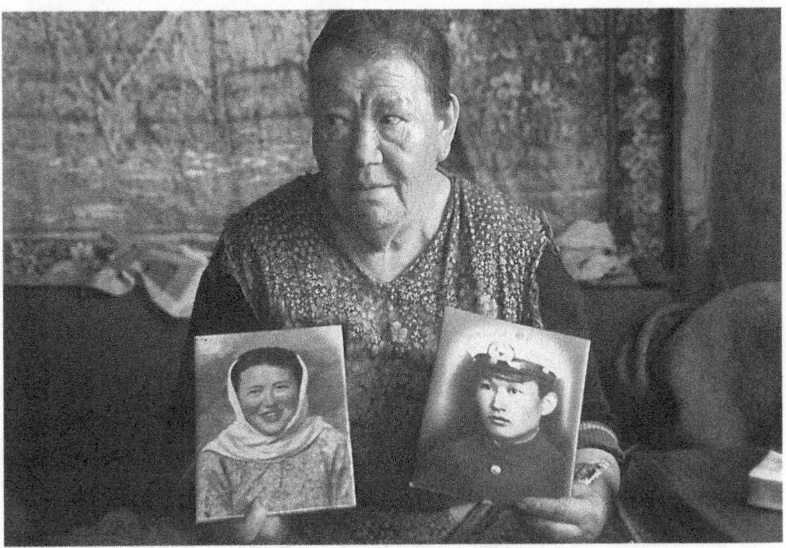

**Figure 3.2**
One of the last speakers of Tofa, "Aunt" Marta Kongaraeva, an expert hunter and former reindeer herder, still knows the Tofa eco-calendar. Photograph by Thomas Hegenbart, courtesy of Contact Press Images

events. This contrasts with our arbitrary English months, which are either inaccurately numbered in Latin or named for Roman gods and emperors with whom we have no connection. Our month names bear no relation to our yearly cycle of activities. Then again, we do not have much of a yearly cycle of ecological activities dictated by nature, apart from the fact that we may have to pay more for tomatoes in December or don galoshes in April.

Ecological calendars tell us a great deal about local natural cycles and their importance to cultural activities. Such calendars or traces of them exist not only in Siberia, where I first became aware of them, but in nearly all indigenous cultures where they have not yet been replaced by the modern calendar. Unfortunately, owing to the replacement of these calendars by the modern systems, we now find them mostly in history books.

An eighteenth-century Swedish ethnographer named Johann Peter Falck, who wandered over great stretches of central Siberia, was clearly impressed by the detailed ecological calendar of the native people he found living along the Chulym River, where he recorded details of each settle-

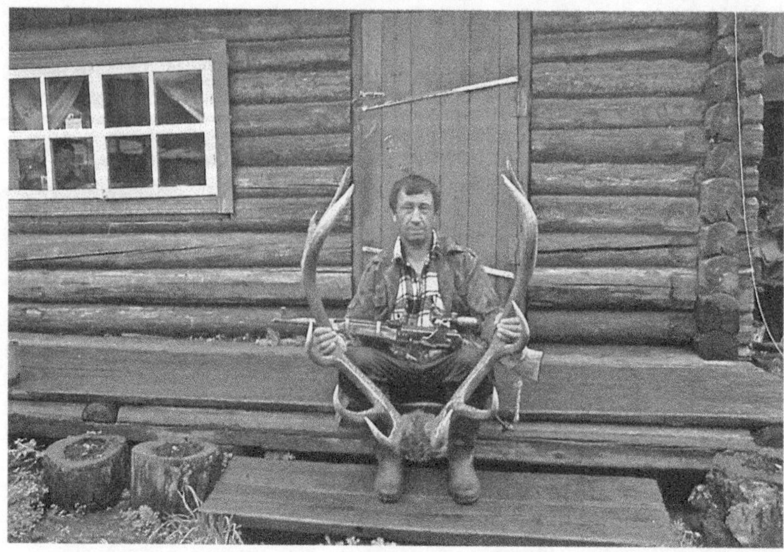

**Figure 3.3**
Sergei Kongaraev, Aunt Marta's son, is also an expert hunter and regularly gathers edible and medicinal plants, but he does not remember the traditional eco-calendar. Photograph by Thomas Hegenbart, courtesy of Contact Press Images

ment he visited: the numbers of birch bark huts and people, and their activities as hunter-gatherers and fishermen. He also recorded their ecological lunar calendar. Falck writes:

> The first snow-fall is their New Year. From there they count 12 months (*Ai*), *Ka-rakal Ai* is essentially our September, *Garisch Ai* October, *Kitscha Ai* (shorter month) November, *Ulu Ai* (bigger month) December, *Jel Serta* (half winter) January, *Tulg Ai* (fox month) February, *Kutschugen Ai* (eagle month) March, *Karga Ai* (raven month) April, *Koi Ai* (cuckoo month) May, *Kitschi Schilgai* (smaller Summer) June, *Ulu Schelgai Ai* (bigger summer) July and *Urgai Ai* (longer month) August, because it lasts until the snow falls.[13]

The name 'longer month' for August suggests it extended to include more than one lunar cycle and might have served as a kind of synchronizing mechanism to reset the calendar year at the first snow.

**Table 3.3**
**Older Tofa month names**

| *Approximate equivalent* | *Tofa month names recorded in 1880* | *Tofa month names recorded in the 1850s* |
|---|---|---|
| January | dry teepee | great cold |
| February | lumber preparation | chasing animals on skis |
| March | dog | snow becomes soft |
| April | greenery | hunting with dogs |
| May | birch | greenery |
| June | *Saranki flower* | birch |
| July | summer migration | *Saranki* flower blooms |
| August | nut gathering | digging *Saranki* roots |
| September | round-up (of deer) | nut gathering |
| October | sable | round-up (of deer) |
| November | short days | sable |
| December | cold | short days |
| 13th month | | cold |

In 2005, I visited native people living along the Chulym River, quite possibly descendants of the same people Falck visited in 1768–73. Their name for themselves is the Ös people, and their lifestyle remains intimately tied to nature. They fish, gather berries and medicinal plants, harvest birch bark and nuts, and carve wooden dugout canoes by hand. I was pleased to find speakers who could tell traditional bear-hunting stories, give eyewitness accounts of shamans performing rituals, sing their grandmother's wool-spinning songs, and relate practical knowledge about harvesting medicinal plants and making fishing lures.

But in interviewing 16 of only about 30 remaining speakers of the Ös language, I found only the faintest traces of the old calendar system. Three elders together recalled only four month names. Three month names *sounded* similar to ones noted by Falck in 1768, but the speakers only reported the same meaning for one—'fox month'. The others they remembered were 'chipmunk month', 'riverbank month', and 'green month'. No living Ös people know that for their ancestors, the new year began in September at first snowfall. The early record preserved by the Swedish traveler Falck and remembered fragments from 2005 remain our only glimpse into the calendric past of this tiny Siberian community.[14]

Not all people who still live off the land in Siberia have abandoned their ecological calendar. Two thousand miles to the east, at the other end of the Siberian vastness on the Kamchatka peninsula (just across the Bering Strait from Alaska) live the Koryak people (3,500 speakers), who herd reindeer and hunt. Some Koryak still observe an ecological calendar based on the life cycle of domestic reindeer and assorted nature signs. Anthropologist Alexander King observes: "The Koryaks think of months as lunar events connected to seasonal cycles, so the correspondences are very approximate . . . depending on how the year is going (late frosts, etc.) . . . February could last six weeks and March only two or three." King also notes that Koryak months have many alternate names, varying from one family or group of herders to the next. In one family he surveyed, December was known as 'snow dust devils month', named for the mini-cyclones of snow that spring up. January is 'middle of the head month', which indicates that it ends one lunar year and starts a new one. March is 'month of false reindeer milk' when the deer near their birthing time and April is 'real reindeer milk month' when milk begins to appear in the deer's udders. August, when the first overnight frosts begin, they dub 'heat goes home month'.[15]

Moving further west across the Arctic, we find the Chilkat Tlingit people (845 speakers) using a mixed calendar with highly specific ecological names for some months, and simple numbers for others. Their year begins in July with 'tobacco drying month', then 'new snow on mountains', 'ground-hog preparing home', 'big moon', and 'digging moon' (when bears dig their winter burrows). One Tlingit month name, 'hair on seal in womb' reflects observations made while hunting and butchering seals. March is 'underwater plants sprout month' but between March and July, when the new year begins, they simply assign numbers—10th through 13th—to the months.[16]

Ecological calendars are being irretrievably lost as languages vanish. The Ainu language was once spoken by the native people of Japan's northernmost Hokkaido Island who were salmon fishers and agriculturalists. Ainu is now reported to have no fluent speakers. In 1905 researchers recorded 13 Ainu month names. But by 1973, with very few elderly speakers left, this had been reduced to only 12 month names. However certain ecological names remained, including 'canegrass' (cut to make chopsticks) month, 'rushes' (woven to make matting) month, 'torchlight fishing of dog salmon' month, and, as we might expect from a Northern people, 'edible-lily bulb month'. These month names and the knowledge they point to can now be found only in books.[17]

## Watermelon Month

The Natchez language, now extinct, was spoken by Native Americans along the lower Mississippi River. Natchez belonged to the Gulf family of languages—now fully extinct—which had no demonstrated relationship to other Native American languages. Had they survived or been documented, Gulf languages would have provided particularly valuable insights into the history of human settlement and migration in North America. The Natchez were considered unusual among Native American cultures for their sun-worshiping, building of ceremonial earth mounds, and social stratification into nobility and commoner classes. A French explorer named Antoine-Simone Le Page du Pratz visited the Natchez in the 1750s and found them using a fruit-based lunar calendar.

The Natchez second lunar period, beginning in April, was named 'strawberries', the third 'little corn', the fourth 'watermelons', the fifth 'peaches', the sixth 'mulberries', the seventh 'great corn', the twelfth 'chestnuts', and the thirteenth 'nuts'. Natchez months not named for fruits reflected a hunting cycle: first month 'deer', fifth 'fishes', eighth 'turkey', and ninth 'buffalo'. At least one lunar month—'chestnut' month in December—was named not for food-gathering activities taking place at that time, but for a dietary necessity. Chestnuts were reportedly an undesirable food for the Natchez, collected in summer but stored away and not eaten until December when all other food ran out.[18]

Curiously, peaches and watermelons are not native plants, but were introduced to the Southeastern United States by Spanish colonizers. While the date of this technology transfer is unknown, domesticated peaches and watermelons had become important enough by the 1750s to have Natchez months named for them. The Natchez calendar, now preserved only in eighteenth-century histories, may still provide important historical clues about diffusion of old-world domesticated plants among new-world peoples.[19]

We see the adaptability of ecological calendars in Natchez and also in Lenape, a language once spoken by Native Americans in Delaware. Although the lunar calendar has likely vanished from memory, the month names once reflected where each tribe lived and what was available in the local ecosystem. If a tribe moved to another environment, or if the ecosystem changed, they could change month names accordingly:

> The months have each a separate name . . . refer[ring] chiefly to the climate of the district, and the benefits and good things enjoyed in it. Thus the Lenape, who lived by the Atlantic Ocean, called March the month of shads, since the shad then came up from the sea into the rivers to spawn; but since in the district to which they afterwards migrated this fish is not found, they changed the name of the month and called it the juice-dripping or the sugar-refining month, since at this time the juice of the sugar-maple begins to flow.[20]

## Staying in Synch

Calendars linked to events like the migration of the geese, the harvesting of birch-bark, or the birth of reindeer fawns offer greater accuracy precisely because they are flexible. Civilizations that try to reconcile the lunar and solar cycles find them to be an unwieldy match. Cultures that have a lunar calendar only and link it directly to events in the natural world without writing it down on paper can avoid getting out of synch with the seasons. Environmentally linked lunar months are not only flexible, but potentially more accurate. The reindeer may be a bit late in giving birth one year, or the wild lilies early in blooming the next, due to weather patterns. Still, these events can be expected to occur within the month named for them, or a preceding month can be extended to make sure that things synch up. Natural events are highly predictable and they recur in a specific order over the year.

Once large, centralized civilizations take over, they have tended to adopt calendars based strictly on astronomical observations. For example, a year can be calculated as the time it takes the earth to orbit the sun. Due to variations in earth's orbit, this amount differs slightly each year. In the year 2000, the earth took 365.2564 days to get all the way around.[21] Alternatively, you can measure a year as the period between vernal equinoxes, the time in March when the sun passes directly over the equator as it moves from the southern to the northern hemisphere. This period also varies by up to several minutes, but usually lasts around 365.242 days.

But no matter how you measure the solar year, you cannot fit a whole number of 24–hour days into it. Similarly, the lunar phases vary in length and may depart from the mean duration of 29.53 days by up to 7 hours. The discrepancies add up, and so any month on the solar calendar maps to a different and uneven portion of the lunar month. Modern calendars—rigid by nature—do not cope well with this astronomical slippage and must confront the same old problem of staying in synch. To do so they require complex calculations and additions of 'intercalary' (or what we call 'leap') minutes, hours, days, or months to keep the solar year or lunar year more or less in synch. But such calculations must be constantly updated by precise astronomical observations, which for most of human history were impossible. Calculations that insert a leap day, February 29th, every fourth year would have been unfeasible just a few millennia ago.

Pre-modern societies devised clever and highly practical solutions. One method was to adopt a 13-month lunar cycle and anchor it to natural environmental events. In this case, it was important to make the units (months) flexible, or to stretch one of them, to stay in synch with nature. The Chukchee of Siberia used the highly predictable birthing time of the reindeer calves to reset their calendar annually. For example, they called the April lunar cycle '*graa-aa-alijn*' referring to the time when reindeer calves are born. But if in a particular year the deer may be born later, say in May, due to the shifting of lunar cycles vis-à-vis the solar year, the Chukchee simply called the May lunar cycle by the same name. By repeating one named month they could easily resynchronize their lunar calendar around a regular event—reindeer birth.[22]

The Nggela people of the Solomon Islands (10,000 speakers) synchronize their lunar calendar using a sea worm they call '*odu*'. This worm is said to begin its swarming and reproduction cycle precisely one hour after dark on the first or second night after the full moon in October. The sea worm itself remains buried in a burrow on the sea bed, but its reproductive organ breaks off and rises to the surface where it spreads the worm's sperm or eggs. The Nggela call the October lunar cycle 'coral sea worm' and the November cycle 'mother sea worm'.[23] Since they live off the sea, the Nggela notice tides and the behavior and migrations of sea life, and they can synchronize their hunting activities to this.

The Yurok people of northern California (fewer than 10 speakers left) traditionally began their year with the first lunar cycle after the winter solstice. As the calendar fell into disuse, Yurok speakers began to disagree over whether their calendar had 12 or 13 months. They did agree, however, on using the acorn harvest to reset the calendar. Anthropologist A. L. Kroeber observed this in 1925, though he failed to understand the utility of resetting a calendar through ecological indicators: "The older Yurok are aware that some of them allow 13 moons to a year and others only 12. When individual reckonings differ, long arguments result. But when the acorns are ripe for picking, disputes end, for then it is unquestionably *Nohso* [the tenth month]. This method of correction by seasonal phenomena is quaint in view of the [year's] unquestionable astronomical starting point."[24]

The Klamath people of Oregon (1 speaker left in 1998) adopted a 10-month cycle and did not name their months but simply counted them using the names of the 10 fingers (so each year had two months called "thumb" two known as "little finger", and so on). Though this is not an ecological calendar with months named for nature, the Klamath did use water-lilies to reset their calendar and fit their 10-month cycle to the lunar year. The Klamath lived in southern Oregon among enormous marshes where the *wokas*, an edible species of water lily, grew in great abundance. Each August they would harvest *wokas*, dry the seed pods, then roast and grind the seeds to make flour.[25]

Since the Klamath water-lily seed harvest predictably ended sometime in September, their new year began with the first new moon following the end of the *wokas* harvest. If by the following July they had used up all 10 fingers counting months, but the water-lilies were not yet ready for harvesting, they simply stretched out the tenth month over a longer period (up to two and a half months). This covered the harvest and seed processing period and ensured that the new year began right on time in October.

Kroeber, the anthropologist who documented the Klamath ecological calendar, failed to appreciate the adaptive advantages it provided. He noted with some disdain that this "quaint" native scheme was "little useful . . . even in the rudest way, for most of the practical purposes of our calendar."[26]

## Anchoring Time

Besides anchoring the lunar year to natural events, people have invented different ways to peg the year or other time units to physical objects or the body. Many cultures give a special name to the month that ends or

**Figure 3.4**
Klamath technologies for harvesting *wokas* (water-lily seeds) helped them recalibrate their lunar calendar. Reproduced from Coville 1902. Courtesy of SODA, Southern Oregon University

begins a year and anchors it to the body or some physical object.[27] The O'odham of Arizona begin their year in June and call December the 'backbone' month because it evenly divides the year.[28] The Koryak of Siberia observe a winter year and a summer year and call January the 'top of the head month' because it falls at the middle of their year, which begins in September. In the highland rice terraces of the Philippines, the Ifugao people call September 'a part in the hair' because it divides their year into two equal parts.[29]

The Chukchee, living at the extreme northeastern edge of Siberia, herd reindeer and have built their calendar around them. According to Harald Sverdrup, an ethnographer who visited the Chukchee in the 1920s, they also employed body-counting techniques to track the 13-moon cycle:

> When they want to explain which 'moon' they mean, they count on the finger joints and knuckles, wrist and elbow joints, shoulder and head. They begin, for instance, with the first Fall moon on the wrist of the right hand . . . then the second moon falls on the elbow, the first winter moon on the shoulder, midwinter moon on the head, and so forth.[30]

Sverdrup also noticed that though the Chukchee observe lunar cycles they do not subdivide them into countable days: "No one could tell me how many days are between two full moons, nor in a year."

The Tundra Yukaghir of Siberia refer to the year as 'all the joints' because they use a special body-counting method to track lunar months. If you make your two hands into fists, then butt your clenched fists together in front of you, so that your knuckles touch, you have assumed the special body position the Yukaghir people use to count months. They first count the crack between the fists where the knuckles come together, then move counterclockwise up the left arm counting the metacarpals, left wrist, left elbow, left shoulders, and so on.

While body-counting, the Yukaghir also name each month for an ecological theme: first month 'middle of summer' (July), second 'small mosquito' (August), third 'fish' (September), fourth 'wild-reindeer buck' (October), fifth 'autumn' (November). The sixth month is called 'before the ridge' because we have reached the shoulder in our body-count and will land next at the spine. The seventh, January, is 'ridge' or 'vertebrae' month and marks the half-year. We then continue down the right arm, once again touching body parts and naming ecological themes (May is 'deer calving month'), until we reach the space between the fists once again and complete one full body cycle of a year.[31] In this way the Yukaghir link moon phases to both the environment and the body.

## Shorter and Longer Time Units

The day and lunar month were the basic units of time-reckoning in most pre-modern cultures. People also kept track of units longer than a solar year in duration or less than a day in length. Judging by the rarity of these units across cultures, we can set them aside as less important than the lunar month. Many languages marked lunar months but did not number days or years. By contrast, cultures that had sequences of days or years typically used lunar months as well.

Prior to the introduction of modern clocks, there was no concept of the hour. But many cultures found it useful to subdivide the day and night into smaller segments. This allowed them to refer to specific times of day or increments of time. The Ifugao people of the Philippines designated a unit of time lasting 30 to 60 minutes called *ubun* or 'sitting' period', the amount of time one might sit down and rest on the trail during a journey.[32]

The Yukaghir people of Siberia (30 to 150 speakers) used a traditional unit they called 'the kettle boiled'.[33] It was originally conceived of as a distance, how far you could travel in the time it took a kettle of water to boil over a campfire. Since travel happens at different speed on foot and on horseback, the unit eventually came to refer to the period of kettle-boiling time (about an hour), not the distance traveled. This unit was so useful that they added another, slightly longer time unit that they called 'the frozen kettle boiled' (about 90 minutes). In that way they could say with some precision how long an interval of time lasted.[34]

The Borôro people of Amazonia (850 speakers) link the progressions of the sun during the day to points on the face and head. As anthropologist Stephen Fabian notes, they employ a very precise, rapid hand and arm gesture, which allows them to specify the angle and location of the spot in the sky where the sun will be at the hour they wish to refer to.[35]

When they position their arm and say the Borôro words for 'the sun here', the person receiving the order interprets the gesture correctly and arrives at the appointed time. The Borôro also anchor sun-time to the body by pointing to or naming locations on the face, head, and neck. Naming or pointing to 'mouth' means just after sunrise, while 'eye level' means early morning, 'forehead' denotes mid-morning, and 'back of the head' early afternoon. Body time is somewhat less precise than the hand-pointing method, but a bit more precise than a system like that of English that only names 'morning', 'mid-morning', and the like.

Units larger than the year are relatively rare. Before the arrival of the modern calendar, most indigenous cultures did not sequentially number years. This yields a different view of history, in which the past may be commemorated in song or epic, but people have no need to say an event took place, say, exactly 57 years ago. Similarly, most indigenous cultures never counted the ages of people in years, but instead used complex age categories based on physiognomy, social status, kinship, and other factors. Occasionally, though, we can find evidence of traditional cultures tracking certain supra-annual events, and periods of time spanning many months or years.

Cultures such as the Koryak of Siberia recognized two 'years'; a winter year and a 'summer' year that made up the solar year. These were usually linked to migration patterns, meteorological periods (dry vs. rainy), and important survival activities.

Anthropologist Harold Conklin describes how the Hanunóo people of the Philippines (13,000 speakers) used agricultural activity (slashing of vegetation to clear new garden plots) to track units longer than a year:

> the slashing period is normally a happy one for the entire community. . . . Since it is at this stage that the new pattern of swiddens and trails for the agricultural year first take shape, it is not strange that the Hanunóo most often discuss the duration of time covering more than a year by enumerating gāmas 'slashing(s)' rather than by other calendric means.[36]

Like many people of the tropics, the Xavante of Brazil (8,000 speakers) divided the year into 'rains' and 'dry season'. They could also keep track of periods of many years by linking these to social rituals. In Xavante society, all members are assigned to age groups that undergo initiation rituals together and move through assigned life stages from childhood to bachelorhood to marriage to old age in multi-year intervals. While individual Xavante do not typically know their age in years, they know what age class every person belongs to. They can use this system to refer to events as far as 40 years in the past by referring to the time when a particular age group was in the bachelors' hut (where the young men reside for 5 years after childhood but before initiation into manhood).

Some indigenous cultures also used the moon to track an extended astronomical cycle. The ancient Greeks' calendar was based in part on the 'Metonic' cycle named for an astronomer, Meton of Athens (ca. 440 B.C.). Meton discovered that it takes 235 lunar months (exactly 19 solar years) for the full moon to align again exactly the same way with any given star constellation. But it was not only large civilizations like the Greeks or Maya—with their mathematics and architecture—that tracked Metonic cycles. The Tupinamba people inhabiting Marajo Island off the coast of Brazil had a festival that occurred every 19 years, corresponding to one metonic cycle. Called the *yamaricura* feast, it was a time when men could behave and dress as women and vice versa.[37] Observing Metonic cycles does not require you keep track of days, or even years, but merely to note the phases of the moon and the position of the full moon in relation to stars. For example, if you see the full moon directly above the head of the well-known constellation Orion tonight, you would next see it that exact location in precisely 19 years. Amateur astronomers, if they do not wish to wait 19 years to observe the cycle, can run a simulation using free Internet-based tools such as "Your Sky."[38] Indigenous cultures had to be more patient to track Metonic cycles, using a lunar calendar that alternated 12- and 13-month years.[39]

The Kewa people (35,000 speakers), hunters and farmers of Papua New Guinea used multi-month cycles to maintain socio-economic relations among clans and villages. Political alliances and kin ties were reinforced by festivals at which large numbers of pigs would be slaughtered and certain key people or groups fed. The major pig-kill feast took place once every 47 lunar months. But as the Kewa did not recognize a unit of the year, they used a body-counting system to count these months. For example, starting at the little finger they would count 10 fingers, the wrist, and the right elbow, and then it was time for the *rake* festival. Continuing the count, up across the body and then down the other arm, the Kewa could determine the appropriate time for each event in the nearly four-year long feast cycle, without ever using a unit of time longer than the lunar month.[40]

| *Kewa festival* | *falls in the . . .* |
| --- | --- |
| *rake* feast | elbow (12th month) |
| *mena rudupu* pig festival | shoulder (15th month) |
| shell and pig festival | between the eyes (24th month) |
| *raguna yasa* dance of the long hats | 'other' shoulder (33rd month) |
| *kega yogo lapo* vegetable feast | 'other' elbow (36th month) |
| marsupial cooking festival | 'other' wrist (40th month) |
| *mena lie* pig-killing feast | 'other' little finger (47th month) |

When the lunar month for a Kewa pig-killing festival had been reckoned the traditional way, using the full body-month count, the ensuing festival took place. It is described by one anthropologist as follows:

> On that particular day, all the men from the various clans kill all of their full grown pigs very early in the morning and cut them up and roast them late in the morning of the same day. At about lunch time the pork is ready to be distributed among the relatives, friends and some other extended family members from other villages. Hundreds of people attend the pig kill and some of them go home without having eaten pork, because of having no friends or relatives.[41]

The elaborate Kewa feast cycle, once scheduled by counting lunar months on body parts, has recently—under outside influence—been held every five years as reckoned by modern calendars.

## Multilayered Seasonal Knowledge without Calendars

Some cultures notice lunar cycles but choose not to build their calendars upon them. The Kaluli people (2,000 speakers), tropical mountain agriculturalists of Papua New Guinea, name three main seasons after vegetative cycles: the fruiting of magnolia trees, the falling of leaves around the bases of trees, and the ripening of the *marita* fruit. Anthropologist Edward Schiefflin notes that "the Kaluli are not counting months or moons or noting changes in the weather, but reading the indications of forest vegetation." The Kaluli tie other seasonal periods to the appearance of specific birds or plants. The season called *ten* that runs from April to September is named for the Rainbow Bee-eater, a bird the Kaluli refer to as '*bili*'. The anthropologist describes how the bird serves as a seasonal harbinger: "at the beginning of *ten* in 1977, I heard several youths running across the courtyard yelling, '*Ten*'s really here; we heard *bili*.' "[42]

Weaving weather, plant, and animal cycles into a complex annual calendar is a common strategy and an alternative or complement to the lunar model. It has the added advantage that it never need be synched up with astronomical observations. The blooming of plants and arrival of animals on which people rely for sustenance unfolds predictably and dependably. These can thus serve as a way to orient oneself within longer time cycles.

One of the more complex environmental calendars described is from the Yanyuwa people (70 to 100 speakers), aborigines of Australia, who keep track of many overlapping cycles of edible fruits, meteorological periods, and game animals. Anthropologist Richard Baker, who studies Yanyuwa ecological knowledge, notes that in contrast to cultures that track lunar months and moon phases, for the Yanyuwa, "the exact date of the onset of seasons is variable. It is *the sequence and not the date* of their occurrence that is recorded in Yanyuwa knowledge of the seasons." He describes how the Yanyuwa construct their calendar by linking ecological events:

> For the Yanyuwa these factors are linked, as they have a detailed knowledge of the interconnections between the animal and plant worlds and seasonal climatic patterns. For example, the flowering times of various plants are known to correspond with specific animal resources. The acacia, *ma-kawurrka*, is known to flower when dugong and turtle move close to the shore and are particularly 'fat'. Similarly, it is known that dugong are easy to hunt at the time of the year when *na-wurlurlu* (cuttle fish shells) are washed up on the beaches, and the arrival of the Torres Strait pigeon heralds the end of the hot *ngardaru* season. In other cases the connections between plant and animal worlds are more directly linked . . . bush honey, for example, is particularly rich and plentiful in the early dry season as a result of the number of plants in flower at that time of year.[43]

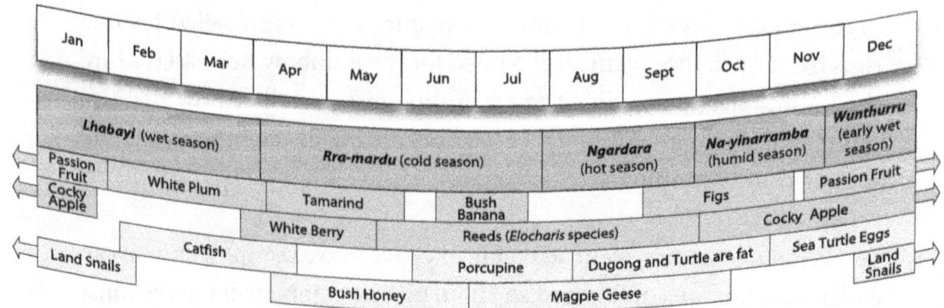


**Figure 3.5**
A partial set of Yanyuwa seasonal ecological knowledge in three domains: seasons, edible plants, and game animals. I have placed the names of English months above this for comparison only—the match is far from exact.

## Linking the Moon to the Fishes

The Marovo people of the Solomon Islands are extraordinary fishermen—they are said to use a greater variety of marine species than almost any other maritime people. As mentioned in chapter 1, the Marovo have a special vocabulary to describe different types of aggregating and swimming behaviors of fish schools. Their word *ukuka*, for example, refers to "the behavior of groups of fish when individuals drift, circle and float as if drunk."[44] Many fish behavior terms are linked to exact days or short periods of days on the lunar calendar. For example, blue-finned jacks, fish that normally swim solo, form groups around the outer edge of the barrier reef during two- or three-day periods precisely at the time of the new moon. When they do this, the blue-finned jacks are full of eggs and easy for fishermen to spear.

Marovo success in fishing and maritime survival is thus directly due to their intellectual achievement in making the tightest possible linkage between the lunar calendar and the rhythms of their ecological niche. This is not surprising, since they are a maritime people, and they survive by applying their deep knowledge of the habits of sea creatures to find sustenance. Much more than land creatures, the lives and rhythms of sea creatures respond to the moon's phases. For the Marovo, who have built up knowledge of these correlations over centuries, specific days of the lunar calendar can be anchored to specific reproductive, aggregating, and feeding behaviors of a multitude of sea animals. This facilitates efficient hunting and gathering, and therefore survival.

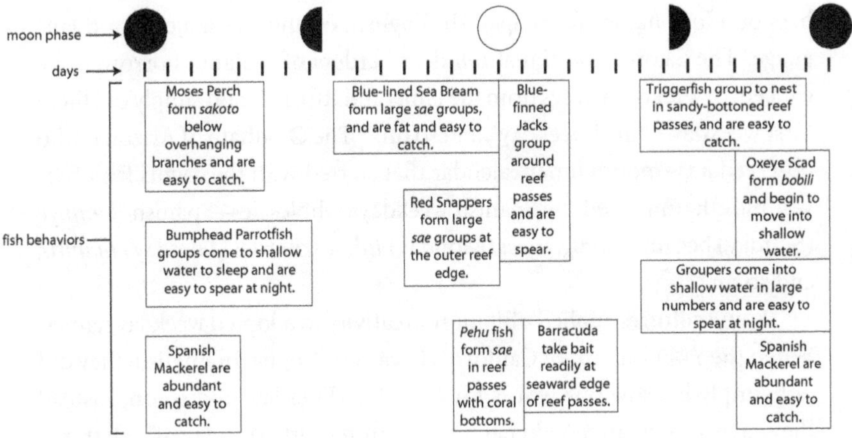


**Figure 3.6**
Traditional Marovo knowledge links lunar periods and fish behaviors.

## Before the Seven-Day Week

Modern societies take the seven-day week entirely for granted. It seems so much a natural category that people express surprise when asked where the seven-day week came from. Some cite the biblical creation account, that God created new things each day for six days then rested on the seventh. But the week is not a natural unit based on patterns observable in the cosmos or bio-rhythms. The week is not perceptually detectable and does not map neatly either onto the lunar year or the solar month.[45]

Linguist Ray Jackendoff has observed that the week, a unit of seven days, is a "completely non-perceptual unit," and one that cannot "be conceived of at all without linguistic anchoring."[46] It follows from this argument that if a language has no word for week (as many languages do not), then the concept may not exist for those cultures, since it is entirely abstract.

Indeed, the notion of the week turns out to be missing entirely from most languages. An early ethnographer who visited the Yukaghir of Siberia noted in his journal: "The Yukaghir used to take no account of weeks, and there were no names for week-days. At present they use the Russian names."[47]

When indigenous cultures adopt weekday names, as they inevitably must to fit in the modern world, they tend to simply assign them numbers or adopt names from Spanish, English, or another major world language. The Saami, traditional reindeer herders of Finland, borrowed the concept of weekday names from the Finns and Russians and simply call them 'first weekday', 'third weekday', and so on.[48] The O'odham of Arizona, who observed a 13–month lunar calendar that started with the cactus fruit harvest month, imported the Spanish weekdays wholesale—Spanish *domingo* (Sunday) became *domig, lunes* (Monday) *luhnas, martes* (Tuesday) *mahltis,* and so on.[49]

Some cultures applied a bit more creativity to adopted weekday names. When the Yuki Indians of California became bilingual in English, they did not simply borrow our words for Monday, Tuesday, and so on, instead they gave days creative Yuki names, beginning with Monday, which translates as 'work get up', then 'work two', 'work three', and so on until 'work one day remaining' (Saturday) and then 'work rest' day (Sunday).[50]

But what have these cultures given up in adopting the modern week? Was there a pre-modern time unit larger than the 24-hour day but smaller than the lunar month? If so, what purpose did it serve in allowing humans to adapt to diverse environments and manage ecological risk and rewards? For clues we turn again to languages like Yuki, now nearly extinct with fewer than 6 speakers left in California. The Yuki used a day-naming system that was limited to today (*ka inái*), tomorrow (*hao,* 'morning star'), the day after tomorrow (*wánk haó,* 'next morning star'), yesterday (*sum*), and the day before yesterday (*husám,* 'before'). So, the Yuki could refer easily to any cluster of five consecutive days. Of course, the Yuki could also presumably say things like '17 days from tomorrow' if they needed to, but what concerns us here is the number of days on either side of today that they regarded as useful to give names to. Their conceptual unit was a mobile, five-day week.

Most traditional calendars seemed to lack the notion of a fixed, sequential week. Instead, they tracked a mobile week, ranging from five to ten days in duration and centered around today. This allowed people to refer easily to 'the day before yesterday' or 'four days ago', or 'six days from today'—arguably for them a more useful temporal orientation than a fixed week. One can imagine getting by just fine in many cultures without ever needing to refer to 'two Tuesdays ago' or 'every Sunday.' English has weekday names, but is oddly deficient in this kind of day-naming. We have no way to express in a single word the concepts 'three days ago' or 'the day after tomorrow'.

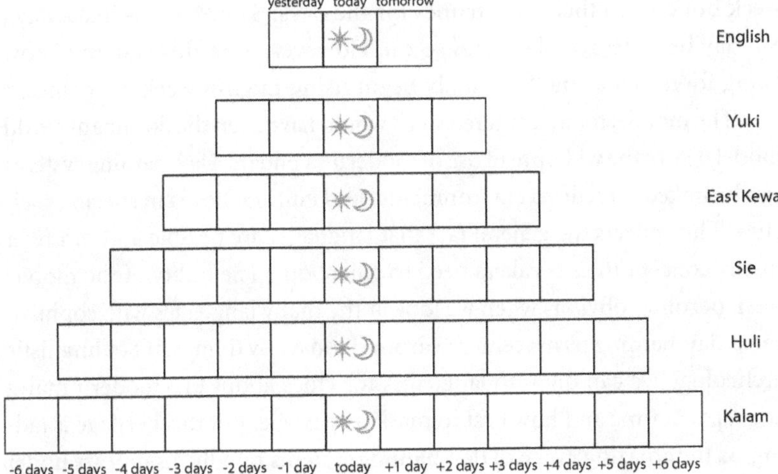


**Figure 3.7**
Days on either side of today that can be expressed by a single word in different languages: Yuki (California), East Kewa (Papua New Guinea), Sie (Vanuatu), Huli (Papua New Guinea), Kalam (Papua New Guinea), and English.

Aneityum (600 speakers), a language of Vanuatu, has a mirror system in which the names for day before yesterday and day after tomorrow are *identical*, and the hearer must decide based on context whether it means past or future.

| | *Aneityum days*[51] | *English* |
|---|---|---|
| −3 | *hovid* | three days ago |
| −2 | *invid* | day before yesterday |
| | . . . | |
| 0 | *inpiñ* | today |
| | . . . | |
| +2 | *invid* | day after tomorrow |
| +3 | *hovid* | three days from now |

The Sie people (1,200 speakers), also of Vanuatu, keep track of a nine-day span centered around today. Names in the past and future are alike, with an extra prefix added to past days: *wimpe* means 'four days from now', while *no-wimpe* is 'four days ago'. Using only this system, the Sie lacked weekday names. After contact with missionaries, they adopted a seven-day week but coined their own names for the days: Saturday was 'bake day', Sunday became 'rest day', and so on. However, even this system is now being forgotten as the Sie simply begin using English weekday names.[52]

The mobile, today-centered week would have been the dominant world model before the widespread use of modern calendars. Day-naming systems can be linked directly to environmental and cultural needs in specific societies. This reflects the general fact that languages are flexible and can refer to any concept their speakers need to talk about. The utility of the mobile week becomes obvious when we look at the many languages with sophisticated day-naming terms centered around today. By doing a bit of linguistic archeology we can dig into languages for clues about pre-modern man's concepts of time and how best to mark its passage. But this heritage is fading, as the amazing range of day-naming systems rapidly disappears under pressure from the worldwide seven-day calendar week.[53]

## Types of Time-Reckoning

As traditional calendars are forgotten, it becomes harder to reconstruct their internal logic and discern what, besides moon phases and local ecological cycles, they may have been tracking. Many anthropologists have documented complex star lore and knowledge of astronomical bodies, cycles, and patterns.[54] We will not explore this topic further here, except to note that lunar calendars form just one small part of a vast body of traditional, never-written-down, astronomical knowledge. For millennia, humans have noticed and tracked both heavenly and earthly phenomena. Using myth, story, ritual, architecture, and the human body, different cultures have forged cognitive links between the two domains. Some of these links contributed directly to survival and subsistence, while for others, the connection is less obvious and may be purely aesthetic.

Through their systems of time-reckoning—whether at the level of hours, days, weeks, months, or years—small and endangered languages provide us a window not only into human cognition but also into prehistory. In the ways they anchor time units to earth, the body, and nature, they show how time-reckoning has served humankind as a survival skill. We find an incredible variety in the different temporal units people kept track of, and vast creativity in the ways of naming, marking, organizing, and numbering them.

People clearly kept track of days and moon phases, which add up to lunar months. Some cultures also synched these up with the solar year or with annual plant and animal cycles. The key to keeping these different cycles on track was flexibility. This was accomplished by having one or more stretchable months synched to specific environmental events, by adding a leap period, or by alternating 12- and 13-month years.

In addition to being flexible, such calendars were highly local and adaptable, tying each month to natural events. If hunting-gathering conditions or agricultural cycles changed, new fruits became important, new animals appeared, or people migrated to a new place, calendars could change to reflect this.[55]

Lunar calendars, whatever their utility, arise out of centuries and millennia of collective thought, of noticing patterns, and of consensus and

**Table 3.4**
**One way to look at the different kinds of months**

| *Type* | *Example* | *Example of calendars which use this type* |
|---|---|---|
| Ecological | 'Crab Season' is defined by when the crabs migrate. The crab cycle interlocks with many other ecological cycles of short and partially overlapping durations. | Yanyuwa |
| Ecological, linked to lunar | 'Crab Moon' is one lunar period during which crabs migrate. | Saami |
| Lunar, linked to ecological | 'Crab Moon' is the name for a lunar period defined by sequential moon cycles. Although the name for the month still may offer ecological predictive power, ecological cycles are no longer used to define or signal the period. | Warao |
| Lunar | 'Third Moon' is now the name for the month, as defined by sequential lunar cycles. | Muslim |
| Arbitrary | 'March' is now the name for the month, which is arbitrary and defined only by sequentiality. | English |

ritual arising within a particular culture. The lunar calendar may have been invented once and then evolved along different trajectories, but more probably has been invented spontaneously over and over among different human populations, few of which saw fit to ignore the moon. Each culture made decisions, refined over time, about to how to link ecological events to temporal rhythms and cycles. We cannot always reconstruct the intricate logic of such systems, just as we cannot reconstruct damaged or destroyed ecosystems. This is why we need to document as many calendar systems as we can in hopes of finding the common or comparable elements.

As the worldwide culture of clocks, timekeeping, and modern calendars marches to dominance, it renders entire bodies of knowledge outmoded, obsolete, and vulnerable to abandonment. And as indigenous people switch over to speaking large world tongues like Spanish and Portuguese, they simply adopt the new constellations, calendar months, and time concepts of these large languages.

## Farewell, Edible Lily Month

We have already lost many (if not most) of these complex, fragile, and highly local calendars, these ingenious time-reckoning devices. One response to this loss is to say that ecological and lunar calendars would have been of little use in the modern world. Surely people are better off abandoning quaint old ways and adopting modern timekeeping. Independently of whether this is true, we may sense the loss of highly developed knowledge that evolved in specific environmental niches and to overcome specific survival challenges. We will never know the full extent of what these calendars may have revealed about domestication of plants and animals, hunting and gathering lifeways, astronomical skills, and early philosophies of math and of the cosmos. We look up at the night sky just as mankind has always done, and we see the sun rise and seasons change. If we are particularly astute, we may even notice the North Star in its fixed position, or the blooming of certain wild flowers at a predictable time of year.

Nowadays we live mostly in blissful detachment from all this, and we leave the calculations to astronomers, botanists, almanac writers, and meteorologists. There is little point in being sentimental, but can we really be so confident that this lost calendar knowledge would have contributed nothing to our twenty-first-century world? I fondly recall Aunt Marta, the elderly Siberian hunter and reindeer herder, and her delight in introducing me to the blooming *saranki* flowers as harbingers of the tenth lunation. I have certainly never experienced a comparable joy in showing someone a calendar page of October. For Marta and her clan, the tiny purple lily's brief appearance on the mossy forest floor was as essential yet banal as the passage of time itself. Natural calendar lore served as a bond firmly connecting humankind to the natural world; this bond weakens when languages die.

## Nomads of Western Mongolia

In the vast, open plains of Western Mongolia, the nomadic Monchak people move freely with their herds across thousands of acres of fence-free grazing lands. Mongolia has fewer than five persons per square mile and less than 9,000 miles of paved roads.[1] A full 40 percent of the population practice nomadic animal herding: they raise yaks, sheep, goats, horses, and camels. Despite the large expanses of land and freedom to roam, the small-numbering Monchak feel crowded—both physically and culturally. One of the smallest ethnic groups in this country, comprising fewer than 500 souls among 2.8 million people, they suffer ethnic discrimination, poverty, and incursions on their traditional grazing lands.

The Monchak are unrecognized by the government as an ethnic minority. They have no schooling, radio broadcasts, or books in their native tongue. They must record Mongolian names on their children's birth certificates. Only about 150 of them still speak the ancestral Monchak language fluently.

When I visited the Monchak community for a fourth time in 2004, I brought them copies of a Tuvan–English dictionary. Monchak is a distant dialect of Tuvan, a language spoken about 150 miles to the north, and shares many words in common. The dictionary was the product of years of painstaking work undertaken with my fellow linguist Greg Anderson. Most of the entries were words we had collected in Tuva but a good number were collected directly from the mouths of Monchak speakers pictured in this section.

Most Monchaks are literate, having been schooled in Mongolian. But most had never before seen words from their native tongue in written form. They were simply astonished to see on paper words they could easily recognize in their native tongue. The dictionary got passed around and people took turns reading words aloud, beginning with 'a'—*aar* means 'heavy', *aari* means 'bee'. Each recognized word evoked chuckles or nods of agreement. The mood turned celebratory, and fermented mare's milk was offered all around. This scene was repeated as I traveled from camp to camp.

Surrounded by Mongolians and sent to Mongolian schools, the Monchak struggle to maintain their own ethnic identity. They consider

Members of the Monchak community reading aloud from the Tuvan–English Dictionary (top) and seeing for the first time words written in their native tongue (bottom) (2004). Photographs by K. David Harrison language a crucial part of that identity, something that marks them as distinct. Horse brands matter too—their unique brand makes their livestock instantly distinguishable from Mongolians' herds. Their yurts—collapsible felt houses—also differ in their structure and interior layout. Beyond language, horse brands, and yurts, the Monchaks differ little from Mongolians in physical appearance or dress. They can easily blend in if they wish, especially in the towns.

A less visible marker of identity is the 'secret' name. Every Monchak has an official Mongolian name written on his or her birth certificate and used in all interactions with outsiders. Within the community, name use depends on what language is being spoken and by whom. If there are three older adults and four younger ones in a yurt, the conversation will be held strictly in Mongolian. If the balance shifts, or, for example, if a visiting linguist speaks Monchak with them, or only older adults are present, the conversation will shift too.

When the language of conversation shifts, everybody gets called by their Monchak name. These names are not written down anywhere, but are more familiar, more intimate, and often express some personal quality: 'Brave', 'Joyful', 'Golden', 'Hunter', 'Cowboy', and so on. Monchak names are held in strict secrecy from outsiders—to fit in, Monchaks need to have Mongolian sounding names.

One young man I met had the Monchak name 'No name'. When I addressed him for the first time by his real name, he was so embarrassed he literally crawled under a nearby bed to avoid answering my question. Later, he became quite talkative and even allowed me to make video recordings of him singing Monchak songs.

"Would a Monchak guy marry a Mongolian girl?" I asked my friend Demdi in 2000. Demdi was then an eligible young bachelor of 24. "No way," he replied without hesitation. "Why not?" I inquired. Demdi answered, without hesitation, *dilivis*, a single word meaning 'our language'. I thought it odd that Demdi would have identified language—especially one that few of his peers spoke—as the most important factor disfavoring inter-ethnic marriage. I wondered, but did not ask, if he would marry an ethnic Monchak who did not speak the language. This seemed a likely scenario, since I observed that young Monchak men continue to speak the language in far greater numbers and with greater fluency than do females.

Ironically, two years later when I visited the same community in 2002, Demdi had taken a wife who was ethnically half Monchak and half Mongolian and was monolingual in the Mongolian language. Demdi still spoke to his own father in Monchak, but his 1-year-old son was spoken to exclusively in Mongolian. His three-generation household was a study in language shift.

The Monchak confront the same dilemmas that minority ethnic groups face everywhere. The younger generation speak the national language fluently and can blend in if they choose. The elder generation feels keenly the loss of community and identity. They discourage their children from inter-marrying. Sometimes they even speak to them in Monchak, and are partially understood, but it is almost impossible to find anyone under the age 18 in the community that can speak back.

Language shift—the process by which younger people in a community choose not to speak the ancestral language and opt for the dominant national language—is well under way here. Under current trends, Monchak will cease to be spoken in 50 to 60 years. The Monchaks will have been linguistically fully assimilated to Mongolian.

I found among the very youngest generation people like 7-year-old Aldin-shagaa (her name means 'golden new-year'). She would not speak a word of her parents' language and showed little sign of understanding it. But one evening in June of 2000 when we sat in the yurt drinking tea by candlelight, she was persuaded to sing—in her parents' tongue—a beautiful song about being Monchak: "I am a Monchak, daughter of the silver snow-capped mountains . . ." It seemed that this little song was all she could produce in her parents' language. In visits to her family in 2002 and 2004, I never heard her utter another Monchak word.

The most important cultural memory of the Monchak is encapsulated in their song called 'Eevi River'. The song mentions several rivers by name and gives descriptive words denoting how the waters look and sound. When the older people sing 'Eevi River', they experience a spiritual joy, and get tears in their eyes. The Eevi lies in the ancestral homeland in China's Xingjian Province where the Monchaks lived before migrating to Mongolia in the 1930s and 1950s. Only the very oldest among the Monchak actually claim to have seen the Eevi, and the song nostalgically commemorates hardship, relocation, identity, and sentiment for the homeland. The young generation I talked to admit the song is important but say they do not know how to sing it. In a community that has no history of its own other than memory, the disappearance of this song foretells a history forgotten.

As I write this in 2005, I can report that almost one-third of the Monchak community—some 200 people—has relocated to the yurt shanty-towns that ring Mongolia's capital city Ulaan Bator. Conditions here are less than ideal—hard labor for menial pay, no plumbing, and a life on the margins of Mongolia's transition from herding culture to information society. Monchak youngsters (like 'No name', whom I met in 2000 out on the plains herding camels) now work in factories processing industrial scrap metal and send text messages on their cell phones. They like city life—"it's beautiful" one Monchak girl told me—and I have no reason to think they will ever go back to herding sheep. Nothing in their urban environment favors the continued use of their distinctive ancestral language. In fact, they are trying their hardest to blend in.

I (center) interview Monchak speakers Tserenedmit (left) and Nyaama (right) in 2004 as they prepare a slaughtered sheep in the traditional Monchak way. Courtesy of Kelly Richardson

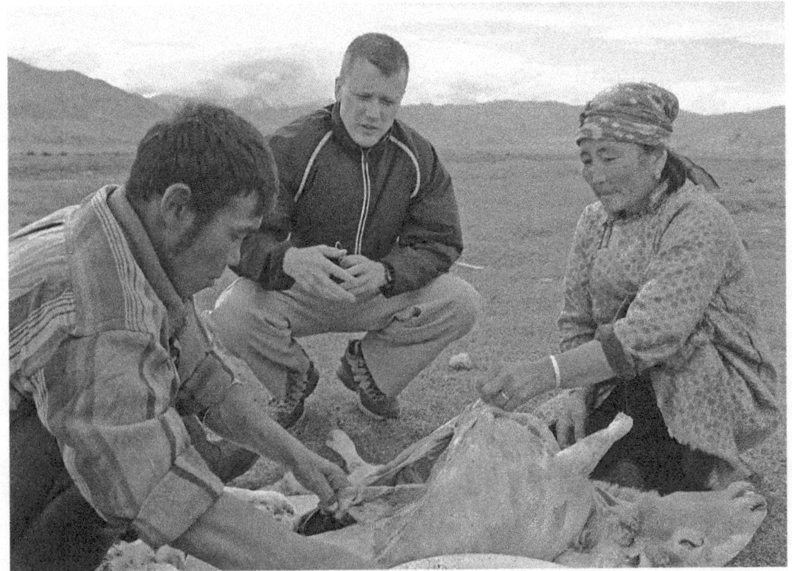

Land, livelihood, and language are intimately connected. What the Monchaks will lose, by relocating to urban areas and giving up their ancestral tongue, is cultural knowledge—how to live the traditional way of life that has sustained them up to now, and how to preserve remembered histories central to their identity as a people.[2]

Many adults know techniques for healing human and animal diseases, rituals for practicing animism, songs and oral histories never put to writing. They may not need any of these things to live in the city. But given the deep attachment many Monchaks have expressed for their history and language, it is hard to imagine they will not miss them. The community is now split: those who have moved to the city cannot imagine going back, and those in the country cannot imagine leaving it. Both factions are undergoing language shift and cultural assimilation, simply at different tempos. The momentum is with the urbanites, as more of those in the country give up the herding life and flock to join them. Those who do stay in the countryside, pressed on all sides by dominant Mongolian culture, are already shifting languages. Globalization and urbanization proceed, and in this particular community, they will soon snuff out the last word of this once vibrant nomadic tongue.

# 4 An Atlas in the Mind

Угаанда тѳнчу чок
Mind has no end.
— Tuvan saying

Language is the most massive and inclusive art we know,
a mountainous and unconscious work
of anonymous generations.
— Edward Sapir, *Language* (1921)

After trekking 12 hours in deep Siberian forests, I felt certain we were lost. We had set out, our party of three linguists plus a native Tofa guide, early that morning on foot from the remote village of Nersa. Set high in the Sayan Mountains, Nersa is the smallest of three villages inhabited by the reindeer-herding Tofa people. Home to just under a hundred hardy souls, the village is accessible only by helicopter, on reindeer-back, or on foot. The Tofa we met there subsisted on small vegetable plots, hunting, and gathering berries and other forest edibles, and a few supplies (flour, sugar, vodka) flown in occasionally on decrepit Russian helicopters. Their domestic reindeer herds, they told us, had long since turned wild and run off. As herding ceased to be a viable livelihood, many villagers sank into despair and alcoholism. Despite the bleak circumstances, our party was warmly welcomed, and we found people eager to share their stories. Perhaps this was because no one else ever asked to hear stories in the Tofa language. Indeed, no one under age 55 spoke Tofa anymore. "We were all sent away to boarding school," explained 35-year-old Valentina S., "and that's why we don't know our language."

For three days we canvassed tiny Nersa village, tracking down anyone who knew even a few words of Tofa. Eighteen-year-old Vova paused from a volleyball game with his buddies to tell us a bilingual joke. It was entirely in Russian except for the key words 'pig' and 'penis', spoken in Tofa and accompanied by loud guffaws. I faithfully wrote down Vova's anecdote in my field notebook, hoping that he might turn out to be a young bilingual speaker. But these two words in a joke about a well-endowed swine turned out to be the entirety of Vova's Tofa vocabulary.

At the extreme other end of the age and wisdom scale, we found Nersa's eldest resident, "Uncle Peter" B. (born 1925) sitting alone in his rustic log cabin that contained nothing but a single cot. A red wooden star affixed to the cabin's front honored Peter as a veteran of the Great Patriotic War (World War II). We sat transfixed on the floor of Peter's rude cabin, brushing away fleas and grasping at his every word. He told us, haltingly but speaking only in Tofa, how in 1946 he had returned alone on foot from the eastern war front where he had been sent as a Red Army conscript to fight the Japanese in Manchuria. The trek, over 1,400 miles long, took him months, tested his superb survival and orientation skills, and left him with a permanent limp. Peter was clearly moved by our meeting. "I can't believe foreigners are talking with me in my own Tofa language," he remarked tearfully. "It's like in a dream."[1]

Two houses down, Constantine M., a hale and deep-voiced 56-year-old, told us a Tofa story of three bothers turned into mountains as punishment after a quarrel over land inheritance. Pointing towards the Sayan range, he indicated the exact three peaks that had formerly been the three brothers. He also told us how he had been punished as a child for speaking his native language, beaten with a switch and held back in the first grade for five years because he could not answer his teacher in Russian. His story of shame and abandonment of the ancestral language turned out to be a typical Tofa tale.

Just across the way we found Svetlana A., a cheery lady of 62 and former elementary schoolteacher, weeding her potato garden. She too was of the generation that had been pressured to become Russian. "I lived in the boarding school dormitory for ten years," she told us. "During that time . . . I never even heard Tofa and wasn't aware that I knew the language. I guess it was forbidden to talk Tofa then—everybody spoke Russian. Such a beautiful, difficult language! Now it's all been forgotten. Everyone's become Russian."

Svetlana told us a poignant tale of a man and woman who lived so deep in the forest and saw no people for such a long time that they came to believe they were the only people left in the whole wide world. They were rescued from their solitude one day when their dog's barking attracted a wandering hunter who offered to lead them back to human settlement. But the hunter needed to depart at once, so the husband, gravely ill, sent his young wife back to live with people and stayed behind alone to die. Svetlana framed this for us as a story of true love. Reading between the lines, we gathered that her story was also about solitude, perhaps similar to the kind that comes from having no one to talk to in one's native language.

Saddened, we departed Nersa, village of mostly forgotten stories. Loaded down with gifts of bread, berries, and our precious videotapes of Tofa stories, we set out with a native guide to return to the main village, Alygdzher, situated 15 miles upstream as the crow flies. The route on foot was winding, but the village mayor, a hardy Siberian German, assured us it was a doable five-hour trek. Our guide was a young man of 25 who seemed reasonably spry and self-assured as he, on horseback, led us, on foot, up and into the mountain forests at 8 a.m. But as midnight that same day approached and we stumbled along through the marshy woods, exhausted, leg-cramped, and bug-bitten, our guide offered little reassurance. He had taken repeated wrong turns throughout the day, his horse stumbled, his confidence evaporated, and we straggled. To our great dismay, we realized he had even set out with a gun but no bullets and no knife—the height of foolhardiness in forests rife with bears.

We grew impatient, but our guide gave a different answer each time I asked him "How many more rivers do we have to cross?" At the bank of one large river, the umpteenth of the day, I actually caught him shaking his head and muttering "There didn't used to be water here." Our guide crossed over high and dry on his horse, taking our packs and leaving us to wade as best we could. We three stripped down to boots and boxer shorts (taking the opportunity to expel wood ticks from our clothing but exposing ourselves to hungry mosquitoes), balanced our clothing on our heads, and waded into the frigid chest-high currents. Drying off on the other side, I cursed our idiot guide and wondered at his sheer ignorance. "What's the name of this fucking river anyway?" I barked at him. "The Uda, probably," he laconically answered. How is it, I fumed, that with Tofa life so tied to forest and landscape, hunting and season, an able-bodied Tofa man could be ignorant of the locations of major rivers?

I did not have to wait too long for an answer. We did finally reach the main village at 2 a.m., shivering and dehydrated. The last river we needed to cross, this time the Uda for sure, was too deep. We were now on the wrong side, but in sight of the sleeping village. By building a huge bonfire and shouting, we awoke the ferryman, who came sleepily to fetch us. The next day our guide blew his entire $30 fee on vodka and got falling-down

**Figure 4.1**
Aerial view of the Uda River as it flows past Alygdzher, the main Tofa village. Photograph by Thomas Hegenbart, courtesy of Contact Press Images

drunk, spreading the news of our fumbled expedition all over the village. We found ourselves the object of sympathy and considerable village gossip. "How could you hire such a guide?" people marveled. Elders shook their heads in dismay. "Our young people don't know their own forests nowadays," Aunt Marta K. said. She had spent decades hunting squirrels in the forests and herding reindeer, and knew by name every tributary and ridge, cave and hollow.

Aunt Marta had a good laugh at our expense, but the very idea that a local could get lost in the woods meant that her world had turned upside down. For her, this was not only a mental but a spiritual decay. In Marta's younger years, the entire Tofa territory was divided into ancestral hunting grounds for exclusive use by individual clans. Boundaries existed solely in memory, passed down from father to daughter and son, and strictly observed. Though one could roam freely anywhere, no Tofa hunter would think of poaching on the territory of another clan, both out of fear of angering that clan, and also of arousing local spirits who might do harm. When hunting on their own clan territory, the Tofa faithfully made offerings of tea, squirrel meat, and reindeer milk to the fire, lake, and river gods to repay them for success in hunting and the use of the land. The land was to be worshipped, and it bestowed blessings in return.[2]

Worshipping the land was not merely a metaphor for the Tofa, it was daily practice. While out hunting, Tofa would collect *kastarma* stones—mysterious and perfectly symmetrical round pebbles, shaped like little spinning tops, flying saucers, or buttons, found along lakesides and riverbeds.[3] Tofa people prized and revered the stones as gifts from *Kastarma*, deity of a local lake. Women sewed them as decorations onto buckskin clothing and saddlebags. Finding a *kastarma* stone meant a blessing bestowed or wish granted, and once taken, it would surely—they believed—be replenished later by the god, but only if he (or she) was satisfied with the balance of proper relations between animal and forest, spirits and people, water and clay. Our lost expedition was understood by some Tofa elders as an omen of imbalance, one requiring a propitiation of the spirits.

Our idiot guide sobered up fully three days after our trek and found that his horse had run away (presumably having no trouble finding *its* way home). Scolding him, I forced a confession that he had last made the trek between the two villages four years ago. I was shocked that between these two villages—the only two human habitations for hundreds of miles—people had ceased to venture. The elders, by contrast, knew every trail, every spring, every mountain ridge intimately and remembered a time when success in hunting and reindeer herding, indeed survival itself, depended on the sober application of such knowledge.

## Mind versus Map

Like most native Siberian peoples, the Tofa oriented themselves first and foremost by rivers and secondarily by mountains. Their basic unit of distance, called a *kösh*, denoted how far one could ride in a day on reindeerback. European observers misunderstood this to be a unit of *distance*, about 25 kilometers.[4] But for people inhabiting mountainous terrain, such as the Tofa, or the Sherpa of Nepal, units of linear distance have little utility.[5] The Tofa *kösh* in fact is a unit of time *and* effort—the actual distance you can cover in a day on reindeer back will depend on terrain, snowfall, and other conditions.

Tofa elders possess intricate knowledge of the rivers, streams, and tributaries of the Uda River basin that drain a thousand square miles of forest. A local Russian who had lived among the Tofa for decades wrote down in a notebook over 600 Tofa geographic names, over half of these being names of bodies of water. Unfortunately, the name collection was lost after being donated to the local museum. But the Tofa themselves never saw any need to write down these names. They simply kept a virtual atlas of Tofa-land in their heads, where it was more useful, but also much more fragile.

After the demise of reindeer herding in the 1980s, and a subsequent decline in hunting, young Tofa ventured less and less often into the forests. Many no longer knew the location of their ancestral hunting grounds and had never learned names of major rivers and mountains. Elders who possess the knowledge are no longer able to roam the forests, while youngsters remain in the villages ignorant of the forests and lacking any need to herd deer or hunt. All this knowledge, an entire atlas in the mind, has vanished in just two generations. We can, of course, view the Uda River basin from satellites or on Google Earth, capturing even the most minute details. But these land features no longer have a *human* geography, they no longer have Tofa names. This remote land, once criss-crossed with human footpaths and well mapped in Tofa stories, has once again become untraversed and largely unnamed territory.

Maps can capture only a fraction of people's mental knowledge of landscapes. Some Siberian native peoples independently developed graphic mapmaking traditions, etching maps of rivers, sky, or mountains onto birch bark or wood, or even sewing star and river maps as designs onto shamans' costumes.[6] Others, like the Tofa, are reported to have lacked any notion of physical maps at the time of first European contact.

Fortunately, we have a historical snapshot of the Tofa mental atlas. In 1908 a Russian explorer named Vasilevich visited the nomadic Tofa reindeer herders. He recounted how they, lacking any notion of maps at all, marveled at his rudimentary maps of their territory. The Tofa had never drawn maps before, either in sand or on the snow, much less on paper. The Russian showed them his maps, then gave them paper and pencil and asked them to map their land. We should keep in mind that in 1908 the Tofa people were living on ancestral territory they had never left, limited to places they could reach on foot and on reindeer, and having trade and cultural contacts only with neighboring indigenous peoples, the Tuvans and the Soyots.

The map the Tofa produced was impressive, given their lack of practice in an unfamiliar medium. It shows a bird's-eye view of the entire Uda River system, but also differs in telling ways from the actual topography.

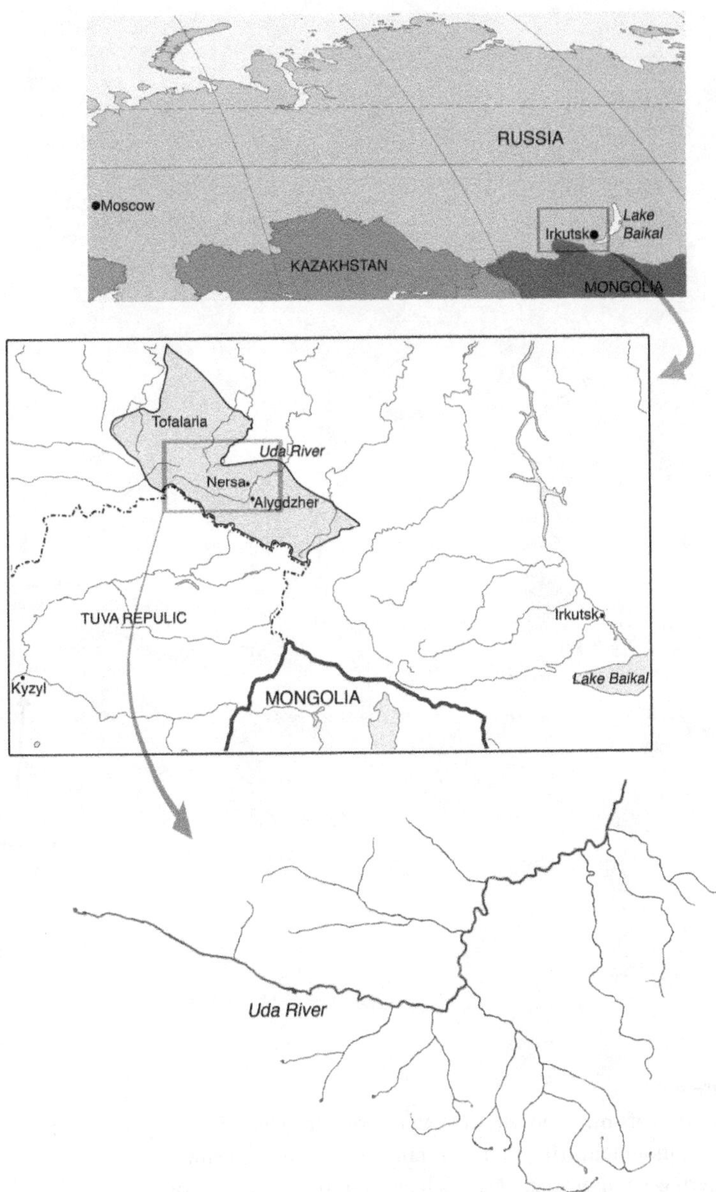


**Figure 4.2**
Northern Eurasia (top), the Tofa territory (middle), and the Uda River basin (bottom). Graphic by Robbie Hart

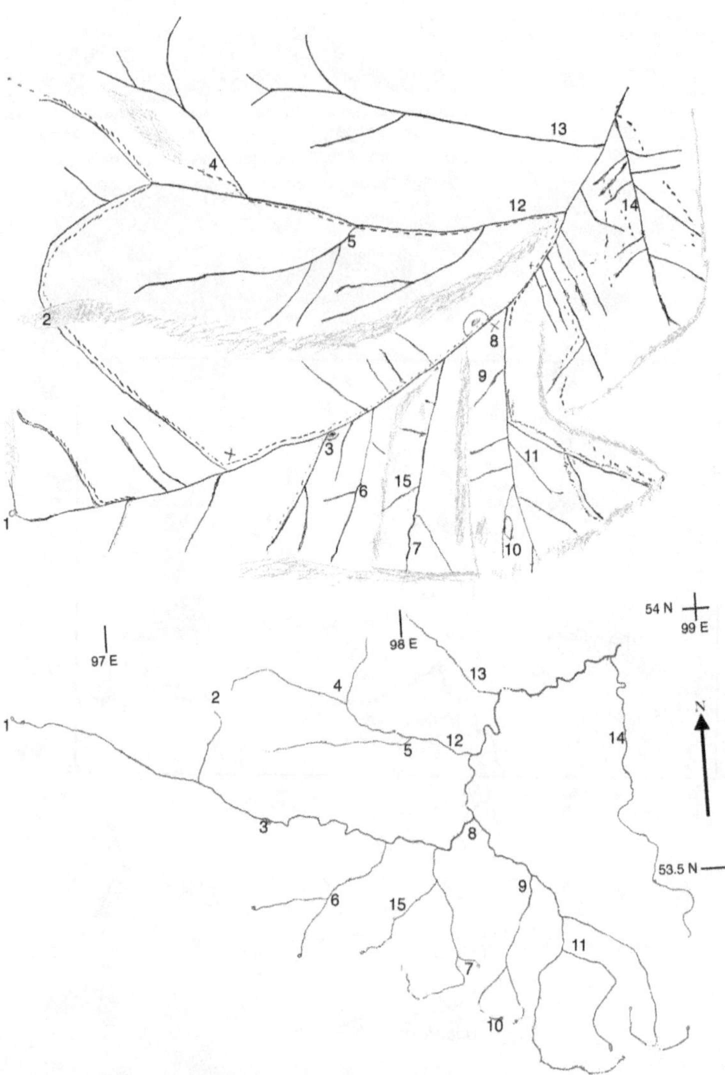


**Figure 4.3**

A 'naïve' Tofa map above (circa 1908) shows the Uda River system, mountains (in gray) and trails (dashed lines). Below is a modern geographic map. Names have been removed here for clarity. Locations have been numbered for comparative purposes. Reproduced from Adler 1910, with additional cartographic elements by Robbie Hart

First of all, it contains a lot more detail than even modern maps: twice as many rivers and four times as many named rivers. The map is not drawn to what we think of as true scale. Instead, it emphasizes important places. The center of the Tofa territory is greatly enlarged, exaggerated even, with commonly used footpaths drawn in. Locations at the edge, though still shown in detail, are greatly shrunk in proportion to the center. One important exception is a lake that lies at the very edge of the territory and is actually quite small, but because of its religious significance (home to the powerful water deity *Kastarma*), it is drawn as if it were enormous. Most strikingly, all the bends and meanders in the rivers are completely straightened out, leaving straight lines and neatly branching forks.

What we have in this century-old native Tofa map may be as clear and direct a view as we can ever get of how traditional Siberian hunter-gatherers and reindeer herders viewed their known world. Topographic knowledge for the Tofa extended beyond mere physical territory: they mapped their mythical world as an extension of their physical world. The Tofa conceptualized the north as off to their left, and associated it with winter, night, and the lower world (inhabited by mythical devils). The south was to their right, connected to the upper world (deities), summer, and light. The east lay out in front, associated with the future, morning, spring; and the west lay behind them, symbolizing evening, autumn, and the past.[7]

Traditional Tofa knowledge of the real earthly landscape (the Uda River basin) and its associated mythological terrain has now nearly faded from memory. The elders who know the land and the belief system lack the strong legs to trek their territory and make the necessary spirit offerings, while the younger generation declines to do so. At the same time Tofa reindeer herds have dwindled to the extent that few Tofa people have the opportunity or skill to ride reindeer anymore, and so they cannot reach remote areas in their land. By a combination of forgetfulness, the decline of reindeer-herding, language shift, and cultural change, the transmission of Tofa topographic knowledge has been fully interrupted. The map has been erased.

## Na(t)ive Maps

When asked by early explorers to draw maps, different native Siberian peoples employed entirely different schemes, suggesting that their culture influenced how they mentally represented landscapes. The Southern

Yukaghir, for example, consistently drew rivers as wide and curvy parallel lines (fig. 4.4). This was completely unlike the Tofa, who drew them as straight, branching single lines. Of course, putting pencil to paper was a novel and unnatural task for these people, and could not have adequately captured the richness of their knowledge. Their ideas about rivers and landscapes were transmitted by a variety of means, including songs, stories, and religious beliefs, but only orally, through language.

The Southern Yukaghir had many songs that narrated the unfolding of a journey along a river (usually the Kolyma). The songs, some collected by linguists, mention currents, notable rocks, tributaries, and point out prominent landmarks associated with myths (e.g., two brothers who turned into rocks). In one song, the river is referred to as being wide and open with people 'sliding' along its middle. Smaller tributaries (e.g., the Oroek) are mentioned, as well as a landmark rock named *Kuntuk* that the river 'flirts' with. One Southern Yukaghir map song went like this:

> Let's tell about our river. A long time ago we used to travel sliding down the middle of our mother Kolyma.
> We used to travel. Our mother Kolyma has many trees here.
> Our mother Kolyma is flirting with Kuntuk.
> It carries us, sitting on the top of mother Oroek . . .
> Many of us are moving in the middle of the river to the river mouth. We are moving away from there, seeing our people.
> Mother earth had bad luck this year. It's bad luck to travel against the stream.
> We are sliding upstream in the middle of mother Oroek on our opened river.[8]

An entirely different view of rivers is adopted by the Tungus people of Siberia. On turn of the century 'naïve' maps, they leave their primary river, the Yana, undrawn as an invisible void at the center of their world (fig. 4.5). Instead, they show only its many branching tributaries. Their main river is so central and obvious to them, functioning as their highway and main route for transport, that they perhaps saw no need to draw it.

Even further east in Siberia, the Nivkh people of Sakhalin Island drew what appears to be each single twist and turn in the rivers (as opposed to the Tofa and Yukaghir strategy of straightening out rivers). The Nivkh, able canoe travellers, did not terminate their drawn rivers at the seashore,

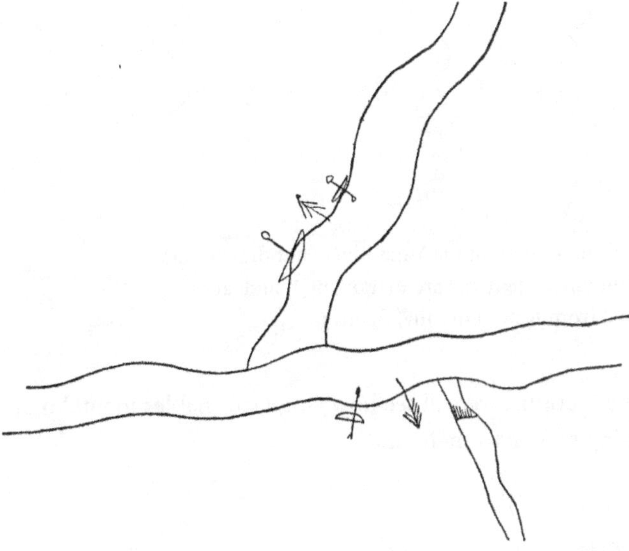

**Figure 4.4**
A Southern Yukaghir naïve map from 1908 shows the confluence of the Kolyma River (center) with the Korkodon "curved" River (top). Also shown are trees, a dam, and three dugout canoes. Reproduced from Adler 1910: 86, figure 21

but drew lines extending far out to sea. The Yakut people drew lakes bisected by rivers (the river passes right through the middle of the lake in a straight line) while the Tungus drew lakes as physically detached from the rivers that feed or drain them.[9] Clearly, Siberians had different cultural strategies for mapping land, lakes, and rivers.

We cannot know to what extent these schematic rivers spring from individual innovation or may be affected by culture and worldview. According to scientists who study patterns in native (or 'naïve') maps, individuals within cultures tend to consistently draw rivers and landscapes in recognizably similar ways.[10] This is, of course, an ethnographic observation, not a firm hypothesis, and it can no longer be tested among native Siberians since these populations have become thoroughly acculturated to Western maps. Nevertheless, such early maps provide valuable glimpses into the mental atlas. Not bound by strict topographic proportion, they can stretch significant features to a greater size, while shrinking more distant or less salient points. Native Siberian maps are also impressive in their level of detail and the intimate association with the land that they reveal.

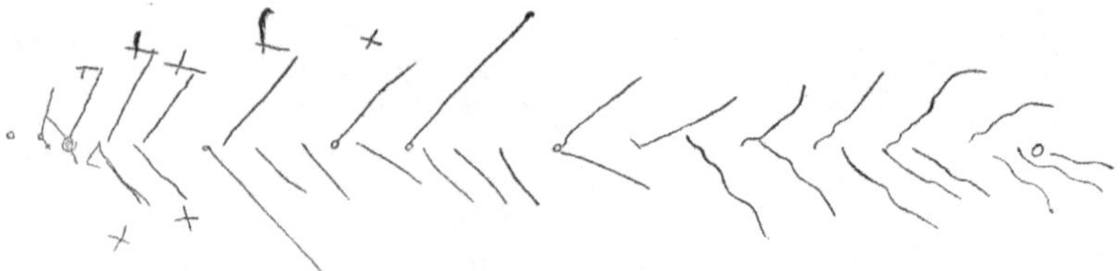

Figure 4.5
A Tungus people's naïve map of the Yana River (not drawn) and its tributaries. Human settlements are marked by X and lakes by O. Reproduced from Adler 1910: 102, figure 30

In the following sections, we will see how language enables mental mapping, thus linking people to their land.

## Topographic Talent

European scientists of the nineteenth and early twentieth century considered native-drawn maps primitive and deficient creations. Some viewed as a shortcoming that in the maps of 'primitive peoples' we do not get 'true' bearings based on cardinal directions, but instead orientations based on rivers, coastlines, and mountains. The Yenisei Ostyak, a Siberian people, had just begun, it was reported in 1910, to use cardinal points, and when shown a modern compass, "at once see its advantages."[11]

A professor exploring German East Africa in the early 1900s admiringly remarked of a native map: "The distances between various places *are wrong* . . . but otherwise it is *wonderfully correct*, considered as the work of an *entirely untrained* man."[12] The German professor declared that the Makonde people possessed a "marked topographic instinct" and enthusiastically drew maps of the southern end of Lake Tanganyika (in what is now Tanzania).

Despite scientists' prejudice against non-cardinal direction systems, they did acknowledge topographic skills. In one encounter, a Russian astronomer on a 1908 arctic expedition asked a native Yukaghir reindeer herder named Nikolai Enkachan to draw a map and provided him with paper and pencils. What the astronomer witnessed next amazed him:

> We simply gasped . . . so outstanding had he [Nikolai] drawn everything: rivers, mountains, the directions of all the ranges . . . We were surprised at such a completely clear presentation

> of a large regions of hundreds of square *versts* . . . moreover, he had probably never seen a geographic map, and likewise had no understanding of reading.[13]

## Horizontal in the Himalayas

American children, when asked to draw maps, tend to adopt a bird's eye view, laying out houses and streets in neat grids as if viewed from above. A study done with Sherpa children in Nepal (<50,000 speakers) showed their strong tendency to emphasize the vertical dimension, better reflecting the *frictional distance* (difficulty in getting from A to B) between points and the importance of the vertical dimension in orienting oneself. A flat map showing only the horizontal is clearly inadequate for life in the Himalayas, as anthropologist James Fisher explains: "In a bird's eye view, two points that may look close together although they are actually far apart—but on a vertical, not a horizontal plane. . . . A destination may be only half a mile away but up a steep and difficult slope. Therefore, as any trekker in Nepal knows, distance is measured in time, not linear units." Fisher goes on to compare horizontal maps drawn by American school children with vertically oriented maps drawn by Nepalese Sherpa children. He concludes: "The Sherpa children thus tend to construct their maps to show the relation of higher and lower, sacrificing that of depth and width, so that the map represents a vertical cross-section rather than a bird's eye view."[14]

Linguist Robbie Hart spent time among the Bantawa Rai people of eastern Nepal, where he witnessed firsthand how a language, Bantawa, can adapt to talking about the vertical dimension. The linguistic habit of specifying relative vertical location made little sense at first to him as a cultural outsider, Hart noted:

> The pages of scratched out words and question marks in my field notes attest to the confusion I felt when I first tried to elicit Bantawa terms equivalent to 'here' and 'there.' Eventually, it became clear that these words each had different forms *depending on the relative altitude* of the place being referred to.

If you are heading down a steep vertical slope along a path, but your destination lies above you on the vertical plane, you would say you are going 'up' even though you happen to be descending at the moment. Speakers

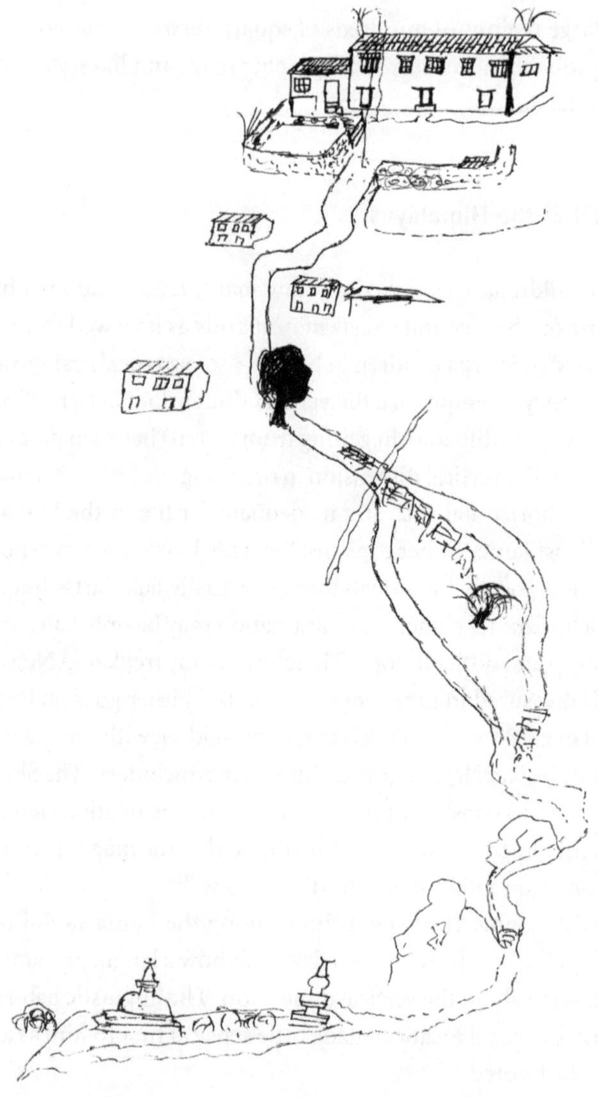

**Figure 4.6**
A map drawn by Ang Rita Sherpa, of the Sherpa people of Nepal, reflects a cultural preference for expressing the vertical dimension when asked to draw two-dimensional maps. Courtesy of James Fisher

of Bantawa and related languages can also indicate whether any person, place, or thing they refer to is higher, level, or lower than the speaker. Their language provides them with the tools to highlight the vertical dimension, which translates into the amount of time and effort required:

> The road was *modu* 'up there,' but the river *moyu* 'down there.' This made perfect sense when one actually walked these paths—though approximately the same distance from the house where the words were spoken, the extreme grade of the Himalayan hills made one a half-hour climb and the other an easy ten-minute walk.[15]

## Culturally Sculpted Landscapes

What people pay attention to in the world, and what they name in the landscape, may be deeply influenced by the language they speak. I present evidence in this chapter that this holds true for many indigenous cultures. By 'indigenous' I mean inhabiting a particular land for as long as collective memory records and being well adapted by cultural habits to surviving on that land. Languages also adapt, quite rapidly, and equip their speakers with specialized tools to describe, divide, and manage the local environment and its resources. But this dynamic is not limited to small or indigenous cultures. If one Manhattanite says "I'm cabbing it crosstown," another Manhattanite will understand perfectly, but outsiders may need a second to process the use of 'cab' as a verb, and figure out what exactly 'crosstown' refers to.

Languages reflect local geography, not only in their vocabulary, but in more deeply structural ways, in their grammar. This knowledge is often accumulated over many centuries, and so geographic terms can represent an ancient layer of cultural knowledge encoded in language. Of course, language change also happens fast. For example, it is easy to think of new words like 'blog' or 'emoticon' that have come into use just in the past few years. But these kinds of adaptations are fresh, they do not reflect hundreds or thousands of years of adaptation to a particular ecological niche, nor the accumulation of wisdom contained in geographic terms. In looking at indigenous cultures we will explore how language helps people adapt to landscapes.

**Figure 4.7**
In Nepal, Bantawa speakers and their neighbors dealing with the precipitous local topography by bridge building (top). The steep, rolling hills of the Bantawa area are carpeted with tea plants (bottom). Courtesy of Robbie Hart

On Mindoro, a lush tropical island in the central Philippines, the Hanunóo people (10,000 speakers) survive by practicing 'swidden' agriculture, in which they constantly clear, cut, and burn small garden plots on steep tropical forest slopes and grow yams and vegetables. The dense and rapidly growing vegetation covers old trails and garden plots quickly and new ones must be blazed. As anthropologist Harold Conklin notes: "In Hanunóo country, no trail is permanent."[16] In addition to trail-blazing, swidden farming requires exceptional skill with the use of controlled burning of vegetation to create new clearings. The Hanunóo, to orient themselves in the dense jungle growth, employ a relatively simple system of directional words on the ground. For all terrestrial directions they use a single system to encode both the upmountain/seaward distinction typical of many island peoples along with the upstream/downstream distinction.

*Hanunóo Terrestrial Directions*

| | |
|---|---|
| *sa bābaw* | above, toward the mountains, upstream |
| *sa lāwud* | down, below, downstream, toward the coast |

But for celestial events, the Hanunóo adopt a much more elaborate six-way directional system, based on how the winds blow. Conklin explains that "Winds are named after, and considered to originate from six cardinal points of the heavens." Each wind direction has a name and one Hanunóo can rapidly orient another by mentioning these names.

Wind direction is part of a larger system of ecological knowledge, as Conklin explains: "Wind direction and duration, like phases of the moon, tides, apparent sidereal revolution, and especially various stages of plant growth . . . are 'calendric' signs and weather signals known to all Hanunóo."

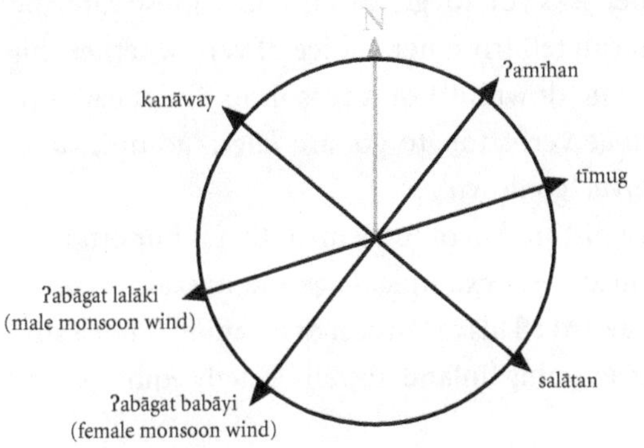


**Figure 4.8**
Hanunóo wind directions (English 'North' shown in gray for comparison). After Harold C. Conklin [1957]1975

Further, "the relations between the six winds and seasonal changes in weather is intimately understood."[17]

Another culture that pays great attention to winds are the Bedouin people of the Middle Eastern deserts. Nomadic Bedouins of Jordan, who live by herding sheep and goats, have verbs for 'to go east' and 'to go west' (these are pronounced *yišarrig* and *yigarrib*). As anthropologist Bill Young observed, there is an important link between linguistic structures and livelihood: Jordanian Bedouins name these directions because "they depend on eastern and western rains for pastoral production." Bedouins of Sudan, by contrast, depend on northern and southern rains to sustain grazing lands for their animals. They have verbs for 'go north' (*yitšaamil*) and 'go south' (*yityaamin*) but lack verbs for 'go west' or 'go east'.[18]

## Dividing Up Small Spaces

Island peoples who sail also care a great deal about wind. They adopt a radically different reference frame than do Siberian forest dwellers, and their languages provide them with tools to describe currents, winds, volcanic slopes, and the topographic patterns unique to islands (e.g., movement towards the sea is generally downwards, away from the sea is upwards). Lolovoli is a dialect of North-East Ambae (5,000 speakers), one of the 113 indigenous languages spoken in Vanuatu. On the small island of Ambae—site of a major volcanic eruption in December 2005—there is more than one way to 'go' and the local language distinguishes these possibilities with three distinct verbs. As in the Himalayas, the terrain on Ambae Island is steep, so clarifying movement as up, down, or across conveys substantially more information about the nature of the 'going'. For instance, if your mother asks you to 'go' to a friend's house carrying a bundle of coconuts, you can tell from her choice of verb whether this task would be a simple favor (downhill) or a reason to disappear (uphill). The three basic Ambae verbs for 'to go' are *hage*, 'go up', *vano*, 'go across / levelly', and *hivo*, 'go down'.

These verbs represent a distinction of movement that is important in all different scales and contexts. For example, *hage* and *hivo* also refer to movement 'inland' and 'seaward'. This extension of meaning is not a surprise, since on conical Ambae, going 'inland' usually exactly equivalent to going 'up' and 'seaward' to going 'down'. But other extended meanings of these verbs do not arise out of a simple correlation of direction and landscape, but are rather products of a culture-specific system to organize space. When talking about movement on different scales, the up/down distinction is applied to other salient oppositions. Take the use of *hage* and *hivo* presented in table 4.1.

Unless the direction of going is unknown (like when asking the question "Where did he go?") either *hage* or *hivo* must be used, no matter how minor the relative change in elevation. Walking around a small village, it is easy to see how a speaker could readily know the height relations between known locations. In fact, this framework extends to very tiny domains, for example, the inside of a hut where the floor is level. In this case, the speaker will think of the general slope of land *outside* the hut, then use the appropriate verb to describe small movements *inside* the hut, for example, to say "Place the dish of meat *hage*" (meaning inland or uphill).

We can imagine however, that as the area over which people 'go' gets larger, and the terrain more varied, it becomes increasingly difficult to decide when to use *hage*, *hivo*, and *vano*. Ambae speakers have resolved this island-specific issue with a linguistic system that has evolved to fill this communication niche. For discussing travel around the island, you compare the known elevations of origin and destination. You then factor in other aspects of the island's landscape and the mode of transport help determine which verb is appropriate. A schematic for this complex decision-making process is shown in figure 4.9. If you begin at the top edge of the diagram with the fundamental question of sea versus land, you can then proceed along the arrowed paths to decide which verb to use.

**Table 4.1**
**Extension of directional terms on Ambae Island, Vanuatu**

| *Smaller* | | | *Scale of movement* <——> | *Larger* |
|---|---|---|---|---|
| ***hage*** | "up" | "inland" | "southeast when traveling to other islands" | "to countries other than Vanuatu" |
| ***hivo*** | "down" | "seaward" | "northwest when traveling to other islands" | "to Vanuatu from other countries" |

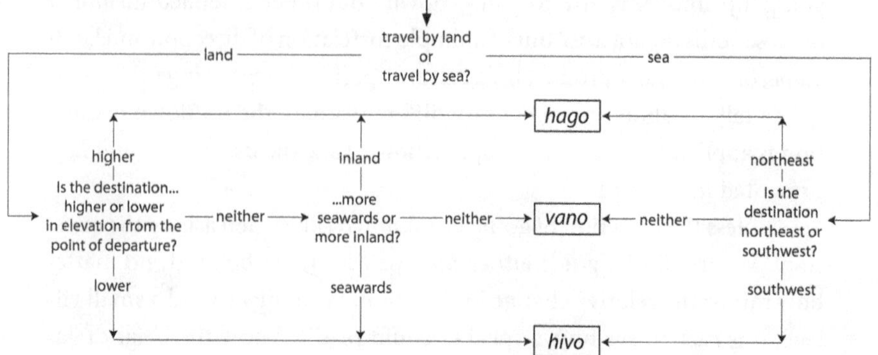


**Figure 4.9**
A decision chart for deciding which directional verb to use in Lolovoli.

When traveling to or from the coast, speakers say *hivo* to describe movement southwest and *hage* for movement northeast; this opposition is neither arbitrary nor based on magnetic fields, but rather corresponds to the logical division of the island along an axis that bisects it. The verbs *hage, hivo,* and *vano* are also used to contrast types of going between islands. In this context, however, the verbs refer to directional movement that is different from the 'going' described when talking about local movement (within a village, say) or movement within one island.

Comparing these different contexts, it becomes increasingly clear that semantically, *hage* and *hivo* describe opposite types of movement and *vano* describes movement that cannot readily be called *hage* or *hivo.* With intra-island travel, when relative height or movement towards or away from the sea is not salient, the axis which determines *hage* versus *hivo* is the lengthwise division of the island; movement across the island's volcanic spine, in either direction, is *vano.*

When the Lolovoli travel in canoes between islands, relative height and landward/seaward judgments are unhelpful. Instead, the use of *hage* vs. *hivo* is determined by the direction of the prevailing wind. Like marching uphill or downhill with a heavy load, specifying sailing direction with respect to the wind tells a lot about the nature of the trip.

Comparing contexts of movement, *hage* trips are difficult (uphill or into a headwind) and *hivo* trips (downhill or with a tailwind) are easy. Interestingly, the one case where *vano* is used for inter-island travel is to Malakula, an island directly to the southwest of Ambae Island, perpen-

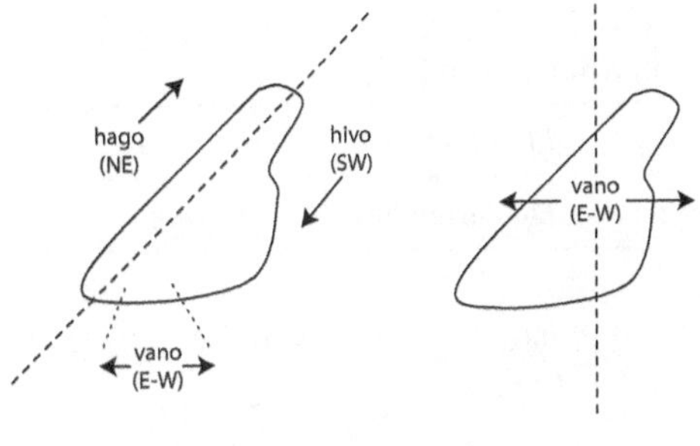


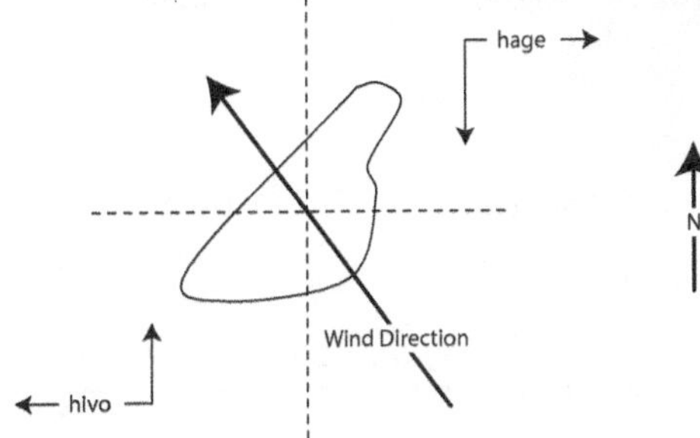


**Figure 4.10**
Lolovoli directional verbs to describe boat trips around the island or hikes across its axis (above) and sailing trips (below).

dicular to the direction of the wind. Trips to and from Malakula are equally easy, each involving sailing perpendicular to the wind.[19]

Culture exerts a robust influence on syntax: if a movement is known to be *hage* or *hivo,* it must be specified as such in order to construct a grammatical sentence.

Directional verbs in Lolovoli encode another layer of spatial description on top of their basic role in specifying absolute direction. By adding suffixes, the up/down/across movement is oriented towards or away from the speaker or item being discussed, or towards the addressee. The suffix for "towards the addressee" also refers to movement toward places in the past or future where the speaker was or will be. Taken together, any mention in Lolovoli of 'going' must include both absolute direction and the perspective of the speaker or item spoken about. This complex packaging of spatial information yields nine distinct verb plus suffix combinations, as shown in the table 4.2.[20]

If you and I both spoke Lolovoli and I used the word *vano-atu* in a sentence, you would understand it to mean that something or someone is either moving levelly across land towards you (my addressee), or sailing

**Table 4.2**
**Verbs of going in Lolovoli spoken on Ambae Island**

| | *Elevation* | | |
|---|---|---|---|
| *Direction* | *Across/levelly* | *Uphill/landward* | *Downhill/seaward* |
| **no suffix** 'Go away' (from speaker or object spoken about) | *vano* | *hage* | *hivo* |
| **add suffix *-mai*** 'Come towards' (speaker or object spoken about) | *vano-mai* | *hage-mai* | *hivo-mai* |
| **add suffix *-atu*** 'Come towards' (the addressee, or a location in the past or future) | *vano-atu* | *hage-atu* | *hivo-atu* |

by sea to your unspecified location on the island of Malakula. If you said *hivo-mai* I would understand that something was moving towards me and downhill or towards the sea (or likely both).

## Yak Herders and Mental Maps

Returning from the South Pacific back to where we started in the center of Siberia, let us consider one more way landscape knowledge permeates language and *vice versa.* In the mountainous ranges of Southern Siberia, Tuvan nomads herd yaks, camels, goats, and sheep. The nomads make no use of maps, compasses, or global positioning devices. In the course of a year's migrations, they may range over hundreds of square miles, crossing many dozens of rivers and streams, passing innumerable mountain ridges and valleys, chasing down straying goats or horses into remote valleys, and climbing above the tree line to hunt marmot and wolves.

The exact amount of roving a nomadic family will do in a year depends on the type of animals they raise. Herders of cattle, sheep, and goats follow a regular seasonal cycle that leads the animals to the best grass and the nomads to a series of four to six campsites. Yak herders migrate greater distances. Their herds wander further seeking cooler, higher pastures in the summer, and unlike sheep and goats they do not regularly return to the camp at night. The yaks must be guarded in two-day shifts by young men—yak-boys—who ride out from the camp on horseback and sleep in the fields.

This constant movement fosters an intimate familiarity with the landscape. Thanks to this knowledge, the herders (and presumably the yaks) never get lost. I spent a great deal of time talking to Tuvan yak herders to understand how this knowledge is constructed and applied. In the following paragraphs, I describe the basic toolbox of Tuvan topographic knowledge.

While out riding or hiking with Tuvan nomads, I noticed that they could almost always identify even seemingly minute features of the landscape. A mountain ridge, for example, would have each visible protrusion along its crest descriptively named: 'white head', 'ice top', 'blue pointy', 'black sister', 'bear head', and so on. Even the tiniest natural spring or stream of water could have a name, or if unnamed, be named for the river it flowed into.

Any known landscape, for Tuvans, is dense with evocatively named places. This allows them to talk easily about exactly where they have been, where the herds are going, or where the neighbors are migrating. Sometimes instead of bestowing proper names, Tuvans will anthropomorphize the landscape, for example, by imagining protrusions of a mountain to be parts of a sleeping bear or a person. This system, highly culture-specific, is very useful for memorizing complex landscapes and using them to orient yourself. Shapes that Tuvans tend to interpret as animal- or human-like may bear no resemblance to New Hampshire's "Old man of the mountains" or Mt. Rushmore's giant presidential heads. Tuvan landscapes are far more abstract and not obvious to the casual outside observer who does not share the same cultural outlook.[21]

In naming landscapes, Tuvans deploy a complex system of mythical and religious beliefs. Many mountain peaks and ridges, bodies of water, and natural springs, are considered sacred and believed to be inhabited by spirits. Mountain passes, the exact point where a trail or road reaches its apex before descending, are of particular significance. One must not pass over without leaving an offering. A strip of cloth tied to a tree branch, a rock stacked on top of a cairn, or a piece of candy laid at the foot of the cairn are offerings to appease the local spirit and ensure safe passage. To

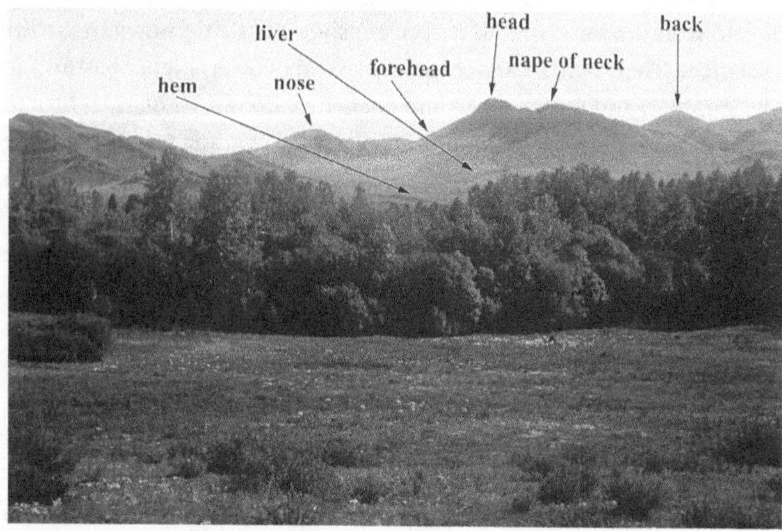


**Figure 4.11**
Tuvan anthropomorphic naming of mountain features. Courtesy of Theodore Levin, topographic data from Anatoli Kuular

visit a spring or cross a pass without making an offering is to risk the wrath of the local spirit who is capable of causing harm if offended. The presence of such spirits, and the places named for them, helps fix the landscape and rules about how to interact with it firmly in the collective memory.[22]

## Senses of Direction

A skill shared by many people who live in intimate connection to their land is an unfailing sense of direction. Tuvan nomads never get lost, even if they have ridden hours away on horseback or traversed many kilometers on foot. Their sense of orientation, as explained to me in many interviews with expert hunters and herders, relies on two distinct systems. First there are natural clues. Tuvan hunters pay close attention to which side of a tree the moss grows on, which sides of an ant hill slope more steeply, which way spiderwebs are oriented, and which side of a marmot's burrow the excavated dirt gets piled on. They can tell subtle slopes of ground from tracks left by falling raindrops in the dust. Such micro-signs provide clues about cardinal directions and local topography. Any of them can be referenced in case the sun is not visible, or even if it is visible, to confirm general directions, to glean information about the coming change of seasons, or the weather forecast.

Second, Tuvans interact with landscapes through senses other than sight, and especially through their language. They use the balance organs of the ear to detect the slope of the ground under their feet. They use their hearing to experience the ambient soundscape. They pay close attention to the texture of the ground, based not only on how it feels but on the kinds of sounds it makes when walked upon. The Tuvan language has a vast and highly creative vocabulary of words to describe specific sounds made in the forest by people or animals. For example, *chyzyr-chyzyr* can be translated as 'the sound of the tree tops moving, swaying, cracking, or snapping as a result of bears marking trees by clawing at them and by scratching their backs up against them'. The word *daldyr* symbolizes the sound of a big horse's hooves, *dyldyr* a big bird's wings flapping, and *koyurt* human feet treading deep snow.[23]

Tuvans pay close attention to and have a rich repertoire of words to describe animal sounds, water sounds, and echoes. The words *hir-hir* are understood to mean either the crackling of a campfire or the sudden rustling of a grouse's wings in the grass. *Shülür* is the sound of water in a nearly dried up river, or of snot being blown out of the nose. Tuvan not only provides many such words ready-made for use but also gives its speakers the tools to make up new *onomatopoetic* words on the fly (more on this in chapter 7).

Place names in Tuva often refer to acoustic properties those places evoke, whether on their own (a burbling brook) or through human and animal intervention (horse hooves clattering over loose rocks and causing miniature rock-slides). And, as musicologist Ted Levin has observed, the Tuvan musical tradition of throat-singing (also called 'overtone singing') springs in part from a heightened attention paid to ambient sounds and acoustic properties of landscapes.[24] For Tuvan nomads, knowledge about physical landscape is thus linked to a whole realm of environmental, biological, aesthetic, and religious knowledge—all expressed with the help of language—and providing a powerful technology for survival.

A third Tuvan orientation skill is the transmission of geographic knowledge, passed on in songs, stories, and lots of everyday conversation. Tuvan nomads talk frequently about where they have been, where the herds are roaming, and where the neighbors are. I was amazed while visiting

**Figure 4.12**
A Monchak Tuvan yurt encampment in Western Mongolia, 2004. Courtesy of Kelly Richardson

Tuvan nomads in Mongolia in 2000 and 2002 to find that my hosts always knew the exact locations of migrating friends and relatives many miles distant.

Nomads migrate on a fairly regular, predictable circuit, modulated by factors such as the condition of the grass, precipitation, weather, health of the animals, and so on. In 2002, I returned to the exact location 'Snakey River' that I had visited on an expedition in June 2000, and I arrived on the same date in June. I felt reasonably sure that friends I had visited in 2000 at that same spot would be found in the vicinity. My friends turned out not to be at that location, but the people camping there knew the exact location of my friends. "They're over on the upper slope of the south bank of Black River Fork," I was informed, "the river is too high to cross at the moment, but they'll be moving in three days down to 'Wet Meadow.'" Both of these locations were more than 30 kilometers away from our present location, across a flooded river.

With tools no more advanced than horses, binoculars, and gossip, the nomads in this tightly knit community managed to keep track of dozens of families, their exact locations, herd movements, and migration schedules. People would answer me with absolute confidence any time I inquired as to the location or migration date of almost any member of this com-

**Figure 4.13**
A Monchak Tuvan yak herder in Western Mongolia, 2004. Courtesy of Kelly Richardson

munity of 1,200 persons. And they did all this in their heads, by daily observations through binoculars, by a great many conversations about migration, by relying on a rich naming system, and by distributing bits of knowledge across cognitive domains (religious, aesthetic, acoustic, linguistic) and among many members of society.

The complexity of the Tuvan topographic naming system goes beyond mere names and extends into the very grammar of the language, for example, verbs. Tuvans live in a land where level spaces are unusual, and nearly every patch of ground slopes in one direction or another. This provides another important system they use for orientation—the directions of watersheds and river currents. The Tuvan language has a general word for 'go' but it is rarely used. Most of the time, Tuvans use a 'path' verb meaning 'go upstream' (*čòkta*) or 'go downstream' (*bàt)* or, as appropriate, 'go cross-stream' (*kes*). You would rarely hear "I'm going to Kyzyl" (the capital city of Tuva) but rather "I'm upstreaming" or "downstreaming" to Kyzyl. Proper use of path verbs demands constant awareness of the nearby streams and river systems and their direction of flow.

We can schematize this knowledge with the decision chart in figure 4.14. Starting at the left edge, the speaker could follow a decision path lead-

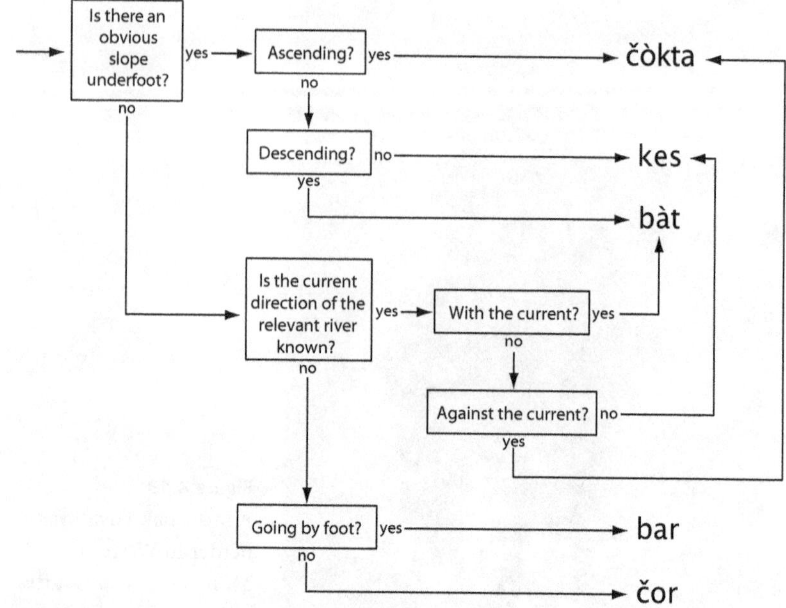


**Figure 4.14**
A decision chart for choosing the appropriate Tuvan word for 'go'.

ing him to the correct choice of the word for go in any given situation. If at any point the topographic information is unknown, he can fall back on the generic words for go: *bar* (go by foot) or *čor* (go by horseback or vehicle). But in Tuvan linguistic custom, topographically oriented path verbs with their richer information content are always preferred.

Tuvan river-based orientation is strictly local, leading to confusion for people (like myself) who know the language but may not know nearby rivers. When visiting the village of Aryg-Üzüü in 1998, I walked along the central dirt road looking for a friend's house. When I asked a local lady for directions, she said (pointing due west) "go *upstream* a bit more, it's the blue house." I thanked her and kept walking west. A hundred yards along the road, another lady pointed west again, but emphatically told me to "go *downstream.*" The crucial difference turned out to be that each lady was referring to an unseen river behind her back as her point of orientation. The first lady stood with her back to the majestic Yenisei River, located 15 kilometers to the north and out of sight over a mountain ridge, but well known to all. The second stood with her back to the tiny (but much

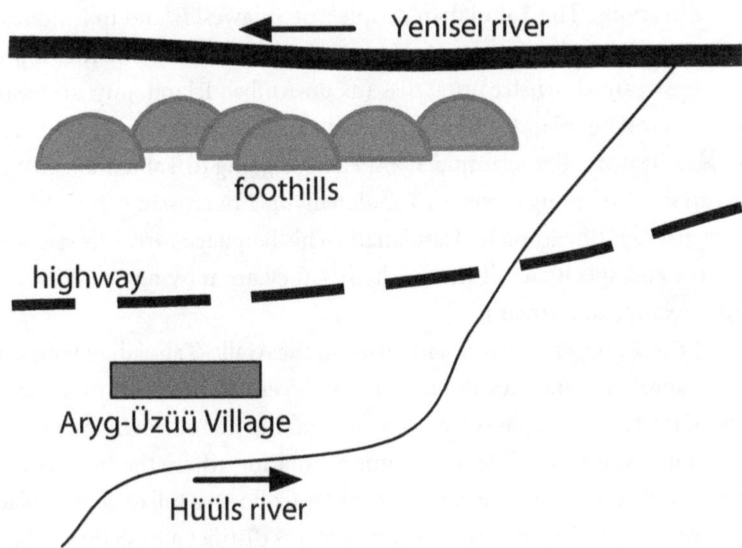


**Figure 4.15**
Two river systems at Aryg-Üzüü village in central Tuva.

closer) Hüüls River (actually a creek), running eastward in a thick woods about four miles south of the village.

My ignorance, as a non-local and non-native speaker, lay in not knowing the local river systems and (even if I had known them) failing to pick up subtle body-posture cues about which river system was being referenced.

I was pleased to find that sedentary villagers had maintained a system of river directional verbs that evolved to suit a purely nomadic culture. But I also noticed that more urban Tuvans, living in the capital city of Kyzyl, used the river directional system only infrequently. Even though the Yenisei River flows right through Kyzyl and everybody knows the direction of its currents, urban Tuvans usually simply say "go," omitting reference to river currents. When they use directional expressions, they are more likely to say "east" or "west." There is some evidence then, that when no longer needed, topographically embedded knowledge can fade from a spoken language, perhaps being exchanged for a more common cardinal direction system.

Systems like Tuvan river-flow orientation may be found in many cultures, where the local landscape takes priority over the more abstract cardinal directions. The Tabulahan people[25] of Sulawesi Island in Indonesia have two overlapping frames of reference for orientation. The first represents upstream/downstream/across (as on Ambae Island, any upstream direction will be inland, and any downstream will be seaward). This system is obligatory. For example, if a speaker is going to Tabulahan village, she can say 'I'm going across to Tabulahan' or 'I'm crossing', but she can never just say 'I'm going to Tabulahan'. This language forces its speakers to know and specify at all times whether they are moving up, down, or across relative to a stream.

The second frame of reference used in the Aralle-Tabulahan language (8,000 speakers) encodes the distinction level/up/down. It might seem redundant to have separate systems for talking about downstream and downhill. But it is possible to imagine a situation where the two systems might conflict: for example, if you have to walk down a hill to get to a place upstream of you. Keeping the two dimensions distinct allows these island dwellers to be very precise in defining not just the destination, but the contour and slope of a journey.[26]

Tuvans and other people I have discussed here use at least three distinct linguistic skills to talk about movement across landscapes. The first is detailed naming of places, including names for even very minute features of the landscape. Topographic knowledge may be fixed in memory by projecting of animal or human features onto the landscape, by assigning religious significance to certain locations (as in Tuvan, done by veneration of local spirits), or by recruiting senses other than sight to interact with the land.

Second, speakers employ multiple frames of reference, including a local one such as island axis (like Ambae) or watershed/river flow (like Tuvan). They may also have a global set of coordinates (south, north), but they tend to favor coordinates tied to local land contour. This local frame gets extended in complex ways to areas outside the traditional territory, or micro-domains such as a chess board, the human body, or the inside of a nomad's yurt.

The third skill is a propensity to talk frequently about locations and landscapes, fixing them in memory.[27] These three skills combined give rise to a powerful mental mapping system. It explains, in part, the fact that nomads never get lost, that they guide their animals to greener pastures, and that they keep mental track of long cycles of migrations that may repeat only every 10 or 12 years. It also explains how, despite my best maps and a global positioning device, I was never able to match even the abilities of young Tuvan children in orienting themselves in their native landscape. My sense of Tuvan nomads' geographic skill is merely anecdotal. I have never conducted experiments to test their actual performance in orienting themselves in familiar or strange landscapes. What I have argued here is that their language, like many indigenous languages, has adapted uniquely to the environment to provide them with enhanced orientation skills.

Some scientists have tested the extent to which linguistic concepts aid in constructing topographic knowledge and achieving real-world orientation success. The Hai||om 'bushmen' people of Namibia (16,000 speakers) (the double bars "||" in Hai||om represent a click sound), regularly traverse long distances on foot for hunting and foraging. They must master a wide variety of landscapes (brush, sand dunes, rock, grassland, etc.) with obscured or long-range views, and diverse flora and fauna. Ethnographer Thomas Widlok noticed the Hai||om's seeming ease in traversing large, varied landscapes and orienting themselves with great skill. Wary that these skills had been over-hyped during a long history of colonial domination that depicted 'Bushmen' as super-human hunters, he decided to test their abilities using controlled experiments.

On a series of walks ranging as far as 40 kilometers, Widlok carried along a global positioning device and asked his Hai||om walkers to point out landmarks, find their way to known destinations along unfamiliar routes, and talk about the journey. Widlok's findings are quite striking: Hai||om fared far better than Europeans asked to perform similar tasks. A study of British people found that they performed poorly when trying to indicate the cardinal direction of their starting point after walking one kilometer through woods. Similarly, Dutch amateur mushroom collectors walking through 'semi-familiar' woods were asked to point out local and distant (but not visible) locations. The Dutch performed little better than at random chance levels in this task. The Hai||om bushmen, in Widlok's experiments, pointed to known but not visible locations with only a 16.4° average deviation.[28]

Widlok concludes that Hai||om "orientation skills are real. . . . Their performance in orientation tasks is at a very high level, though not at the mythical level constructed by some observers, . . . and are far beyond the skills of Europeans." What mental tools do the Hai||om use to achieve this mastery of the landscape? Widlok noticed that their language has a large number of landscape terms. They also use a cardinal (north–south–east–west) direction system in which they talk about landmarks independent of the location of the speaker or hearer. Third, they engage in a great deal of pointing and what Widlok calls 'topographic gossip', or discussion of the landscape and how to traverse it. "Since they do not use any material maps," he concludes, "the communication of spatial information is of crucial importance, there is a continual flow of talk about places and where people and resources are located. This topographic gossip makes little use of person- or body-centered terms but uses a widely shared system of landscape terms."[29]

A skeptic could argue that this ability is no different (and no more special) than my own ability to orient myself in Manhattan, and to walk, almost without thinking, from the corner of Fifth Avenue and Fifty-ninth Street on the upper east side down to Twentieth Street and Eighth Avenue in Chelsea. Or my ability to distinguish uptown–downtown–crosstown and east–west–north–south directions. But comparing Tuvans' to Manhattanites' topographic knowledge is very superficial, and we would be missing something important if we stopped here.

The architecture and layout of cities is an organic thing that evolves over time—one can see the history of this by looking at archeological digs of say, medieval London and its development into the present day. Cities do not spring up overnight, they accrete over centuries, based on thousands of decisions. Apart from conscious planning decisions, there are emergent or self-organizing factors, for example, merchants of similar goods will cluster together, butchers, tailors, car salesmen. Streets, when they are not planned in a grid, also evolve organically, just as footpaths appear on grass where people walk, and then get reinforced by more walkers until they define the most efficient trajectory from A to B.

So how is a New Yorker's knowledge of Manhattan different from a Tuvan's knowledge of the steppes? The difference is that we do not keep all these centuries of accumulated information about urban organization in our heads: we outsource the facts onto signposts, street names, streets, addresses, maps, atlases, tour guides, history books, and computer navigation systems.

In a vast open place like Tuva, where humans leave only a minimal footprint upon the environment, the landscape itself must be committed to memory, since no signposts, permanent buildings, or roads will be built. This memorization is of course easy for Tuvans. They spend their lives observing the face of the land, and easily commit to memory its smallest wrinkles and features. But their language has also developed ways to encode space and package topographic information. These aid memory and are uniquely suited to the local environment. Since the language represents the accretion of knowledge over hundreds of generations, it is only grossly comparable to a mental map of Manhattan or terms like 'cross-town' we may use. The Tuvan knowledge is older, much more detailed, more embedded in language and memory. But is it also more ephemeral and less sticky. It depends for its survival on a continuous and intimate interaction with the land, and on oral, unwritten transmission of knowledge.

Another difference is how the entire system is integrated. Topographic terms are not just used for orientation in Tuva. They carry over into the spiritual realm and the practice of animism. Terms like 'upstream' and 'downstream' can even be extended to locations on the human body, parts of objects, and abstract concepts. Tuvans conceptualize the future as being to the north, behind their backs. They talk of the past as being out in front, to the south. Time concepts are built up out of spatial concepts. This is true of most languages: in English, when we say things like 'Spring break is approaching' we conceptualize it as being out in front, moving towards us in a linear direction. An English expression like 'Spring is just around the bend' could also be read as referring to a road or a river, but these expressions in English have become detached from their topographic metaphors and are simply understood as stock phrases.

So it is not that the Tuvan system is special, it is just that it is still part of everyday talk, it is highly specific to the landscape, and it is fully integrated with many behaviors such as migration, hunting, worship, and so on. The Tuvan nomads have inhabited the Siberian steppes for centuries, even millennia, and the knowledge they possess has been memorized, passed down, and cared for over centuries. It is the accumulated wisdom and keen observations of hundreds or even thousands of minds, pared down to its essence by continual testing and improvement over time. That is what makes these knowledge systems special.

## Endangered Knowledge

Linguistic-topographic knowledge systems like those we have examined in Tofa, Tuvan, Bantawa, Ambae, and other languages differ greatly but also share many features. I will briefly summarize here five ways in which these systems are similar to each other, and in which they may differ (by degree or by quality) from those found in large global languages.

First, each of these languages names a great density of points on the land, not limited to features mapmakers may think important, but extending to very small and subtle features as well. Many of these languages seem to name more topographic points than do languages of people living in Western industrialized societies. And names tend to be transparently meaningful, in a way that a name like 'Mississippi' is not (at least in English; to the 35,000 remaining speakers of Ojibwa it still means 'great river').

Second, these cultures use anthropomorphizing strategies—naming landmarks after parts of human or animal bodies as a way to retain them in memory. In some of the languages examined here, naming is assisted by a belief system that assigns sacred, historical or aesthetic significance to points on the landscape.

Third, they may use senses other than sight to aid memory in coding the landscape. There is great attention paid to rivers and watersheds, wind direction or to some essential local features of the environment. In the case of mountain and island cultures, this is often supplemented with attention to ground slope or the land/sea axis. Absolute directionals (North/South), when they are used in these cultures, are a secondary and often optional system, rarely the primary day-to-day one. What people pay attention to and name in the landscape often reflects their subsistence needs: hunting, gathering, herding, and navigation. Directional knowledge may be highly integrated with daily activities. But it can also reflect purely aesthetic concerns, such as how sounds echo in certain types of landscapes or what spiritual entities are believed to reside there.

Fourth, directional systems never stand alone in these cultures. They are always part of an integrated body of knowledge that includes meteorological patterns, animal behavior, nature signs, human migrations, and mythology.

Fifth, which properties of the landscape people ultimately notice, name, and keep track of can be both enabled and mandated by the language they speak. Certain languages, due to a process of long adaptation to a landscape, will force their speakers to notice and specify certain properties such as direction of river flow. They provide both greater efficiency and a greater cognitive burden. The efficiency comes by the fact that when knowledge is automatically encoded, it is always available to the learner and thus learned without effort. The burden comes from the fact that speakers may be required to notice a certain property (e.g., direction of river flow) in order to be able to express the thought at all.

Each of these examples was chosen because it represents a culture that is intimately tied to a particular environmental niche. That does not imply that big, dispersed languages, such as Spanish, cannot equally adapt to a niche and encode knowledge of the land. But a language spoken in only one niche by a small population may adapt more intimately and rapidly to that niche, and may thus encode more information about human–environment interaction. If the small culture in question is also indigenous to its land, then the language reflects centuries of accumulated observations and generations of geographic wisdom.

Geographic knowledge and its cultural content is passed on in songs, stories, prayers, and many other ways of speaking. In a purely or primarily oral culture, like Tofa, Ambae, or Tuvan, that traditionally made no use of drawn maps, speech is the only means of transmission. Speakers of such a language, if they were to suddenly in the span of two or three generations give up the language and start speaking Spanish, would lose much of that environmental knowledge. Just as we cannot easily recover 'naïve' map drawing skills once people have been familiarized with modern maps and bird's-eye views, we cannot easily recover topographic knowledge—whether a place name like "Mississippi" or an entire mental atlas—once it is lost in translation.

## Wheel of Fortune and a Blessing

I never imagined that one of the last speakers of an endangered language would nearly be drowned out by the din of the TV show *Wheel of Fortune*. I was sitting in the living room of a modest wooden house in a tiny village in Lithuania in 1994, with Mr. Mykolas Firkovičius, a man I believed to be one of the last remaining speakers of the Karai language.

I had no idea what Karai might sound like and strained to hear Mr. Firkovičius over the household din. In the living room, three young children were having a spirited argument in Lithuanian, their first language. The television was on, playing a Russian version of the famous American game show. Mr. Firkovičius' elderly sister bustled in and out of the room serving us tea, exchanging words with him in a language I had never heard. I spoke to him in Polish, the one language we shared fluently. Four languages at once gave rise to a modest Babel.

It was by sheer chance I met Mr. Firkovičius that day. He did not live in the tiny village of Trakai where I met him, but in the capital city of Vilnius, 25 miles away. He had just happened to drive out that day to visit his sister. I had come to Lithuania with a summer study group and was on a day trip to Trakai. As my group headed out to visit the spectacular medieval castle set on an island in the lake, once home to fourteenth-century Lithuanian kings, I had a different agenda. I set off with my tape recorder, telling my friends I planned to seek out members of Lithuania's smallest linguistic minority.

Walking along the village's central road, I was met by an enormous, swarthy man. Standing at least 6' 6", he walked swaying on his feet and seemed in a celebratory mood. Testing out my beginner's Lithuanian, I greeted him and then blurted out: "I want to meet Karaim people." His reaction was not quite what I expected . . . he embraced me in a huge bear hug, and then said, "Let's go." Arm in arm we marched (swaying) along the empty road, watched by bemused village folk. We came to a tidy log house with a porch, and he shouted out something. A lady of about 70 appeared at the door and let loose what sounded like a scolding in our direction. Big Man hung his head and started walking off. Taking my cue, I marched up the steps, and said, "I've come to talk with Karaim people, I'm from America." "Wait," she said, and shut the door. A few seconds later, the door sprang open and a very small, wiry man with large thick glasses greeted me warmly. "You've come to meet the Karaim?" he asked.

We quickly established a rapport, and Mr. Firkovičius began telling me, over tea, of his childhood in this medieval village of Trakai. "We all used to speak Karai here, everybody. But at school we spoke Polish because that was the language of education. And I speak Russian and of course fluent Lithuanian." I paused to compliment him on his multilingualism, and then asked how many people spoke Karai. His face fell noticeably at the question. Leaning towards me for emphasis, he said "Sir, our language is disappearing." I pressed further, wanting to know exactly how many speakers were left. Doing some mental estimates and naming some names, a brother, a sister, and so on, he said he was not sure, but perhaps a few dozen, scattered around the country in different communities.

Not wishing to impose, I prepared to say goodbye and asked Mr. Firkovičius if he could record a blessing for me in the ancient Karai tongue. He had told me how he occupied a position of political and spiritual leadership as the "great *hazzan*" for the community and officiated at weddings and other occasions by reading prayers.

The Karaim are ethnically Turks, not the ones of Turkey, but of the greater Turkic family that includes Azerbaijanis, Kazaks, Uzbeks, as well as the Turkish Turks. The Karaim of Lithuania descended from several dozen families of Crimean Turks who were brought to Lithuania in the year 1397 by the Lithuanian Prince Vytautas.

The Karaim adopted a form of Judaism in the fourteenth-century and practice a Judaism-derived faith up to the present day. Karai was for centuries written in the Hebrew syllabary, but now has a writing system that uses Latin letters, thanks to Mr. Firkovičius and others who introduced new ways of writing. Whatever letters are used, the Karaim prize their ancient literary tradition. It may soon be all that is left of their once vibrant spoken language.

Removing his thick glasses, Mr. Firkovičius motioned me to start my tape recorder: "I am Mikhail Firkovičius," he intoned, "a Karaim, born in Trakai in 1924, in our local Karaim community, which we call

*Jimat* in Karai. All the Karaim who lived here in Trakai spoke Karai." Then he began to sing, in a slightly wavering voice, but one full of vigor and conviction. The first text he sang was Psalm 1, a passage I knew by heart in English. "And he shall be like a tree, planted by the rivers of water. . . ." The great *hazzan* sent me on my way with a small brown prayer book, prefaced with these words: "Praying these prayers our god-fearing fathers and forefathers worshipped the only Mighty God of Heaven—*Tieńri.*"

Along with the prayer book, tucked deep in my pocket I carried a cassette tape with two songs he had sung to me. It would be years and much more study until I would be able to translate the second song, which went like this

*Once there was a man . . .*
*He stood on the ice, and asked:*
*'Oh, ice, whence is your strength?'*
*Ice said:*
*'If I were so strong, the sun would not melt me'*
*The man asked the sun:*
*'Oh sun, whence is your strength?'*
*Sun said:*
*'If I were strong, the clouds would not cover me.'*
*The man asked the cloud:*
*'O cloud, whence is your strength?'*
*Cloud said:*
*'If I were strong, the rain would not fall from me.'*

As each character in the song was found to have a force more powerful than itself, a view of the universe—and man's proper place in it—was revealed.

This little song about strength and weakness came to my mind when I learned Mr. Firkovičius had passed away in autumn 2000. At his funeral, a friend gave the following eulogy: "When it had become impossible to believe in God, and impossible to pray, Mykolas saw further than the rest of us. He studied our faith and our traditions . . ." The small Karaim community has been hard pressed to replace the great *hazzan*, their spiritual leader and one of the last who knew the ancient traditions.[1] Some members of the Karaim community in

Lithuania, Poland, and the Ukraine have taken an interest in reviving their language and passing it on to their grandchildren. They organize yearly gatherings and even a language summer school for their children. Lacking learned elders to recite prayers in their ancestral tongue, they can use a recorded voice from the past, the deceased hazzan on DVD, to help them communicate with their deity.[2]

# 5 Silent Storytellers, Lost Legends

In the beginning . . . was the first duck.
— Tofa creation myth

Even though they didn't have a writing system, the Inuit stories were kept alive by telling them to others by memory. The Inuit had such stories and memories in their minds for a long time.
— Lypa Pitsiulak, Inuit storyteller and artist, quoted in Maria von Finckenstein, *Nuvisavik: The Place Where We Live*

Nobody wants to hear the old stories anymore . . .
— Shoydak-ool, Tuvan epic storyteller

But I can't tell my stories to *that* thing," protested Shoydak-ool, pointing to my video camera sitting ready on its tripod. "I've got to have an audience—I only tell my stories to people!" I had arrived in the tiny village of Aryg-Üzüü, in the Republic of Tuva, a remote enclave in Russia's southern Siberian mountains, famed for its throat singers and colorful horse-riding nomads. The village was located just a stone's throw off Tuva's main east–west road, which runs through the republic from east to west. Passing tourists and travelers rarely give the village of Aryg-Üzüü a second glance, even though it is clearly visible from the road.

What brought me to Aryg-Üzüü village on a hot August day in 1998 was a report that a splendidly talented Tuvan storyteller, one not yet known to the scholars who collect traditional stories, lived and practiced his ancient craft here. My Tuvan guide brought me to the small, unassuming log house where we found Shoydak-ool the storyteller, tending two cows and shushing the angry dog he kept on a short chain in the yard. He motioned us to enter the house while he held back the dog.

A vigorous, cheerful man of seventy-two, Shoydak-ool had retired from his job driving a combine on a collective farm to practice his avocation—storytelling. Every once in a while, he would perform a story at the village 'cultural center' or be invited to the local school. In recent years, opportunities had become less frequent. "People are not interested in the old stories," he lamented. "Kids just want to watch Jackie Chan movies nowadays." Not an inappropriate analogy, I thought to myself: heroes of Tuvan myths often represent the same archetypal character found in Hong Kong action flicks.

In Tuvan tales, there is a poor lad named 'Orphan boy', who lacks any obvious advantages or clear goal in life but possesses wit, persistence, and strength of character. Orphan boy outwits and ultimately vanquishes an evil khan to gain a prize (perhaps a bride or wealth). Along the way, there is typically a moment of self-doubt where he receives sage advice from a wise old man or woman, or a clever animal helper. This advice is always cryptic, and only later at some crucial moment in the plot line does its meaning become clear. The hero is often required to give up his sole possession in order to gain the ultimate prize.

To find Shoydak-ool the audience he required, we set out at 7:00 a.m. the next morning in a jeep, bumping our way over something that resembled parallel ruts and churning up great billows of dust. We arrived at the nomadic summer camp of Shoydak-ool's relatives to find the family still in bed. He roused them with his announcement: "I'm going to tell a story." Tousled heads peered out from under the covers. The young men washed their faces and went to let the sheep and horses out of their stockades to graze. One horse was missing, and appeared to have been stolen during the night, much to the dismay of the entire camp.

Twenty minutes later, with the salty milk tea boiled and morning chores nearly complete, Shoydak-ool opened a battered leather suitcase. Out came his props: a bright pink robe with sash and a red, pointed, rather Santa Claus-like hat. From the matron of the yurt, he requested a tea bowl and ceremonial perforated wooden spoon (called a *tos-karak* 'nine-eye') used to sprinkle tea as an offering to the spirits. No Tuvan story can be properly told unless prefaced with this religious ritual. Then the story began, and it was a real cliff-hanger.

In this tale, the heroine, a girl named Bora, sets off on a quest to bring her dead brother back to life. Along the way, she must use magical powers, carry out feats of strength, and rely on advice from her magical talking horse. The horse informs her that to resurrect her dead brother, she must win the hand of a princess in marriage. So Bora uses her shape-

**Figure 5.1**
Shoydak-ool Khovalyg (born 1929), Tuvan epic storyteller in 2003. Courtesy of Katherine Vincent

changing abilities to disguise herself as a man. Once changed into a man, she finds that although she now has a beard and big biceps, she still has certain anatomical features of her girlhood. Her clever horse helps her complete the transgender disguise by gluing bear fur over her breasts and attaching a goose's head as a fake penis.

Once fitted out with her faux male body parts, Bora enters the khan's archery, wrestling, and horseracing competitions and wins them all. This allows her to win the hand of the princess, who subsequently uses her own, even more powerful magic to bring Bora's brother back to life. In a truly happy ending, the princess marries Bora's brother, Bora changes back into a girl and marries her own suitor, and they live prosperously on the high grassy plains with their sheep and camel herds.[1]

As Shoydak-ool told his tale, funny and ribald parts were greeted with laughter and suspenseful parts with expressions of anticipation. Our little group—an entire family of nomads aged 7 to 75 who had been roused from their sleep, and I, an American linguist—were together experiencing something quite rare. Most Tuvans have never heard a live performance of a traditional epic story, or even a recording of one. What made this encounter even more moving was a sense that this kind of story might soon be lost to history.

Long ago, in the wandering nomadic past of the Tuvan people, the art of storytellers (called *tooldžu*) was a prestigious and popular form of entertainment. Upon arrival at a campsite, a *tooldžu* would begin his or her tale around dusk, as the nomads settled in to drink their salted, milky tea and stoke the fire. Just as the light in the yurt faded to twilight, and the stars became visible through the large round opening in the roof, the words "*shyaan am*. . . " ('Once upon a time') would be heard, spoken in the special singsong voice used by tellers of tales. A story might continue for several successive evenings, late into the night.[2]

Such storytelling scenes now exist only in the memory of elderly Tuvans. Storytelling is no longer a profession, and it is barely even an avocation. Few young people with talent are attracted to it because it does not offer anything in the way of a career. When Shoydak-ool won a storytelling competition in 2002, his only prize was an empty thermos and 12 tea bowls. A master practitioner of a vanishing art, he lives in penury.

## Writing Is Not Language

It is some consolation that many Tuvan stories have been written down in books, and a few have been recorded on audio or videotape. After the

**Figure 5.2**
An exceptional young Tuvan storyteller, Aidyng Byrtan-ool (born 1988), singing an epic tale, 2003. Photographs by K. David Harrison

living tradition of storytelling fades, the tales will persist in some form.[3] But written stories are only a very impoverished form of spoken ones. Nowhere in a written text can you discern the tone of voice, loudness, excitement, gestures, facial expression, or tempo . . . all those things that make a story come alive.

Once a story is written down, it is fixed, canonized in a rigid form. It no longer invites successive generations of storytellers to play freely with the text, embellish it, or change it. It ceases to be a living tradition and becomes an embalmed one. This has been the fate of most oral traditions in the world's major languages. We know of the Greek Homeric epics not because they are still a living tradition, recited by blind bards, but because they have been captured in writing and may be found in books.

While writing allows epic traditions to persist in some form, it paradoxically undermines the environment verbal arts need to thrive. Oral traditions are robust, they have served over many centuries and for many cultures as the sole medium of information transfer. But they are also fragile and may survive the transition to writing only in a greatly changed form. Nora Dauenhauer, a scholar and native speaker of the native Alaskan language Tlingit (845 speakers), describes how writing alters oral traditions:

> The writing down of oral literature, no matter how well-intentioned or how well carried out, petrifies it. . . . A petrified log may look like wood, but it is actually stone. . . . Petrification is not entirely without its benefits: we have the *Iliad* and the *Odyssey*. But, as magnificent as they are, the Homeric epics as we have them are petrified fossils, not the oral performance experienced by the ancient Greeks.[4]

Writing is not the ideal medium for traditional stories, nor is it by any means the norm for the world's languages. Though writing is thousands of years old, it is new to humanity. The ancient art of storytelling has been throughout history a purely verbal practice. Most of the world's living languages and storytelling traditions make no use of writing at all.[5] While we have no solid estimate of how many of the world's 6,912+ languages have a written form, a reasonable estimate would be less than one-quarter, or about 1,700. Even for many of these, the only writing that exists is a system invented or bestowed by outsiders (missionaries, Bible translators, scholars) and not widely known or adopted in the community. Languages can and do thrive without literacy.

We have no current, accurate estimate for how many of the world's languages have *both* a writing system and widespread literacy. Walter Ong asserts that

> Language is so overwhelmingly oral that of all the many thousands of languages—possibly tens of thousands—spoken in the course of human history only around 106 have ever been committed to writing to a degree sufficient to have produced literature, and most have never been written at all. Of the some 3,000 languages spoken that exist today only some 78 have a literature.[6]

Ong's numbers, taken from a 1972 source, are a bit outdated compared with the figure given above of almost 7,000 languages spoken in the world today. Whatever the exact numbers are, it is clear that only a tiny minority of the world's languages have a written form used by the speech community. The lack of widespread writing may actually be a boon for verbal arts—many of the world's smaller languages lack writing but maintain vibrant storytelling traditions and epic genres.

In our own English-speaking culture, we suffer from a strong literacy bias, assuming writing to be the norm when it is not, and viewing literature as something existing primarily on paper. As anthropologist Elizabeth Buck observes: "It is difficult for those who have internalized the processes and assumptions of writing to understand the thought and social processes of cultures in which *words, once spoken, have no residue except for their trace in the human memory.*"[7] She goes on to note that throughout colonial history people in literate (colonial) societies have tended to see unwritten cultures as 'primitive' or 'inferior' and utterly failed to appreciate verbal arts of these societies as the pinnacle of creativity they were. This is ironic, given that the Western canon itself springs from works like the *Iliad* that could only have emerged in the absence of writing (though writing has helped these survive to the present day). Yet we continue to view non-literacy as a social deficiency.

## The Power of Oral Tradition

We might profit from taking a few moments to think about what it means to be a purely oral, non-literate culture. No grocery lists, no letters or e-mails, no memos, no text messages on cell phones, no books, no report cards, no instructions on how to assemble artificial Christmas trees, no owner's manuals, no dictionaries, no newspapers, no libraries. This is the *normal* state of affairs for most human languages.

Yet oral cultures lacking writing manage to transmit, remember, and build upon vast systems of traditional knowledge of the kind explored in this book. They do so without the benefit of any physical medium such as writing that could make this knowledge stick around. This astounding feat of collective and individual memory should make us aware how powerful a tool language is for packaging and transmitting information.

Without writing, all linguistically encoded knowledge is always only one generation away from extinction. If it is not passed on verbally, it is lost. This means that what does get passed on is somehow essential, important, and not frivolous or tangential to human life. It also means that there is only received wisdom, and that each person who passes on information must modify, embellish, and filter it through their own experience. Everything is like improv comedy, subject to individual memory and creativity, nothing is set in stone.

In 'primary oral' cultures, people draw on an impressive arsenal of speech strategies: narrative, talk, gossip, conversation, pauses, intonation, silence, loudness, word-choice, story, and myth.[8] They rely solely on social learning to transmit and receive everything that can be encapsulated in language. Information must also be structured for ease of memorization. There are many devices, such as alliteration, rhyme, and parallelism, that aid in remembering long texts. In English and other large languages with literary traditions, such devices are more an art form than a daily cognitive necessity. For unwritten languages, relying on such mnemonics allows people to accumulate and recall large bodies of everyday or esoteric knowledge.

Such knowledge tends, for efficiency, to be socially distributed. People who command restricted or privileged bodies of knowledge in such societies are not librarians or web-masters, but shamans and storytellers. And knowledge is passed on in ways that divvy it up among people that need it, and who bear the responsibility for remembering. For example, among the Batangan people of the Philippines (8,000 speakers), only boys are taught folk medicine, while only adult males are taught religious chants and rituals.[9]

Once societies make the transition to letters, writing may come to seem indispensable to them. But do a people sacrifice something to gain this prize? Is something essential lost when a purely verbal culture gives way to writing? This question goes well beyond the literary or linguistic realm, raising fundamental issues of thought, culture, and psychology. Scientists have only just begun to explore how contemporary oral cultures function (socially, cognitively, artistically, and psychologically) and what we (as literate cultures) may be lacking due to our heavy reliance on the written word.

Due to our long engagement with writing, it is hard for us even to imagine how our day-to-day life (in thought, speech, and interaction) would change in the complete absence of writing. Our use of language would have to be much different if we became a purely oral society. What would be different in the domains of information flow, small-talk, conversation, grocery shopping, even grammatical structures? Would our memory be up to the task? How might we adapt?

We do not have good historically documented examples of societies that went from having writing to not having it. But we do have many contemporary examples of entire societies that have not yet acquired writing or have only recently done so. We might learn a great deal from such societies, but the window of opportunity is closing as literacy becomes the global norm.

Governments and non-governmental organizations worldwide have prioritized literacy. UNESCO reports that worldwide adult literacy reached 81.8 percent in the period 2002–2004. This is markedly up from the World Bank estimates for 1970, at 55 percent literacy, or even 1990, at 71 percent literacy.[10] The increase is largely due to national campaigns, like one conducted in India that brought Indian literacy from a mere 18.33 percent in 1951 to 64.84 percent by 2001.[11] Such campaigns, while laudable, cast non-literacy in a wholly negative light with the use of slogans such as "Literacy is Freedom" (implying that non-literacy is a kind of slavery or prison).[12] Hidden behind such statistics is the fact that 'literacy' usually means ability to read and write solely in the dominant national or regional language (e.g., Hindi or English). Many small languages will vanish without ever having literate speakers; small languages are seldom included in national literacy campaigns. Regrettably, literacy in large national languages is often the beginning of an educational process that leads to abandonment of small languages.

While having literacy is certainly a good thing from our modern point of view, it is also worth exploring the natural, non-literate state of human society while we may still observe it. In the following sections I will describe the case of a small language that has only recently acquired writing, and the impact this has had on its society.

## Present at the Creation

On a 2003 expedition to visit the remote Ös people of central Siberia, linguist Greg Anderson and I witnessed firsthand the emergence of a brand new writing system in a language that had never before had one. The Ös people inhabit a few scattered villages in a remote marshy forest of Siberia, where they continue their traditional livelihood of fishing and hunting and gathering. The eldest Ös people, now in their nineties, can still recall a time when their parents or grandparents lived in birch bark teepees. They now live in small log cabins in villages where they grow vegetables, fish, hunt moose and bear, and collect berries and edible plants. The Ös are extremely poor, and lack many basic necessities such as health care, plumbing, and roads.

The Ös have also suffered a catastrophe of cultural forgetting. Their language has been oppressed: Today's adults were as children forced to speak, read, and write Russian only. If the Ös people ever had an epic storytelling tradition, myths, folktales, or songs, these are long forgotten. Only fragments of their folklore and oral tradition survive. In expeditions in 2003 and 2005, we collected just two wise sayings, one wool-spinning song, and a couple dozen brief stories about hunting moose and bears. We also collected plain old everyday speech: people talking about their lives, their pastimes, hunting, and personal history. But we found no poetry, no epic tales, no creation myth, shaman's healing chants, or riddles.

Mr. Vasya Gabov (born 1951), the youngest fluent speaker of Ös and our expedition guide, felt particularly pained by the fact that Ös had never been allowed to have an alphabet. Like Sequoyah, the native Cherokee scholar who invented writing for his people in 1809, Vasya was determined to bring the technology of writing to his people in their own language. In the Soviet Union, alphabets were designed and bestowed by Russian scientists, and the political decisions about which minority peoples could have letters were made in Moscow. It would have been a punishable offense to invent your own alphabet, so the Ös did without.

Vasya and his peers told us how they had been made fun of for being dark-skinned native children among blond Russians in elementary school.

They had also, he recounted, been made to feel ashamed of their language and forbidden to speak it. Under such pressures, he and his generation made the decision (one that they now regret) to avoid using Ös and speak exclusively Russian. Ös children like Vasya made this decision at the very young age of 5 or 6, not realizing it presaged the loss of their ancestral language. They were concerned with how to fit in, be accepted, and avoid ridicule for being different.

Vasya grew up to be a successful worker in Soviet society, married and had children, and worked as a truck driver. A born outdoorsman, he never lost his love of hunting and would spend weeks at a time out hunting bears, moose, and other animals. At night, sitting alone in a small log cabin in the forest, he made an audacious decision—he would keep a hunting journal in his own native Ös language. Of course, he—like all Ös adults—knew how to read and write in Russian. But Ös has four sounds not found in Russian. Since Vasya was not a trained linguist, he decided that he would not invent four new letters for these sounds, but would simply use new combinations of Russian letters he already knew.[13]

After some time Vasya worked out his new writing system and began to make regular entries in his journal. He was motivated in part by some-

**Figure 5.3**
Vasya Gabov writing the first surviving Ös text in his own invented orthography, 2003. Photograph by K. David Harrison

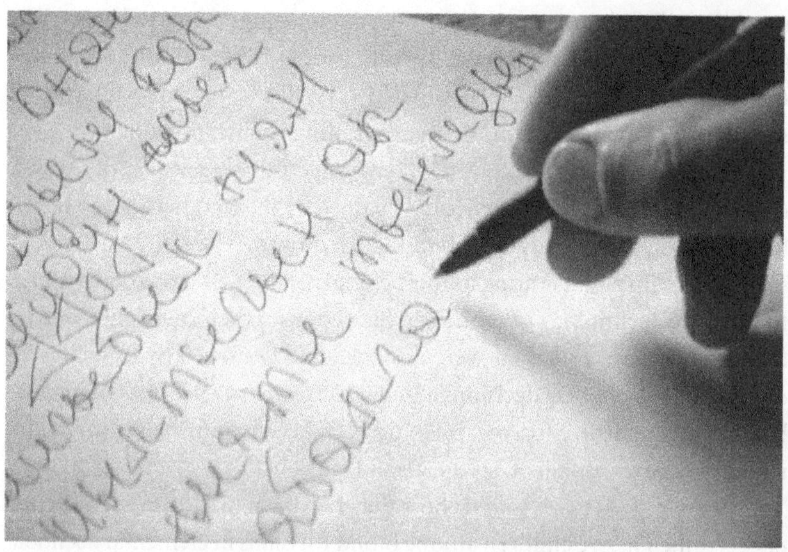

thing his mother had said to him as a young boy: "My mother told me that it is necessary to speak our Ös language. . . . Let the Russians speak Russian and let the Ös speak Ös." This expression of linguistic pride inspired him to keep writing and perhaps to even dare to think that Ös might be passed on to his children's generation. But Vasya's journal was ill fated.

One day Vasya got up his courage and showed his journal—containing three years' worth of entries painstakingly written—to a Russian friend. The Russian's reaction was devastating for him. "What are you writing there, in what language?" the friend demanded. "Why would you write Ös?" When Vasya heard these disdainful words, he felt as if he had done something wrong. The shame of the schoolyard and stigma of being different came back to him. In a fit of pique, he threw his journal—the first and only book ever written in his native Ös tongue—out into the forest to rot. "I might have wanted to show it to you," he told me in 2003, "but it's not here, it's still there where I threw it away."

Despite this prior discouragement, Vasya agreed to sit down in 2003 and demonstrate his writing to visiting linguists. He wrote a simple story and filmed an interview in which he talked about his writing system. He felt secure enough to express pride once more in his ancestral tongue. "I have always loved the Ös language and I have spoken it . . . I will never throw away my language, I still speak it."

In the hope that we might encourage Vasya to propagate his writing system in the community, we agreed to a request from the Ös tribal council to produce a storybook. We commissioned local Ös children—none of whom speak the language—to draw illustrations for it. Their efforts, and Vasya's brilliant orthography, led to the very first Ös book. While prospects are very slim that Ös will be revitalized and passed to another generation, this first (and possibly last ever) Ös book attests to one man's love for his language and determination that it not fade away without a struggle.

## Glimpses of Prehistory

Despite my exhilaration at seeing Vasya's writing system, there were many things I had hoped to find in Ös that may already have faded from existence. I had wanted, for example, to collect stories about religious rituals. Like all Siberian peoples, the Ös would have practiced animism,

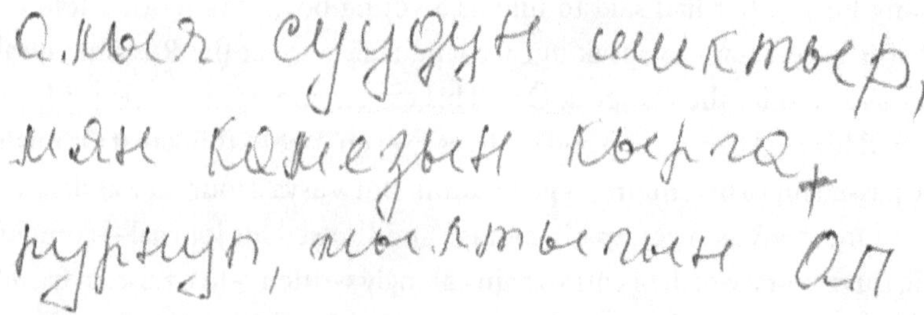

**Figure 5.4**
Fragment from the first surviving text written by Vasya Gabov in his own Ös native orthography, 2003. "The moose came up out of the water, I brought my boat to shore, grabbed my gun and . . ."

a religion based on the belief that spirits inhabit objects and places, and that they must be appeased. Animist beliefs often invoke an elaborate cosmology, with multiple upper and lower layers of the world inhabited by different beings wielding different powers. In many such societies special practitioners—shamans—can mediate between the invisible and visible worlds.

The Ös indeed had shamans and practiced animism, as we know from historical sources. When Swedish explorer Johan Falck visited the Ös in 1786, he noted they had been forcibly baptized but were half-hearted converts: "In 1720, the Archbishop of Tobolsk baptized . . . almost all of the Chulym without much event . . . [but] they still have many shamanistic superstitions and are so ignorant of the [Christian] religion that one almost only notices their Christianity by the crosses they wear."[14]

As far as we know, no Ös shaman's chants, incantations, or rituals were ever recorded. Only one living member of the community—Varvara Budeyeva, aged 92 when we met her in 2003 and since deceased—had witnessed shamans healing people in traditional ceremonies. Varvara described a shaman's divination ritual to visiting Russian researchers in 1972. The telling itself was a courageous act: expressions of religion were severely frowned upon in Soviet society, and many shamans had been brutally repressed in the 1950s and 1960s under Stalinism.

When Varvara reminisced of shamans in 1972, the researchers dutifully wrote it down in their notebooks. Her account then lay dormant for over three decades in the archives of the local university. As the last surviving shred of evidence of now-forgotten shamanic rites among the Ös people, Varvara's story is now seeing the light of day for the first time. We present here an English translation:

*When the shaman shamanizes, there is a plate of meat and three liters of alcohol sitting nearby.*
*Around her neck hang nineteen strings of beads, and a white scarf is tied on her head.*
*She holds twelve rings in her hand and beats on them with a wooden spoon.*
*Then she takes the spoon and shamanizes with it.*
*If the wooden spoon lands right side up, it augurs good.*
*If the wooden spoon lands upside down, it augurs bad.*[15]

This firsthand account is a glimpse backwards into unrecorded prehistory—perhaps the only one we will ever have—at a now vanished religious tradition. No living Ös person knows how to perform such a ritual, and only one or two persons still living when this text was first written down in 1972 had actually witnessed one. The modern-day Ös seem to get by without their traditional animistic religion, and some have converted to Orthodox Christianity. But with the loss of any religion, people lose a part of their heritage and scholars of religion and culture worldwide are impoverished in their field of study.

Given that so much of world history is about the forcible replacement of some belief systems by others, we should be sensitive to the impending loss of so many more religions and worldviews as languages die. As indigenous beliefs approach the vanishing point due to language shift, the best we can do, perhaps, is to write down or record texts or first-person accounts of what people once believed in and how they talked to and about their gods.

## What Good Are Books?

Why make books for people who cannot read them, and whose language is nearly extinct anyway?[16] I wondered about this after our meeting with the Ös tribal council in 2003. Of eight council members, only one speaks Ös fluently, while two others had latent knowledge (they could understand an overheard conversation, but not speak). The other five professed no knowledge of Ös at all, but hoped that the production of a storybook might lend the language some prestige and perhaps help revitalize it. My colleague

Greg Anderson and I, having worked in many endangered language communities, considered this latter scenario highly unlikely, but expressed support for the idea anyway.

Ös is already moribund, with no children speaking it. Vasya Gabov at age 55 is the youngest fluent speaker. Even elderly fluent speakers who live side by side in the villages rarely speak it to each other. We found only one household where the husband and wife used Ös daily with each other (see fig. 1.1, chapter 1). The younger generation, schooled in ethnic shame, shows an active disinterest in knowing Ös. It would take a near-miraculous convergence of circumstances for Ös to once again become a vibrant, spoken language of daily communication. "It's going to be very difficult," remarked Vasya, "but I think it's still possible to correct the situation."

## Writing and Cognition

Capturing all the sounds of a language in letters—an orthography—is a very complex task. When untrained speakers of languages invent 'naïve' orthographies, the choices they make give scientists new insights into the psychology of language. For cognitive scientists, such writing systems provide a natural laboratory to study the ways the human brain perceives speech sounds, similarities and differences among sounds, and other linguistic structures. I will give two brief examples here of how these writing systems shed light on what is going on in the brain when speech is translated into written symbols.

Vasya Gabov, when he invented his Ös writing, had to decide how to represent in writing three vowels Ös has but Russian lacks. The first vowel is 'a' as in 'apple', which linguists call a 'low front' vowel because the tongue is pushed downwards and forward in the mouth. The other two Ös vowels are not found in English, but sound like the 'ü' in German *kühl* ('cool') and the 'ö' in German *schön* ('beautiful'). Linguists dub these last two 'front rounded' vowels, because the tongue is pushed very far towards the front of the mouth and the lips are tightly puckered into a rounded shape. Vasya could have done what trained linguists would have done: invent new symbols for these distinctive sounds. But this would have been risky: people who already knew how to read and write Russian might have balked at using unfamiliar letters, and this might have dampened enthusiasm for the new writing.

<u>Алыч</u>

Артян туруп, кун гарагы шикпанча,
мян мылтыгын ап чердюпскем кольге.

Кольдя мен камям полган.

Камя олуруп амьда парыдым.

❦ ❦ ❦

<u>Лось</u> – Я утром стал, до восхода солнца, взял своё ружьё и отправился к озеру.
У озера был обласок мой. Я сел в обласок и отппавился.

<u>*Moose*</u> – *'I got up in the morning before the sun rose, took my gun and set off to the lake.'*
*'My boat was at the lake. I sat in my boat and set off.'*

**Figure 5.5**
The first book ever published in the Ös language (2005). This story about moose hunting was told by Vasya Gabov and translated into Russian and English by me with linguist Greg Anderson. Courtesy of Living Tongues Institute for Endangered Languages

A second solution would have been more like our English alphabet, where we make a single vowel symbol stand for more than one sound. For example, the words 'fat' and 'father' contain the same letter 'a' but are pronounced differently: 'fat' contains the same vowel as 'cat', while 'father' uses the same vowel as 'bother.' Our English writing imperfectly captures actual speech sounds. There are many exceptions that must simply be memorized, which is why events like spelling bees pose any sort of challenge. So, the

English-style solution (one letter represents multiple sounds) would also have been undesirable for Ös, and Vasya Gabov wisely rejected it.

Vasya instead came up with a clever solution using materials already available to him in the Russian alphabet. Russian has a special letter called the 'soft sign', which tells you to add a 'y' sound (as in 'yes') after a consonant. For example, you can say 'la' in Russian, or you can add a soft sign and say 'lya'. It is important to note that 'y' is not a vowel here, it is what linguists call a palatal glide and it gets added onto the 'l' sound to make it distinctive in Russian, while still sounding like an 'l'. Ös, unlike Russian, lacks palatalized consonants, so the soft sign is of no use. But Vasya noticed that the tongue motion required to produce 'y' is very similar to the tongue motion needed to produce the three special vowels. Both 'y' and the vowels require the tongue to be pushed very far forward in the mouth, almost to the point where it bumps against the palate.

Most people are not aware of what their tongue is doing when they produce vowels. In fact it takes professional training by a phonetician or speech therapist for most of us to become aware of which tongue motions produce which sounds. We learned to make speech sounds in infancy, by babbling, and have never thought about it consciously. Vasya figured it out on his own, with no professional help, and wove this solution into his writing system in an ingenious way, one that even a professional linguist might not have thought of.[17]

In his writing system, he placed the soft sign (which signals the speaker to push their tongue towards the front) after the first consonant following one of the three special vowels. He also decided, economically, that he would put in only one soft sign per word. Since Ös has a rule of *vowel harmony* which requires all vowels in a word to be pronounced either in the front of the mouth or in the back, only a single soft sign is needed to clue in speakers that all the vowels in a word are pronounced towards the front of the mouth. What is surprising to linguists is that Vasya figured out the intricacies of tongue position and the system of vowel harmony all without any technical training, and then fitted his writing system perfectly to both.

## To Survive, Be Memorable

Oral culture may also hold keys to understanding how human memory works. In order for anything to be passed on, it must be memorable. We

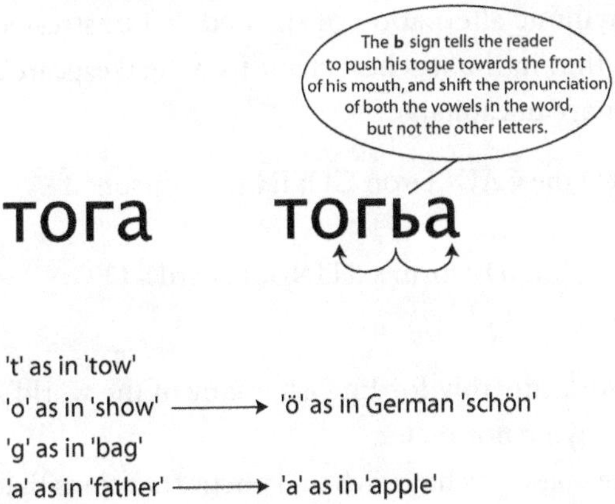

The **b** sign tells the reader to push his togue towards the front of his mouth, and shift the pronunciation of both the vowels in the word, but not the other letters.

тога тогьа

't' as in 'tow'
'o' as in 'show' ⟶ 'ö' as in German 'schön'
'g' as in 'bag'
'a' as in 'father' ⟶ 'a' as in 'apple'

**Figure 5.6**
Vasya Gabov's naïve orthography for Ös cleverly uses the Russian 'soft sign' {ь} to signal alternative vowel pronunciations.

can view the diversity of human verbal arts as a kind of survival of the fittest. Let us start by taking examples from American culture. Speech forms like rap and song lyrics, limericks, jokes, ghost stories, hopscotch counting rhymes, and cheerleader chants do not often get written down. They are passed on mostly by oral recitation and memorization among young people. To survive and be passed on to successive generations, speech genres in a given culture must offer memory a number of easy hooks to hold onto. Hard-to-memorize genres will not survive long unless they are written down. In a non-literate culture, writing is not an option, and so all verbal speech forms must allow for easy memorization.

Verbal arts that come down to us through purely oral cultures resemble well-polished rocks.[18] All the rough edges have been smoothed as the rock has passed through many minds, and through generations of transmission, repetition, and memorization. What is left is the essential core, finely wrought and perfectly fitted to its niche (human memory). Scholars of oral epics have explored how verbal art forms succeed in getting memorized and passed on, and shown how works like Homer's *Iliad* are "elaborately adapted to the constraints of oral transmission and human memory."[19]

All languages have virtuoso wordplay we would recognize as poetry, but in most languages these are never written down. Languages use different strategies to create poetry and to render it memorable in the absence of writing. In the Western tradition, we are used to thinking of rhyme as the best aid to memory in poems, as in: "The rain in Spain stays mainly in the plain."[20] A second common strategy of our Western literary canon is meter, especially the rhythmic alternation of stressed and unstressed syllables. We hear this rhythm in the witches' chant from Shakespeare's *Macbeth* (stressed syllables are in capitals):

> "ROUND and ROUND the CAULDron GO; IN the POIsoned ENtrails THROW
> . . . ADder's FORK and BLIND-worm's STING, LIZard's LEG and HOWlet's WING"

While these devices work superbly for English, many of the world's languages care for neither rhyme nor meter.

Nonetheless, these languages may have rich oral poetic traditions that use an array of different strategies to aid memory. Languages like Tuvan, for example, lack rhyme almost entirely. How can a language lack rhyme? When building words in Tuvan, you add suffixes. Since there is a limited set of suffixes, it is trivially easy (and uninteresting) to make words rhyme. For example, it is easy to rhyme *bar-gan* 'went' and *al-gan* 'took' or *ur-gan* 'lifted'. These all rhyme automatically with the past tense suffix '*-gan*' attached. While rhyming is thus possible in Tuvan, it presents no creative challenge to a poet and no unique pattern to memory. Simply put, for some languages rhyming is neither poetic nor memorable: other cognitively salient patterns must be found.

Similarly, Tuvan makes no use of rhythm or meter because the language has only very light stress, unlike in the lines from *Macbeth* above, where the stressed syllables get great emphasis. Tuvan stress can only appear on the last syllable of a word. So there is nothing creative or memorable to be done with stress either. To create poetry, Tuvan, like many small languages, must look elsewhere, beyond rhyme and meter. Tuvan poets employ cognitive strategies like alliteration (repeating first letters of words), assonance (repeating vowels within words), and parallelism (repeating words or phrases). All three of these powerful memory hooks figure prominently in Tuvan poetics.

The study of oral traditions in small languages, especially ones that have not been part of the canon of literature studies at universities or high schools, forces us to re-examine our notions of poetry and memory. What counts as poetry may be entirely different in Ainu, Tuvan, or Makah and may not resemble at all our received notions of what poetry looks like.

What we do expect to find in common in all oral traditions is a set of powerful devices that facilitate memory and a flair for playing with intricate structures of sound and meaning. We find verbal masterpieces that have survived the harsh test of time to emerge as well-polished pebbles of speech. These provide insights into how human memory works. They also tell us what kinds of mental hooks survive the test of forgetfulness, since the success of certain memory strategies can be judged in part by the survival of verbal art forms that employ them. As anthropologist Brad Shore notes: "Conventional oral genres were finely tuned to the cognitive requirements of retention and transmission."[21] Though humans all share the same memory device—a brain—the cognitive fine-tuning we see in poetry manifests itself differently in each human language.

## Our Vanishing Cultural Heritage

As languages fall out of use into forgetfulness, entire genres of oral tradition—stories, songs, and epics—rapidly approach extinction. Only a small fraction have ever been recorded or set down in books. And the tales captured in books, when no longer spoken, will exist as mere shadows of a once vibrant tradition. We stand to lose volumes: entire worldviews, religious beliefs, creation myths, observations about life, technologies for how to domesticate animals and cultivate plants, histories of migration and settlement, and collective wisdom. And we will lose insight into how humans fine-tune memory to preserve and transmit epic tales.

In our so-called 'information age', knowledge tends to be deep but narrow. At American universities you can enroll in entire courses of study devoted to the works of a single author or even a single work (for example, a course on the *Canterbury Tales*). It is ironic, then, that the collective wisdom of entire human societies languishes for lack of any attention from outsiders, for lack of use by the culture bearers themselves, and lack of interest on the part of their children.

It takes a decent amount of money and a lot of time and effort to go out and document small languages and their story traditions. But it is doable, and it deserves our urgent attention. Imagine a course at an American university on Kayapó entomology, on Tuvan epic tales, or on Papuan mathematics. We do not even know what it is that we stand to lose when these traditions fall into disuse without being recorded. As scientists and humanitarians, we are absurdly failing to notice the forest for the trees. If we can get beyond our book bias and appreciate the creativity and beauty of purely oral cultures, we open a portal to entire new vistas of the world and mankind's place in it. But that door, still ajar as I write this in 2006, will soon slam shut, and vast domains of human creativity will be forever closed to us.

## New Rice versus Old Knowledge

Rice harvest days have arrived in the tiny hamlet of Baynīnan, a village in the mountains of Luzon, the largest of the Philippine islands. I am sitting in the communal space under a thatched house raised on wooden posts, enjoying the shade, the fermented rice beer, and the smell of cooking pork and rice.

Next to me sits Mr. Puggūwon, a traditional shaman of the Ifugao people (the Ifugao language has 167,000 speakers). Sitting on his haunches, the shaman is wearing a loincloth and a bright red shawl. He chants in a singsong voice, swaying slightly back and forth. I begin to feel dizzy from the chanting and the rice beer I have drunk.

The host family themselves are not harvesting—they have hired day laborers who will work for a lunch of pork with rice and about a dollar. The head of the household, a young man of 26, now lives in the nearby town and only visits his elderly mother at important times such as rice planting and harvest. She lives alone, keeping an eye over the family's rice fields. "Nobody wants to be a rice farmer anymore," her

An Ifugao youth carries bundles of freshly harvested rice to the granary, 2001. Photograph by K. David Harrison

son explains to me in decent English, talking of his plans to learn computers and pursue a career in the city.

His elderly mother, stooped and quiet, sits gazing out over her family's rice field below (see fig. 1.6). Rice paddies are sacred in these parts, inherited and passed down, and the object of many ritual and religious observances. The family invited Mr. Puggūwon, the local shaman, to sacrifice a chicken, drain its blood into a wooden platter, and then 'read' its entrails for signs of an auspicious year, season, and crop. After the sacrifice, he began chanting their genealogy, an activity deemed essential to invoke the spirit world of deceased ancestors in support of a successful harvest.

Young men and boys tread a constant circuit from the paddies down below up to the house yard, carrying wooden yokes laden with bundles of rice. Each yoke weighs upwards of 80 pounds, and the boys' bare feet leave deep impressions in the mud. Younger children heft single bundles of rice on their heads, taking frequent breaks to play.

Down below, in the pond fields, women harvest rice as they have for centuries: by hand, with small metal blades. Ankle deep in muddy water, they progress slowly across the paddy. As they work, an occasional hum of song breaks out. Traditionally, an epic song, the *hud-hud*, was sung by women while harvesting rice. The *hud-hud* has fallen into disuse in recent years and is now known only in fragments. It may soon be forgotten as radio and TV assume a more important role in Philippine rural life.

Some distance from the harvesting women, one woman toils alone. She is a seed selector, trained from early youth in rice knowledge. At harvest time, certain foods, social contacts, and activities are taboo to her. As the women make their way across the field cutting rice stalks by hand, the seed selector moves out in front collecting the plumpest healthiest seeds for replanting next season. The well-being of the community is in her hands. If she fails to pick correctly, the crop will suffer, stomachs will be empty, and the genetic vigor of the plants may deteriorate. If she picks correctly, the strains of rice will mix their genetic material, become hardy, grow plump, and feed many.

I have come to this village with renowned anthropologist Prof. Harold Conklin, who has devoted more than 40 years to understanding highland Philippine rice cultures.[1] He speaks fluent Ifugao, and even helped devise a writing system for the language. But only a handful of people read and write Ifugao, and our seed selector is not among them. Her knowledge resides only in her head, and Professor Conklin has spent years interviewing her to record that knowledge. Much of what the seed selector knows involves subtle qualities of rice stalks and grains: color, plumpness, texture, crunchiness. She commands a very large set of terms for rice varieties and qualities, and these serve as the conduit to allow her to pass on the knowledge to girls who will be seed selectors after her.

The Ifugao language, documented by Conklin and others, has an intricate vocabulary of rice technology. Their language has 27 different names for pottery vessels for storing rice wine, 30 names for types of woven baskets used to carry foods, and 130 phrases describing in detail payments made for the use of rice pond fields.[2] It has many expressive words like *tiwātiw*, a verb meaning 'to frighten animals, birds or chickens away from drying rice'.

The entire existence of the Ifugao revolves around rice and its cultivation. In a myth now mostly forgotten, the Ifugao were first given rice and instructions for its planting by unearthly beings they called 'Skyworld people'. The Ifugao people have quite literally moved mountains to grow their rice. Living on the steepest of hillsides, they have covered every available square foot with massive stone-walled pond fields. To irrigate these, they have developed unparalleled expertise in hydrology. Hardly a drop of rain falls on their mountain that is not channeled, controlled, and put to the service of rice irrigation. The massive stone terraces are served by a network of thousands of channels, weirs, pools, and aqueducts. Walking along one path, I spotted a single leaf, the size of my palm, that had been pinned down with twigs in such a way that it would channel a tiny trickle of water into a nearby pond field.

Rice knowledge—including seed selection, cultivation, hydrology, and so much more—is on the wane, as scientifically engineered modern varieties of rice and planting and fertilization techniques advance up from the lowlands. Driving up from Manila, my driver swerved constantly to avoid beds of drying rice, called *palay*, lining the highway. Looking at the rice paddies, I noticed that every single one bore a metal placard touting the brand of hybrid rice or pesticide being used. As we reached the highlands, the areas the Ifugao people inhabit, these signs vanished, indicating that more traditional varieties of rice were still being planted, and with fewer pesticides.

An Ifugao shaman, Puggũwon, blesses the rice harvest with chanting, offerings of rice, rice wine, and chicken entrails. Photograph by K. David Harrison

It is hard to argue with progress: as modern (genetically engineered) high-yield rice varieties have been introduced, along with modern fertilizer and pesticides, crop yields have increased. But what is the downside?

Modern rice is the subject of intense research including production of new genetically modified strains. Paradoxically, the international seed industry, which does an estimated $15 billion a year in trade, derives much of its genetic technology from crops "selected, nurtured, improved by Third world farmers for hundreds, even thousands of years."[3] Farmers in the Philippines now find themselves under pressure to abandon traditional rice technologies and even the strains of rice bred over millennia by their ancestors. The Philippine Rice Institute—known as 'Phil Rice'—advocates hybrid rice strains, pesticides, and fertilizers to increase yield. Phil Rice openly belittles traditional knowledge as useless folk-beliefs that hinder effective farming. Under traditional beliefs, farmers were "forbidden to plant when there was no moon and when the *ipon* or million fish is in season, since this will be the time when insects will also multiply." Phil Rice debunks such beliefs, blaming farmers' low rice yields on the "superstitions that bound them for years."[4]

An ideological struggle is underway, pitting peasant farmers with traditional knowledge and technologies against the global cartel that manufactures pesticides, fertilizer, and rice hybrids. The cartel seems to have the upper hand because it can claim, in the short term, higher yields and more income for farmers who abandon old ways and take on modern technologies. Hybrid rice growing is aggressively promoted to farmers by radio, training workshops, even brochures and cartoons. Written in the national language Tagalog, this propaganda ignores specialized local knowledge of rice found in the 170 smaller languages spoken across the Philippines.

Recently, a few farmers have begun to resist the pressure and organize protests against the new rice. "Hybrid rice promotes farmers dependency on chemical inputs that are harmful to human health and the environment," declares Danilo Ramos of the Philippine Peasant Movement. "Contrary to the claim of Phil Rice that it serves the interests of farmers, it actually protects the interests of agrochemical

A propaganda cartoon from the Philippines Rice Institute (PhilRice) depicts a modern farmer bestowing hybrid rice grains on a traditional, loincloth wearing farmer. The modern farmer says in Ilocano: "We harvest a lot here in the North." Courtesy of PhilRice. Ilocano translation courtesy of Dante Obcena

transnational corporations because hybrid rice promotes the heavy use of pesticides and commercial fertilizers."[5]

It is not clear if traditional rice technologies will survive modern agro-technology and cultural shifts. Lost in the debate is the role of traditional knowledge and the many small Philippine languages that contain it.[6] Just as the right to practice a traditional livelihood may be seen as a human right, so too may the right to speak your own ancestral language, and to tap into the knowledge it contains. This right must be safeguarded even if small languages and folk knowledge seem inefficient in our modern world. Must it be a choice? Isn't there something that could be learned from traditional knowledge that might inform modern genetics and crop science? We can only answer this question if these languages and knowledge systems get the chance to stay around for the future.

# 6 Endangered Number Systems

## Counting to Twenty on Your Toes

We have no word for "thousand."
—Anna Badeyeva, a last speaker of the Ös language of Siberia.

These Esquimaux are no great proficients in the science of arithmetic, their numerals extending in general only to five . . . In counting even as far as three they must use their fingers as auxiliaries, and before they arrive at seven generally make some mistake.[1]
— Captain William Parry, 1820s Arctic explorer

Human languages, when counting, not only have different names for the numbers but also use a wide diversity of mathematical strategies. In almost all languages, speakers build larger numbers by combining smaller numbers, called bases. Most large, global languages use ten as a base. In this chapter, we explore unusual counting systems found in small and endangered languages. Some may have no numbers at all, or such limited counting that scientists have questioned whether counting is even necessary to human cultural and intellectual life. Many languages have the capability to go on counting forever, while others stop at thirty-six, five, or even three. Others employ unusual number bases, counting by combining twos, threes, or even fifteens. Some languages require their speakers to master complex calculations in order to simply count to ten.

All humans appear to be born with an innate 'number sense', and even 5-month-old infants show sensitivity to number and quantity. But languages differ enormously in the kinds of counting systems they choose to build (or not build) upon this cognitive foundation. Many of the more unusual counting systems are found in endangered languages. These are likely to disappear before scientists can discern the full range of possible counting systems. If this happens, we stand to lose important insights into

## Languages Featured in Chapter 6

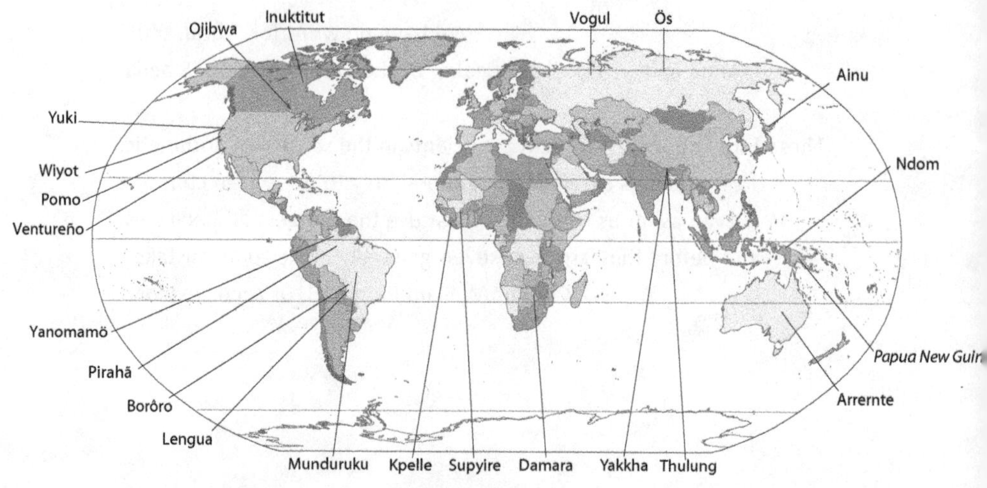


Papua New Guinea Language Hotspot:
Aiome, Yagwoia, Baruga, Bukiyip, Huli, Kaluli, Kewa, Kobon, Loboda, Vanimo, Wampar, Yupno

how humans count, why they count, and how our innate number sense reveals itself in our culturally defined counting habits.

Humans have probably always counted, to keep track of people, animals, possessions, units of time, and other countable things. Numbers and quantities matter to us, and they are one fundamental way we interact with our physical environment, view the world, notice patterns, and find our way. Early *Homo sapiens* left behind bones with carefully carved notches that resemble our use of stick figures to tally items in groups of five.[2] An intricately carved eagle's bone from Le Placard, France dated 13,000 to 17,000 years old, bears carved notches that have been deciphered as numbers corresponding to lunar cycles.[3] This eagle bone thus represents one of the earliest counting devices and at the same time is the earliest known calendar. (The connection between counting, time-reckoning, and calendar systems is a topic dealt with in chapter 3.)

Whether counting with the help of words, fingers, toes, body parts, or objects like the notched eagle bone, humans have a wide variety of counting strategies and routines available to them. These depend—to a surprising extent—on what language they happen to speak.

## Tallying Sticks and Stones

Objects can serve as an aid to mental counting. Just as we offload mathematical tasks onto a calculator, many societies developed mechanical devices to assist computation. The Kpelle people of Liberia (487,000 speakers) count with piles of pebbles. They are reportedly so adept at this specific task that they performed better than a group of Yale undergraduates at estimating numbers of pebbles (ranging from 10 to 100) in a pile. But those same Kpelle—living in a tiny village of 97 souls in 41 grass huts—performed poorly when asked to report the precise number of huts and people in their village. The fact that this was a highly unusual counting task and not done with the aid of stones may have contributed to their incorrect answers.[4]

The Pomo of California (less than 60 speakers),[5] who excelled at basket-weaving, hunting, and fur-trading, counted with sticks. An early twentieth-century anthropologist described with admiration Pomo calculations of large sums: "The Pomo are great counters. . . . They counted their long strings of beads. Their arithmetical faculties must have been highly developed. The Pomo . . . are well able to continue counting indefinitely."[6]

Below twenty, the Pomo had unique names for numbers—for example, *k'áli* meant 'one'. However, for twenty and above, they combined number names with 'stick' or 'big stick'. For sixty-one, the Pomo would say *xómk'a-xày k'áli,* combining *xómk'a* meaning 'three' with *xày* 'stick' plus *k'áli* 'one'. Pomo counting thus took place both in the mind, using linguistic labels, and on the ground, by laying out sticks.

*Some Pomo numbers*

| | |
|---|---|
| 20 | '1 stick' |
| 61 | '3 sticks and 1' |
| 100 | '5 sticks' |
| 400 | '1 big stick' |
| 500 | '1 big stick and 5 [small] sticks' |
| 4,000 | '10 big sticks' |

A Pomo myth reveals that the Pomo did have occasion to count quite high. When a 'bear shaman' accidentally caused the death of a person, he feigned sympathy by counting out forty thousand beads (used by the Pomo as currency) in recompense.

Use of objects (pebbles, sticks, toes) for counting begs the question: which came first, object counting or mental concepts of numbers? Claudia Zaslavsky, an expert in African mathematics, surmises object counting came first:

> The development of a number system depends upon need. In a small, self-contained economy in which all or most of the necessities of life are produced within the community—typical of large sections of Africa—there is little need for an extensive reckoning system. The names of numbers are frequently connected with the objects to be counted, just as we have special names for certain sets—flock, herd brace, etc., dating back from a pastoral or agricultural society.[7]

While language may facilitate counting, it need not strictly limit it. For example, a language may have no word for 'thousand' but that does not mean its speakers could not devise a way to count that high if they needed to. If the need persisted over time, then speakers would surely invent a word for 'thousand' or borrow it from another language they came into contact with.

Using objects is one way to extend a counting system higher, as the Pomo discovered. By offloading counting tasks onto physical objects, people having limited linguistic number repertoires count much higher. Math historian Karl Menninger imagines a more extreme example:

> It is a mistake to think that a tribe that has only three number words can count only to three, by physically representing the number by a quantity of pebbles arranged element by element, they can count much further. As the use of counting devices became commonplace, a language might adopt a word for higher numbers that was simply the name for the object used to tally them, so, 'pile' (of pebbles) could come to mean 'twenty'.[8]

Both language and cultural practice shape counting ability and influence the specific set of number words that a language may invent. This influence also works in the other direction: once a set of counting objects is agreed upon, the names for those objects no longer need refer solely to a 'stick' or 'pebble' but may become completely abstract, linguistic labels denoting numbers. Countable objects like sticks, pebbles, and fingers become hooks upon which people hang certain cognitive operations and help reinforce the links between objects and concepts.

## Body Parts as Numerals

Our earliest human counting device must have been our fingers and toes. Using fingers to count is a nearly universal trait of humankind. Many languages simply use finger names ('pinkie', 'index finger') instead of having number words at all. The Borôro language (850 speakers) uses complex phrases referring to fingers as numbers. Borôro number nine is 'the one to the left side of my middle finger', ten is 'my fingers all together in front', thirteen is 'now the one on my foot that is in the middle again' (by which the speaker means that he has counted all his fingers, started counting toes on one foot, and has reached his middle toe).[9]

Some languages extend body-counting far beyond fingers and toes, naming other body parts (arm, elbow, left and right nostril) to count as high as seventy-four. Body-part counting requires much more than just noticing the fact of ten fingers and toes and using these to tally up objects in the world—it presupposes an abstract understanding of numbers. The fact that the body has ten fingers and toes might seem to encourage counting to twenty and using five, ten, or twenty as a base, and in fact these are the most common combinatory number bases worldwide. But many body-based counting systems turn out to be limited and often do not use numerical bases to create larger numbers.

Of course, the body may be interpreted in different ways. Though languages spoken as far apart as the Oceanic islands and the Himalayan mountains use the word for 'hand' to mean 'five', the fact of having five-fingered hands does not force your language to count in units of five.

For the Kewa people (35,000 speakers) of Papua New Guinea, who omit the thumb, 'four' is expressed as 'one hand', 'five' is 'one hand and one thumb', six is 'one hand and two thumbs'. Kewa speakers can go further—they are not limited to the actual number of hands and thumbs they have. 'Twelve' is 'three hands', while 'three hands and three thumbs' means 'fifteen'. Since nobody actually has three hands or three thumbs, this shows how a body-based system can morph into a purely mental counting system with abstract bases.

Linking counting to the hands provides efficiency and aids memory. The Aivilingmiut dialect of Inuktitut (14,000 speakers) has unique number words for one through five and for ten. Six is expressed as 'the one at the edge of the right hand', while seven and eight re-use the number words for two and three plus the expression 'at the edge of the right hand'.[10] Aivilingmiut children might learn to count to ten more easily than English-speaking children do because they memorize fewer unique labels to reach ten and because memorization gets anchored to the body.

Counting on the body is so 'handy' that it can emerge in a language that did not previously use it—hands and feet serve as natural points of reference. The Yakkha people are subsistence farmers who number only a few thousand and inhabit the lower Arun valley in eastern Nepal. The Yakkha numerals as recorded in 1857 were based on the Tibeto-Burman ancestor language and similar to those in many related languages.[11] But many of the neighboring languages have since replaced their higher numbers with words from the dominant national language, Nepali. Similarly, by this century, the Yakkha had preserved the ancestral numbers only up to three.

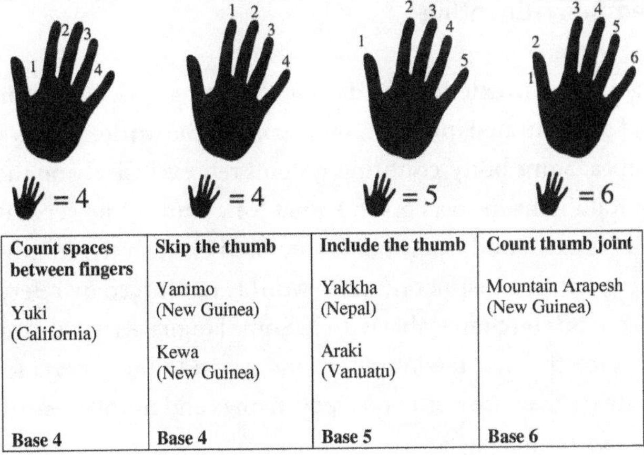

= 4
= 4
= 5
= 6
Count spaces between fingers
Yuki (California)
Base 4
Skip the thumb
Vanimo (New Guinea)
Kewa (New Guinea)
Base 4
Include the thumb
Yakkha (Nepal)
Araki (Vanuatu)
Base 5
Count thumb joint
Mountain Arapesh (New Guinea)
Base 6


**Figure 6.1**
Four different ways to count the hand: Yuki counts just the four spaces between the fingers; Vanimo and Kewa count to four by omitting the thumb; Yakkha and Araki, like English, tally all five digits; Mountain Arapesh gets six by including the thumb joint. Yuki data from Kroeber 1925, qtd. in Hinton 1994: 118. Kroeber, who studied the Yuki Indians of northern California, connects the origin of their base-4 system to the way they used their hands in stick counting: "they did not count the fingers but the spaces between them, in each of which . . . two twigs were laid. Naturally enough, their 'hundred' was 64" (4 hands holding 8 sticks each). Yakkha data from Gvozdanović 1985. Vanaimo, Kewa, Araki, and Mountain Arapesh counting systems data from Lean 1992

But when linguists visited the Yakkha in the 1980s, they found numbers above three had been replaced not with Nepali numbers, but with terms based on Yakkha words for hand (*muktapi*).[12] Four and the numbers above five were all produced by adding or subtracting from five. By introducing the word 'hand', to mean five, along with addition and subtraction, the Yakkha avoided borrowing any Nepali numbers. They gave up a simpler but less transparent counting system to adopt a more mathematically complex and transparent (and perhaps more learnable) body-part based system. The Yakkha innovation opposes an overwhelming global trend of giving up native ways of counting to borrow numbers from politically dominant tongues.

## Extended Body-Counting

Languages that use extended body-part counting systems are small, isolated, and concentrated in a few remote parts of the world, mostly in Papua New Guinea. Some body-counting systems rely exclusively on the human body. In Kaluli (2,500 speakers in Papua New Guinea) no separate words for numbers exist: body-part names are used exclusively. In other body-counting systems, a distinct number word is reinforced by reference to a body part or is interchangeable with it. Some languages use abstract number words for the first few numbers and move to body parts for higher figures, others may use both body-part names and number words for the very smallest numbers.

Although there are examples of body-counting from around the world, the forty or so systems in the mountains of Papua New Guinea (an area about as big as California) exhibit the most diversity. They differ in how high they count on the body (ranging from just twelve all the way up to seventy-four), which direction they count (top to bottom, left to right), how much of the body they employ (upper body only or upper and lower), and which body parts (nostril, elbow, penis) get assigned values.

In Kaluli you count by naming or pointing to a body part. Kaluli counting (fig. 6.3) starts with the pinkie finger at the lower left. By eighteen, the Kaluli counter has arrived at the nose, the midpoint, and moves

**Table 6.1**
**Yakkha numerals being replaced by body-counting**

| *Yakkha numbers in the 1850s* | | *Yakkha numbers in the 1980s* | | |
|---|---|---|---|---|
| *ik'ko* | 1 | *kolok* | 1 | |
| *kicchi* | 2 | *hitci* | 2 | |
| *sum'chi* | 3 | *sumci* | 3 | |
| *líchi* | 4 | *sumcibi usongbi kolok* | 3+1 | |
| *gnáchi* | 5 | *muktapi* | | 'hand' |
| *tuk'chi* | 6 | *muktapi usongbi kolok* | +1 | 'hand and one' |
| *núchi* | 7 | *muktapi usongbi hitci* | + 2 | 'hand and two' |
| *phang'chi* | 8 | *muktapi usongbi sumci* | + 3 | 'hand and three' |
| *yecchi* | 9 | *muckcurukbi kolok hongbi* | -1 | 'hands one less' |
| *ik'bong* | 10 | *muktapi hita* | | 'hand two' |

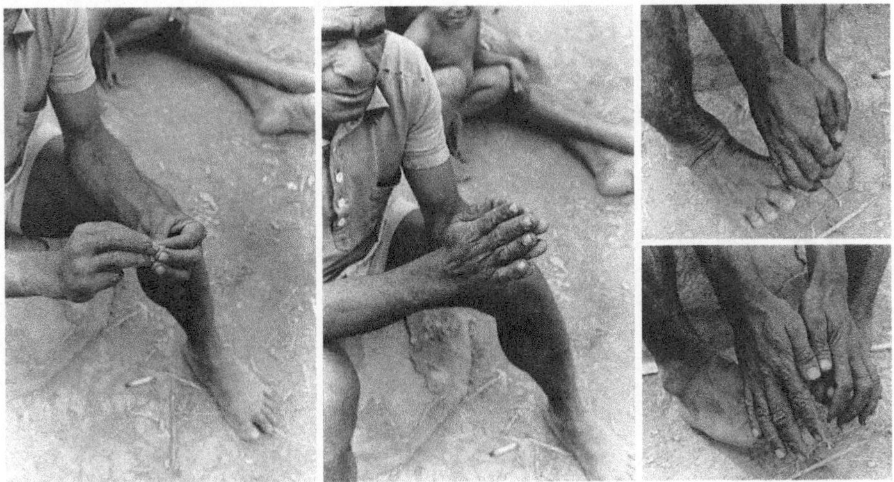

**Figure 6.2**
Mr. Omalyca-Taqalyce of the Iqwaye people demonstrates counting on his fingers and toes. 9 = all the fingers but the right pinkie; 10 = all the fingers; 11 = all the fingers and the big toe; 20 = all the fingers and toes. Yagwoia-Anga language, Yalqwaalye village, Papua New Guinea. Courtesy of Jadran Mimica

symmetrically back down to the right pinkie for a full cycle (to thirty-five).

As the modern world encroaches, the Kaluli are reportedly abandoning body-counting. Their counting needs have changed now that they participate in the national economy and school system and have paper money to count. Being bilingual in Tok Pisin, the national language, the Kaluli now use Tok Pisin numbers to count money and large sums and limit their use of body-counting to small numbers up to twenty.[13]

If counting systems like that of Kaluli go extinct, or survive only as museum relics, entire philosophies of mathematics may be lost. Some may not lament this loss. After all, it could be argued that humans likely would not have invented nuclear physics or algebra using only Kaluli body-counting. But we need not claim every mathematical system is equally complex to acknowledge that each is a unique achievement of human thought and reasoning. Each sets forth a unique philosophical viewpoint, which, once lost, may never be re-imagined.

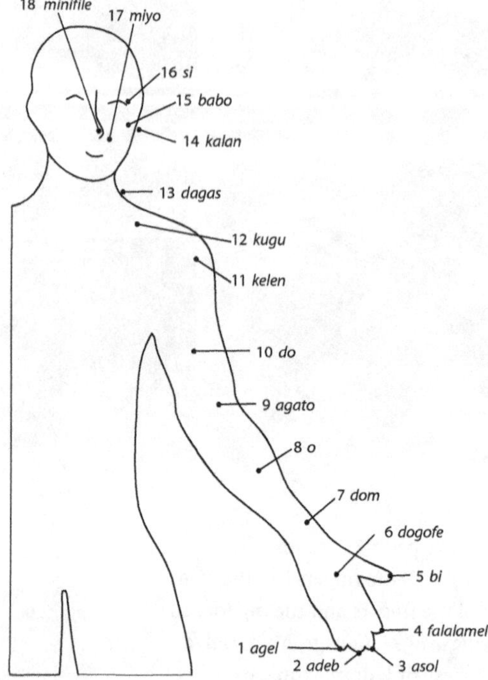


**Figure 6.3** Kaluli names for body parts also serve as numbers. Kaluli counting. After Schieffelin and Feld 1998

Like the Kaluli, the Kobon (6,000 speakers) have no words for numbers and count by naming or pointing to body parts. I invite the reader to count aloud to ten in the Kobon way. We will start at the left pinky and we will point to and name the countable body parts in order: *little finger, ring finger, middle finger, forefinger, thumb, wrist, forearm, inside elbow, bicep, shoulder.* We have reached ten, now we will go a bit higher on the body: *collarbone.* Next is the mid-point, twelve, the hollow at the base of the throat. In English, we have no name for this spot, but the Kobon call it '*mögan*'. After the midpoint, we proceed down the right side of the body, but here the count gets a little more difficult. We use the same set of words but add the word *böng,* meaning 'other side' after each one. Here we go: *collarbone böng, shoulder böng, biceps böng, inside elbow böng, forearm böng, wrist böng, thumb böng, forefinger böng, middle finger böng, ring finger böng, little finger böng.* Now we have reached twenty-three, which is one complete cycle in Kobon body-counting.

It may seem odd to have a counting system that stops at an odd number, but the Kobon seem to be more interested here in symmetry (eleven on each side, plus a mid-point) than divisibility. But they do not stop here; Kobon speakers can continue back in the opposite direction (fingers of right hand up to chest then down to fingers of left hand), thus counting all the way up to 46. Here the counting gets really complex because on the way back across the body, you have to say a phrase that means '*hand turn around go back*' before naming each body part. This means the hand is retracing its steps in the other direction. When you get past the midpoint, you have to say both '*hand turn around go back*' and '*other side*'. So, in order to say 'thirty-nine' you have to say the equivalent of '*hand turn around go back, inside elbow other side*'. As awkward as this sounds, the Kobon can count even higher using multiple circuits around the body. To count sixty-one seashells, they will say '*hand turn around second time go back biceps other side seashells*'. Now try saying that really fast and imagine you are counting seashells.[14]

## Doing the Math

Can people who have only or primarily body-counting also do arithmetic? For most of the body-part systems, we have only scanty ethnographic accounts of what people actually do with the numbers, what they choose to count, and whether they add, subtract, multiply, or use them in transactions. Speakers who are adept at body-counting may use it only infrequently or with difficulty to perform larger calculations.

But calculations in indigenous cultures are not idle schoolroom exercises; they emerge in response to environmental needs. As counting systems evolve to meet local needs, people who inhabit similar environments may select very different scenarios for counting. While the number-obsessed Huli people (70,000 speakers) reportedly count nearly everything, the neighboring Loboda (less than 8,000 speakers) apparently count nothing but money. The nearby Yupno (7,200 speakers) count 'string bags, grass skirts, pigs, traditional string money, and modern paper money', but do not count 'days, people, sweet potatoes, or betel nuts', perhaps in observance of some taboo or simply because they regard it as unnecessary.[15]

Body-counting constitutes a closed system and poses difficulty in generating larger numbers because it never evolved to fill such a need. The Iqwaye people (2,500 speakers of the Yagwoia tongue) do a lot with a very limited body-count system. They have number words only for 'one' and 'two'. For all higher numbers they use only the words 'one' and 'two' plus the toes and fingers grouped into base units of five (fig. 6.2). Five is 'hand', ten is 'two hands'. Eleven is '(two hands then) down to the leg then one'. Here, the phrase referring to hands may be omitted because any Iqwaye speaker knows that once you get down to the feet you have already counted the hands. Fifteen gets expressed as 'half of the legs' meaning that you have counted the toes on one foot. Twenty is 'one man', meaning all a person's fingers and toes. One hundred is expressed as 'five men' (5 x 20). The system becomes unwieldy with larger numbers, which are infrequently used.[16] Five hundred gets cumbersomely expressed as "this many persons [as] me, this [one] person all their legs and hands and then to another person's hand all their legs and hands." Let us break it down into parts and paraphrase it:

| | |
|---|---|
| 'I am one person, count me' | 1 |
| 'Now count all digits of my legs and hands' | x 20 |
| 'Now count the digits on that other guy's hand' | + 5 |
| | = 25 |
| 'Now count all digits on the legs and hands of that many people' | (20 * 25) = 500 |

The body-counting systems of the Kaluli, Kobon, and Iqwaye constitute some of the more colorful of those reported from Papua New Guinea. In his survey *Counting Systems of Papua New Guinea and Oceania*, Glendon Lean documented diverse body-counting systems that counted up to 12, 14, 18, 19, 22, 23, 25, 26, 27, 28, 29, 30, 31, 32, 33, 35, 37, 47, 68, and 74, respectively. Clearly, such systems have proven adaptable and useful to the lifeways of hunter-gatherers and subsistence agriculturalists of New Guinea. They also tell us something about the history of the region and cultural contacts among New Guinean tribes. And they may provide insights into how the human mind grasps numbers.

But body-counting that extends beyond the hands is not confined to Oceania. Over and over, cultures have hit upon the same idea of anchoring mathematics to the body. The Lengua people of Paraguay (6,705 speakers), hunter-gatherers of the swampy Chaco region, used a mixed system with names for one, two, and three, and the use of hands and feet as base units of five. They adopt a concept of symmetry to describe the number four as two identical 'sides' of two each.

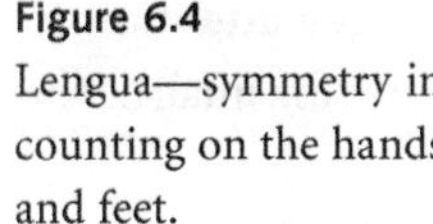

**Figure 6.4**
Lengua—symmetry in counting on the hands and feet.

| | | |
|---|---|---|
| 1 | 'one' | |
| 2 | 'two' | |
| 3 | 'two (and) one' | |
| 4 | 'two sides alike' (fingers are symmetrical--two sets of two) | |
| 11 | 'arrived at the foot one' | I |
| 12 | 'arrived at the foot two' | II |
| 13 | 'arrived at the foot two and one' | II+I |
| 14 | 'arrived at the foot two sides alike' | II II |
| 20 | 'finished the feet' | |

**Figure 6.5**
Lenguas of Paraguay playing the dice game Hăstáwa. Reproduced from Hawtrey 1901

Games with dice, a favorite pastime, reflect the Lengua attention to symmetry, the use of hands and feet to count, and preference for small bases:

> A characteristic game . . . *Hăstáwa* . . . played with dice . . . four pieces of wood, round on one side and flat on the other. Two are held in each hand, and brought smartly together, and then are swept off the under hand on to [*sic*] a smooth piece of hide. Even numbers, flat or round, score variously, and allow another throw; odd numbers give the next man his turn.[17]

## The Counting Baby

Infants, long before they talk, show evidence of innate abilities to grasp numerical concepts. Dubbed the 'number sense' by scientists, this mental faculty seems able to perform not only simple counting and estimates of quantities but also elementary mathematics with no training at all. In experiments carefully devised by psychologist Karen Wynn, 5-month-old babies were shown simple addition and subtraction operations performed with puppets. First, a single puppet inside a small box was shown to a baby. Then a screen was raised in front of the box to hide the puppet. The infant would then see a hand reach out from one side and deposit a second puppet in the space behind the screen. If the screen was then lowered to reveal not the expected two puppets, but just one, babies gazed at the scene longer. They paid significantly greater attention whenever the lowered screen revealed an unexpected number of objects: two instead of three, two instead of one. Babies' directed gaze indicated increased attention to illogical or impossible results of addition or subtraction, compared to the lesser amount of attention they devoted to numerically logical results. Wynn concludes:

> In sum, infants possess true numerical concepts . . . the existence of these arithmetical abilities so early in infancy suggests that humans innately possess the capacity to perform simple arithmetical calculations, which may provide the foundations for the development of further arithmetical knowledge.[18]

This and other research reveals that infants have a mental representation of number available to them at a very early age. They can discriminate sets of individual objects on the basis of number, and they also represent the correct results of additions and subtractions. Amazing as this ability is, it is not unique to humans. We share at least some of our innate 'number sense' with animals. Zoologist Marc Hauser and his colleagues performed Wynn's puppet experiments with wild Puerto Rican rhesus monkeys, substituting eggplants for puppets, and achieving similar results. The monkeys gazed longer at mathematically unexpected outcomes.[19]

Some animals can even learn symbols to represent numbers. Chimpanzees in a lab at Ohio State University were taught number symbols up to seven. One of the chimps, Sheba, was trained at first on numbers one, two, and three only. When she saw one of these flashed on a television screen, she had to select a nearby object bearing the matching number of dots. Sheba achieved an 85 percent success rate, well above random chance. In later experiments, Sheba was shown sets of objects (three oranges, two batteries, six balls) and had to select an arabic number written on a card to match the amount of items. Sheba again achieved significant success, indicating an ability to build learned behavior upon a foundation of an innate number sense (or pattern matching ability).

Whether Sheba was actually counting is not clear, but a more ambitious set of experiments attempted to teach her addition and subtraction. Sheba was presented with a card that read '1' then a card that read '3', and required to select a card that read '4' as the answer. She performed correctly 81 percent of the time. Most impressive were Sheba's subtraction skills. She would be shown an array of objects, say, four oranges. Then a box was placed over the oranges to hide them. With the oranges hidden from view, the experimenter reached his hand into a hole in the box and, in plain view of Sheba, removed items one at a time. Sheba was asked "How many are left?" which was her cue to pick an arabic number on a flashcard. She eventually performed correctly about 70 percent of the time, indicating she could couple symbolic knowledge of numbers with her ability to do simple subtraction.[20]

Training of non-primates, ranging from rats and raccoons to parrots and canaries, has succeeded in teaching them modest cognitive abilities that resemble human counting. Animals can be taught to recognize abstract, numbered quantities, independently of what specific objects they see. But they seem limited to low numbers and dependent on long training.[21] Animal researchers such as Marc Hauser remain wisely cautious in interpreting such findings, suggesting that "nonhuman primates such as rhesus monkeys may also have access to arithmetical representations, although alternative explanations must be considered."[22]

Science awaits many more important discoveries about the ability of human infants to grasp number concepts. Attempts to teach animals to count, while somewhat less mainstream, will provide us glimpses into the minds of other species. Since humans and animals share elements of an innate number sense, what is the point at which they diverge? Why and how do human beings construct upon these modest number abilities elaborate counting systems and entire mathematical philosophies? Can we identify cognitive and cultural building blocks for math? These are questions that will require many years of research to answer, but some preliminary proposals in this area hold promise.

Linguist George Lakoff and psychologist Rafael E. Núñez have suggested that humans evolved math through a process of metaphor-building. Humans, they claim, view the world in terms of innate concepts called 'image schemas'. These include notions like distance, proximity, containment, and solidity. Human infants come equipped with these basic notions about how the world works. For example, babies react with surprise (and heightened attention) if they see one supposedly solid object pass clean through another object. They are similarly surprised if one object magically morphs into another, for example, if a bottle is placed behind a screen, then the screen is raised to reveal a ball.[23]

Image schemas like those proposed above lead us to expect the physical world to behave in predictable ways: objects are solid, they retain their shapes, they can be added or subtracted. These notions provide the base upon which we build more elaborate concepts, or what Lakoff and Núñez call 'primary metaphors'. These include metaphors such as 'similarity is closeness'; 'motion is change'; or 'up is more, and down is less'. Languages transmit and reinforce these notions in thousands of everyday figures of speech: "He's *up* to his ears in debt" (= a lot of debt); or "Turquoise is *close* to blue" (= similar). When coupled with our innate number sense, basic metaphors may provide all the tools we need to develop full-blown mathematics. Lakoff proposes basic metaphors that allow humans to build arithmetic on top of our innate number sense. One such metaphor sees "arithmetic as motion along a path." It is fairly obvious that if zero can be conceived as the starting point of a path, addition is motion away from the origin and subtraction motion back towards it. If you are standing at position five on a line and you take two steps forward, you have added two and find yourself at seven. Or you can take one step back, subtracting to reach six.[24] Important numbers serve as signposts along a metaphorical math path and come to be used in number systems as combinatory bases.

In a few rare cases, endangered or extinct languages seem to visualize increasing numbers as motion along a path. Vogul (3,184 speakers in western Siberia) uses this strategy for many of its numbers. Vogul speakers look ahead to the next ten-unit and express how many one-unit steps they have moved towards it from the previous ten-unit. For example, Vogul twenty-two is expressed as 'thirty-towards two' (or 'two towards thirty'): starting from twenty, you take two steps in the direction of thirty and find yourself at twenty-two. No simple mathematical operation we could perform with thirty and two would get us twenty-two, but this process, termed "overcounting," makes perfect sense when thought of as a visual metaphor, in the manner suggested by Lakoff and Núñez (fig. 6.6).[25]

Old Turkic, a now vanished language we know only from ninth-century runic inscriptions, also overcounted. Twenty-seven was expressed 'seven thirty'. Languages descended from Old Turkic, including modern-

**Figure 6.6**
The overcounting procedure envisions integers as steps towards a destination.

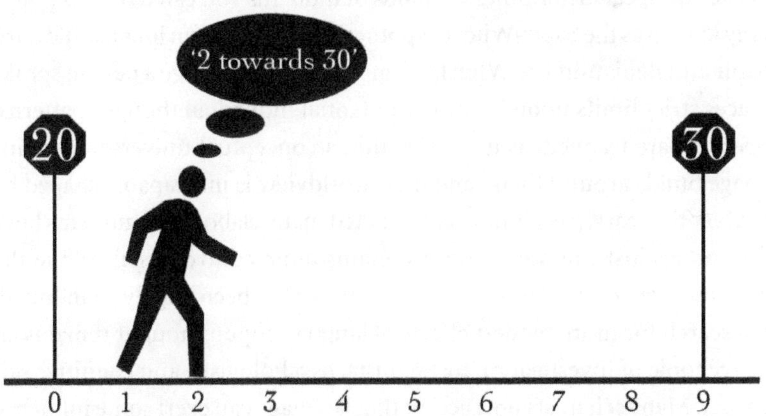

day Turkish, Kyrgyz, and Uzbek, have completely restructured their counting systems to look more like a standard base-10 system with addition—twenty-seven is now expressed as 2 x 10 + 7. While addition and subtraction are common in the world's number systems, overcounting is vanishingly rare.

## Does Language Shape Numerical Thought?

There must be intricate connections between the innate human number sense, cognitive metaphors, linguistic counting systems, and the emergence of mathematics. Despite having comparable cognitive abilities at the start, adult humans do not all end up speaking the same language or counting in the same ways. Languages differ in several key ways in the tools they provide their speakers for counting. First, they differ in how many numbers they give unique names to. Second, they differ in how high they count. Third, languages differ in the complexity of number names, for example, whether they encode concepts like addition and subtraction directly into number words. Fourth, to look at the big picture, languages presumably differ in their use of metaphorical extension, or to what extent they build elaborate, open-ended counting and numbering routines upon the modest foundation of innate human abilities. This last area—driven by language and culture—is perhaps where the most dramatic differences arise.

Does saying that languages differ in their counting and mathematical conceptions commit us to linguistic relativity? This notion—that the language you speak determines the kinds of thoughts you can have—is popularly known as the Sapir-Whorf hypothesis after American linguists Edward Sapir and Benjamin Lee Whorf. It holds that the language a person speaks places strict limits upon his or her potential individual thought patterns. Speakers are trapped, as it were, within a conceptual universe their language builds around them, and their worldview is inescapably shaped by it. Over the years, people have constructed many elaborate arguments both for and against this view, and it remains quite controversial. While the extreme form of the Sapir-Whorf hypothesis has been largely abandoned, the search for more modest effects of language upon thought remains an active topic of investigation by linguists, psychologists, and cognitive scientists. Many scientists now accept that language can exert some influence on thought, though they remain unsure as to how much influence and in what areas precisely.

One thing that languages can do is to direct speakers' attention to certain aspects of the world by forcing them to talk about these. For example, in Spanish, it is impossible to use any noun (even a made-up word) without first deciding if it is masculine or feminine gender. Though most non-living objects lack true gender (is a teapot feminine or masculine?), Spanish requires everything in the world be sorted into these categories.[26] In English, it is similarly impossible to use nouns in most circumstances without first deciding if it is definite or indefinite ('a' vs. 'the'), a distinction that is crucial in English but completely absent in many languages.

Language strictures like these lead scientists to wonder to what extent language and culture may influence human cognition. I use the term 'culture' here to mean simply knowledge that is learned from others and is not innate.[27] If language turns out to shape mathematical abilities at all, and these abilities differ across cultures, then it must be due to that part of language we learn from our parents, and not that part of language that is innate.

Linguists believe, based on a large body of research, that humans come genetically pre-programmed with elements of language, allowing them to learn any language to which they are exposed. There is much about universal linguistic structure that babies do not need to learn by inference or trial and error. For example, humans seem to have innate notions of word categories such as nouns, verbs, and so on. But we must learn by experience the particular facts about our mother tongues, for example, that 'dog' is *hund* or *chien*, that adjectives precede or follow nouns, or that nouns can have gender.

If your language has the particular quality of forcing you to sort even non-living objects into abstract categories of 'masculine' and 'feminine', do you come to think of them at some abstract level as possessing such qualities? A series of experiments by Psychologist Lera Boroditsky shows that speakers of 'gendered' languages like Spanish do come to associate typically feminine qualities (beauty, elegance) with even inanimate objects (bridges, tables) that their language assigns to the feminine gender, and associate different qualities with masculine-gendered objects. If true, this shows some small way in which an arbitrary linguistic category like gender can influence thinking. This is a promising beginning to understanding the subtle yet pervasive influence language and culture—and counting systems—may exert on thought.[28]

If linguistic structures can indeed influence thought, what role might culture may play in shaping mathematical thought? One effect of culture seems to be to determine if people need to count at all, and a further effect is on how high and complex the numbers can get.

## Life without Numbers

Linguist Daniel Everett has documented the lack of numbers in the Amazonian language Pirahã.[29] After living among the Pirahã, learning to speak proficiently in their tongue and appreciate their worldview, Everett startled the scientific world by claiming that the Pirahã lack numbers and counting altogether.[30]

Intrigued by Everett's claims about the Pirahã, psychologist Peter Gordon devised experiments to explore their concepts of numbers and counting.[31] He began with the assumption that the Pirahã, having an "impoverished" number system, might not perform so well at certain nonlinguistic cognitive tasks requiring counting. For example, he arrayed six batteries on a table, and then gave Pirahã speakers a handful of batteries and asked them to place more batteries on the table in a similar layout. The subjects performed correctly only about 75 percent of the time. The Pirahã performed much better if they only had to duplicate a set of two or three objects. If the task got complicated (duplicating a set of batteries with a set of nuts), they performed miserably on all sets greater than three objects.

Gordon concludes the "impoverished" counting system of the Pirahã "truly limits their ability to enumerate exact quantities when set sizes exceed two or three items." He notes, however, that their wrong answers tended to be *close* to the right number, indicating that they were relying not on counting (a skill with which their language does not equip them) but on estimating (which comes from the innate number sense) and were indeed attempting to answer correctly. Gordon interprets the results as evidence of a specific cognitive limitation imposed on the Pirahã directly by their language. If true, it would provide some evidence for how language can constrain thought. The claim is that the language's lack of numbers prevents the Pirahã from performing what ought to be simple counting of sets of objects. But since the Pirahã did show an ability to estimate, Gordon proposes that estimation is a separate area of cognition "immune" to the effects of number deprivation.

Gordon's research stirred up considerable controversy.[32] Another team of linguists studied the nearby Amazonian Munduruku people, who have a similarly impoverished linguistic counting system, and found similar results. However, this team interprets their results very differently from Gordon, stressing the Amazonians' estimation prowess. They write that while "language plays a special role in the emergence of *exact* arithmetic . . . we conclude that sophisticated numerical competence can be present in the absence of a well-developed lexicon of number words."[33]

The Yanoama (14,000 speakers), another Amazonian group, reportedly lack words for any numbers higher than three. Anthropologist Hans Becher, who documented the restricted Yanoama system, explains that their lack of number words in no way impairs their ability to detect small differences among quantities: "If twenty arrows are standing together and one increases or reduces the bundle by only one during the owner's absence, he will notice this change at once upon his return."[34] In other words, the Yanoama exercise a keen 'number sense', even without apparently being able to count above three. The distinction between counting and the number sense remains an important and culturally mediated one.

If claims about Pirahã, Munduruku, and Yanoama hold up under scrutiny, these may represent the lower limit of what a language can build upon the innate number sense. Very small languages such as these may thus hold vital clues to the possible limits of human mathematical thought—clues that will disappear as these languages cease to be spoken.

## Getting to Bases

No language with a large inventory of numbers assigns a unique, simple name to every one of them. Imagine if, in English, we had a word 'blark' that meant 'four hundred eight-seven' a word 'frep' meaning 'four hundred eighty-eight', and so on all the way up to one thousand. Though this would be quicker and more efficient to say, it is a significant burden to memorize 1,000 distinct words. Instead, we combine basic words to express big numbers, which requires more talk but less memory.

The units or building blocks we combine are called bases, and they seem to be a nearly universal property of number systems.[35] As soon as you have bases in a number system, you also get arithmetic because bases must be added, multiplied, or subtracted to generate other numbers. But you do not have to have very large bases or count very high to start using arithmetic. Aiome (751 speakers, New Guinea) employs only base-2 counting, yielding one of the simplest known systems known to include arithmetic operations.[36]

| | *Aiome numbers* | *Meaning* |
|---|---|---|
| 1 | *nogom* | 'one' |
| 2 | *omngar* | 'two' |
| 3 | *omngar nogom* | 'two and one' |
| 4 | *omngar omngar* | 'two and two' |
| 5 | *omngar omngar nogom* | 'two and two and one' |
| 6 | *omngar omngar omngar* | 'two and two and two' |

Few languages that have numbers fail to take advantage of this combinatory principle. However, in extremes, it does not seem practical. A theoretical number system with only one numeral (and therefore maximal combinatorics), makes the operation 7 + 7 formidable: "one one one one one one one plus one one one one one one one". Aiome, and languages like it, get by with the simplest inventory of numerals (two), and the greatest use of the combinatory system. At the other end of the spectrum are the larger body-counting systems, with almost as many unique names for numbers as they have body parts, but almost no combinatorics. English falls between those two extremes: one through twelve are simple numerals, as are hundred and thousand, but the vast majority of numbers gets expressed combinatorially.

When and what people choose to count is not necessarily constrained by their numeral system or its bases. This runs contrary to the assumption that individual details of a numeral system could make people in some cultures less eager to count things. The Loboda of Papua New Guinea have a base-5, base-20 system—one of the more common in the world—yet, as mentioned above, they seldom use it. For the Loboda, enumeration is simply not a traditional cultural practice.[37] Only a few hundred miles away, the Huli have a rare base-15 system that seems to be a regularized form of body-counting and incorporates complex classifiers that denote exactly what they are counting. Despite all this complexity, the Huli are reportedly avid counters, for example, using precise numbers in situations where English speakers might report a vague quantity.[38]

## We Have No Word for 'Thousand'

Even with the combinatory power of bases, counting systems can impose limits. Many languages with perfectly good combinatorial numbers simply lack a word for 'thousand'. I first became aware of this fact while visiting a small village built near a mosquito-filled bog in Central Siberia. I had come here with linguist Greg Anderson to verify whether there were any speakers left of a very small and little-documented language called Ös (35 speakers), discussed at some length in chapter 5.[39] After locating several elderly speakers, we were eager to elicit as many words and sentences as possible, including numbers. I still recall the perplexed look on the face of one speaker, 68-year-old Anna Badeyeva, when I asked her to say 'one thousand' in her native tongue. Up to that point, Anna had been counting up a storm, easily rattling off the twenties, sixties, hundreds, even large numbers like eight hundred and sixty-six. But when I asked for 'thousand' she seemed utterly stumped. There was a long silence. As a bilingual speaker who knew and regularly used the Russian word for 'thousand', she felt that her own language *ought* to have such a word, but it did not. She seemed momentarily disappointed. Then she smiled and remarked, "in the olden days, our people never needed to count a thousand things . . . so there's no word for it." I believe Anna's insight to be correct. Most languages get along fine with limited counting. Speakers can easily invent new labels or borrow them from other languages they may come in contact with. The Ös eventually borrowed the word *tisyach* (1,000) from Russian.

## Back-Door Math

Another way languages differ is in the complexity of their number words. For example, in English the word for 'eleven' is a simplex numeral—it is not formed through the combination of bases. An observant English speaker might be exposed to the notion of addition when she learns 'sixteen'. But since 'sixteen' does not really sound quite like 'six, ten' an English speaker could easily overlook the internal structure of the word and treat it as an opaque label. But in Ainu (a language still spoken by a few indigenous people in the far north of Japan) the word for eleven—*shine ikashima wa*—is complex and can be broken into parts that literally mean 'one added to ten'.[40] By simply learning the word, an Ainu speaker is exposed to the notion of addition, and the idea of ten as a base.

| | *Ainu numbers* | *Math formula* |
|---|---|---|
| 31 | *shine ikashima, wan e, tu hot ne* | |
| | 'one add, ten subtract, two twenty' | $1 + (2 \times 20) - 10$ |
| 39 | *shinepe-san ikashima, wan e, tu hot ne* | |
| | 'one minus ten add, ten subtract, two twenty' | $(10 - 1) + (2 \times 20) - 10$ |

Speakers of languages like Ainu get extra math knowledge essentially for free, without having to learn the concepts of addition, multiplication, subtraction separately from numbers or in a classroom. And why should they? Research on infants has shown that the brain possesses these notions from birth and with no explicit instruction. Some languages build much upon this natural mathematical foundation. Others build next to nothing. And as we have seen, even some of the very simplest systems, like Aiome, can include mathematics.

We do not fully know the cognitive consequences of exposure to hidden math. Research comparing the skills of children who speak English with children who speak Mandarin Chinese (which builds complex numbers upon base-10) suggests that the Chinese children, speaking a language with a 'transparent' counting system that includes more obvious mathematical operations, learn to count higher more quickly. The Chinese children also grasped the idea of a base and how to break larger numbers, for example fourteen, down into ten plus something. [41] Similarly, Welsh children were found to grasp how numbers are built of bases more quickly than do their monolingual English peers. They do so, it is claimed, because twelve in Welsh is pronounced *un deg dau* or literally "one ten two."[42] In other words, when exposed to a counting system that sneaks mathematics in through the back door, children may benefit cognitively.

## Unusual Bases

A language's choice of a base is not trivial and has far-reaching consequences for expressing numbers. Any choice is a trade-off, yielding greater efficiency in one area and less in another. Non-base-10 languages make it very difficult to say numbers that we decimal counters think are important. For example, in Supyire (364,000 speakers in Mali), 'one thousand' gets cumbersomely expressed as (400 x 2) + (80 x 2) + (20 x 2).[43] But non-decimal bases make it easy to say other numbers. In base-15 Huli, 225 is expressed simply as *ngui ngui* (15 x 15). Compare this to the relatively complex English expression 'two-hundred and twenty-five': (2 x 100) + (2 x 10) + 5.

Though the world is now dominated by base-10 systems, less common bases may still be found. Aiome employs base-2, Yuki base-4, Huli base-15, and Pomo base-20. Ndom, spoken by 1,200 people in Papua New Guinea, uses six as a base. In the Ndom number table given below we can see how six, called 'mer', gets used in addition and multiplication to build larger numbers:

| | | | |
|---|---|---|---|
| 1 | *sas* | 7 | *mer abo sas* |
| 2 | *thef* | 8 | *mer abo thef* |
| 3 | *ithin* | 9 | *mer abo ithin* |
| 4 | *thonith* | 10 | *mer abo thonith* |
| 5 | *meregh* | 11 | *mer abo meregh* |
| 6 | *mer* | 12 | *mer an thef* |

The Papuan language Bukiyip (also called Mountain Arapesh, with 16,233 speakers) has two different counting systems, one base-4 and another base-3. According to Bukiyip custom, which system you use depends on what objects you are counting.

The Bukiyip word for hand, *anauwip*, appears in both counting systems. In the base-3 system, *anauwip* means six, because they count all five fingers plus the thumb joint. In the base-4 system, *anauwip* means 'twenty-

**Table 6.2.**
**The two counting systems of Bukiyip**

| *Mountain Arapesh things counted by fours* | *Mountain Arapesh things counted by threes* |
|---|---|
| coconuts | betel nuts |
| small yams | big yams |
| bundles of firewood | single sticks of firewood |
| days | moons (months) |
| eggs, birds, lizards, and fish | wild game |
| breadfruit | bananas |
| bows and arrows | shields |

four', because it implies multiplying each of the six points on the hand by the base. So, the same word *anauwip* can refer to six betel nuts or twenty-four coconuts! Despite having two counting systems, both unusual, both partially based in body-counting and both having a low base, the Bukiyip people are said to excel at counting.[44]

## Counting Universals

Linguist Joseph Greenberg surveyed a large number of the world's counting systems and proposed certain shared, universal properties.[45] Exceptions to some of these universals can be found in very small or endangered languages. There is evidence that counting systems on a worldwide scale are rapidly becoming more uniform and more decimal-based. When the quirky exceptions disappear, we may falsely assume certain principles to be universal simply because all evidence to the contrary has vanished. Finding such exceptions thus becomes more urgent as languages disappear.

Greenberg's universals encompass all the issues I have raised thus far: bases, the combinatorial nature of numbers, the use of simplex versus complex labels, and hidden arithmetic in counting. Among his many proposed universal principles we find:

- A Every language has a numeral system of finite scope.
- B Zero is never expressed as part of the numeral system.
- C In complex numbers, the subtrahend never precedes the minuend.
- D All bases in a system are divisible by fundamental base.
- E The only numeral expressions deleted [i.e., understood by the speaker and hearer, but not mentioned in speech] are those for one and for bases of the system.

Ventureño, an extinct language of California, used base-4, with additional bases 8 and 16. In Ventureño we find a good example of Greenberg's principle E. Explicit reference to bases 4 and 16 could be omitted in speech because the speakers easily understood from the context what base was being referred to. For example, in the additive expressions for five, six, and seven, the underlying base '4' was understood but not mentioned. Fifteen was simply expressed as 'one less' with no need to mention the base-16.

Four could also be omitted in multiplicative expressions: for example, in the term for twenty-eight, 'three comes again' $(4 \times (4 + 3))$.[46]

Since Greenberg's work, a great many more number systems have been documented. Interesting and quirky exceptions to universal tendencies often turn up in very small or endangered languages.

| *Universal* | *Language* | *Nature of exception* |
|---|---|---|
| A | Pirahã | no number system at all |
| B | Tongan[47] | expresses zero |
| C | Ainu | expresses 'eight' as 'two ten' |
| D | Wampar | larger bases indivisible by smaller |

Greenberg's universal C predicts that if a language uses subtraction, it will not simply place the number being subtracted (*the subtrahend*) before the number being subtracted from (*the minuend*). In other words, a language will not rely on the sequence alone to signal this relation, without including some mathematical expression (like 'subtracted from') in between the two numbers. Ainu, on the very brink of extinction, presents an apparent exception to this:

| | | |
|---|---|---|
| 1 | *shine* | |
| 2 | *tu* | |
| 8 | *tu-pesan* | 'two [subtracted from] ten' |
| 9 | *shine-pesan* | 'one [subtracted from] ten' |
| 10 | *pesan* | |

One final universal to which we can find exceptions in endangered languages is D: if a language has multiple bases, all bases are divisible by the smallest base. This universal would predict the occurrence of English, with bases of 10 and 100, but would not predict, for instance, base-3 base-20 languages. Wampar (5,150 speakers) along with more than one hundred other small Papuan languages, uses both base-2 and base-5.[48]

| | | |
|---|---|---|
| 1 | *orots* | |
| 2 | *serok* | |
| 3 | ***serok** orots* | 2 + 1 |
| 4 | ***serok** a serok* | 2 + 2 |
| 5 | ***bangid** ongan* | 5 once |
| 10 | ***bangid** serok* | 5 x 2 |

## Counting as Cognitive Ecology

Counting systems shed light on human evolution and reveal how cognition and culture adapt to changing environmental demands. On the one hand, we see that many societies throughout history have functioned well without precision counting or even without any kind of counting at all. On the other, we have seen that there are multiple ways to conceptualize numbers, to organize them, and to apply them to mental tasks. As far as human language is concerned, there is no absolute or correct or necessary mathematics, instead there are many alternate models of mathematical thought. We turn first to the notion that counting is not essential for accurate quantification.

Kayardild is an Australian language with number words only up to four. To describe larger groups, they might use terms like *ngankirra* 'mob, aggregation', *mumurra* 'big mob of people', or *jardiya* 'complete group'.[49] Outside observers (who may have been biased) concluded that:

> in traditional Aboriginal society, precision was rarely important. . . . They could count when they needed to but such a need was rare. . . . Rather [than being stymied by their lack of an ability to enumerate a herd of animals] a person would use a descriptive phrase such as 'a huge herd' or 'a very big mob' . . . and everyone would be so familiar with the animals' herding habits, that they would have a very good understanding of the size of the herd.[50]

This judgment echoes that of Francis Galton, a century earlier and half a world away, who writes of the Damara of South Africa (56,000 speakers): "In practice, whatever they may possess in their language, they certainly use no numeral greater than three . . . yet they seldom lose oxen: the way in which they discover the loss of one, is not by the number of the herd being diminished, but by the absence of a face they know."[51]

Second, we take up the issue of how math as a system is distributed across different parts of human cognition and culture. The human-environment interface that results in numbers and counting systems may be conceptualized as three interacting domains. First, humankind's latent (inborn) cognitive abilities; second, the demands and pressures of the external environment; and third, the cognitive system of language (to a great extent culturally determined) that mediates between the first two. Cultures do as much math as they need to, but they differ in the tasks they need to perform. Damara nomads must be able to detect a single goat missing from the herd, Micronesian navigators must have an unfailing sense of nautical distance they have covered as expressed in subtle astronomical movements,[52] and the Pirahã, as reported, have little need to do any types of calculations.

Languages (and cultures) differ in how they divide up the labor among the three domains. Some, like the Pirahã or Yanoama leave more work to the latent (non-linguistic) capacity: cognizance of quantities, amounts, and individuals; ability to estimate; ability to detect patterns in time and space. Other cultures offload arithmetical tasks onto the environment, by use of body-counting, pebble-and-stick counting, or (as we do) calculators, compasses, and odometers. Still others do *more* math than they might need to, by building extra arithmetical functions into their number names. Clearly, latent human mathematical ability is quite rich, and culture adds even greater capacity. While the basic tools are up to almost any task, the pressures of the environment vary widely across cultures. Languages adapt to facilitate counting, allowing our innate human capacity to answer the environmental demands put to it.[53]

As in any evolutionary system, you have to work with what you have: what you have inherited and what has evolved over time. At the same time, you have to respond to new environmental pressures as best as you can. Languages do all this and also add their own quirks and idiosyncrasies, by evolving many diverse strategies to accomplish counting tasks. The number systems that languages evolve thus give us insights into universal human capacities, specific demands that have arisen in different times, places, and environments, and how languages and speech communities have evolved differently to meet these demands. As linguist Leanne Hinton observes, "Each number system seems strange and exotic if you are seeing it for the first time. But . . . each people has a way of counting that seems just right to them."[54]

## Losing Your Numbers

The world's number systems—and with them much of human mathematical thought—are now rapidly eroding. The extinction of unusual counting systems has been evident for some time. Alfred Kroeber, who studied

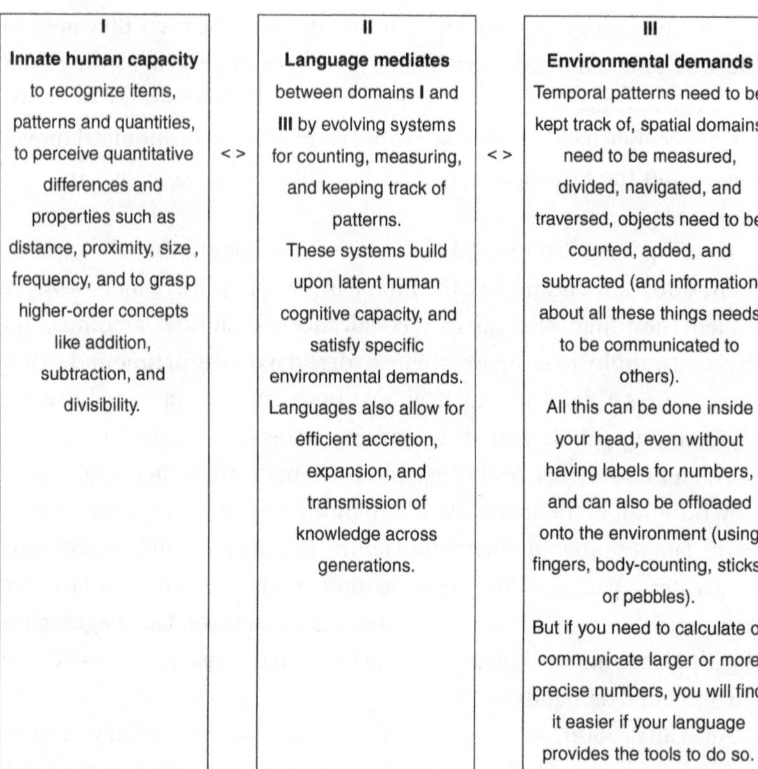

I
Innate human capacity
to recognize items, patterns and quantities, to perceive quantitative differences and properties such as distance, proximity, size, frequency, and to grasp higher-order concepts like addition, subtraction, and divisibility.
< >
II
Language mediates
between domains I and III by evolving systems for counting, measuring, and keeping track of patterns.
These systems build upon latent human cognitive capacity, and satisfy specific environmental demands.
Languages also allow for efficient accretion, expansion, and transmission of knowledge across generations.
< >
III
Environmental demands
Temporal patterns need to be kept track of, spatial domains need to be measured, divided, navigated, and traversed, objects need to be counted, added, and subtracted (and information about all these things needs to be communicated to others).
All this can be done inside your head, even without having labels for numbers, and can also be offloaded onto the environment (using fingers, body-counting, sticks, or pebbles).
But if you need to calculate or communicate larger or more precise numbers, you will find it easier if your language provides the tools to do so.


**Figure 6.7**
The Cognition/Language/Environment interface.

the Yuki Indians of northern California in the 1920s remarked that "The younger men, who have associated with the Americans, seem not to realize that their fathers thought by eights instead of tens."[55] Nearby in California lived the Eastern Pomo people, for whom twenty was 'one stick' and one-hundred 'five sticks', or *lé·ma-xày*. This base-20 word for one-hundred was elicited from native Pomo speakers as recently as 1926, but by the second half of the twentieth century, it had been forgotten.[56] In its place, the Pomo borrowed the Spanish word *ciento*, adding a superfluous 'one' in front of it (in Spanish, the term for 'one hundred' is just *ciento*).

Ventureño, also once spoken in Southern California but now extinct, had a unique base-4 counting system. The only historical record of this appears, ironically enough, in an eighteenth century handbook that counseled Spanish missionaries to teach the Ventureño how to 'count by tens'.

Under Spanish influence, this shift from a base-4 to base-10 occurred across the entire Chumash language family to which Ventureño belonged. At a later date, but still well before their extinction in the mid-twentieth century, the Chumash languages gave up their own unique number words entirely in favor of Spanish numbers.[57]

For Ainu, now teetering on the brink of extinction, it was reported as early as 1905 how "the simpler Japanese method of numeration is rapidly supplanting the cumbrous native system." The reader will recall that Ainu packs an incredible amount of mathematics into its counting system. All this got lost in the switch to Japanese.[58]

The Thulung language of Nepal (33,000 speakers) has been steadily losing speakers as people switch to the national language, Nepali. Even those Thulung who do continue speaking Thulung have begun to replace their numbers with Nepali ones. Lower numbers seem to survive longer—in some communities, only native numbers up to three remain (similar to Yakkha, a related language discussed above). The steady pace of Thulung number replacement has been observed over the past half a century.[59]

Huli, with its unusual base-15 system, has recently developed a decimal system, originally inspired by the necessity of dealing with British money, but now being introduced into other areas of Huli life. Even as decimal systems replace the original Huli system, they are also taking over worldwide.

**Table 6.3**
**Thulung numeral reduction over half a century**

| | *1944* | ⇒ | *1975* | ⇒ | *2000* |
|---|---|---|---|---|---|
| 1 | *ko* | | *ko* | | *ko* |
| 2 | *ne* | | *ne* | | *na* |
| 3 | *sium* | | *sium* | | *su* |
| 4 | *ble* | | *ble* | | Nepali numerals used above three. |
| 5 | *ngo* | | Nepali numerals used above four. | | |
| 6 | *ru* | | | | |
| 7 | *yet* | | | | |
| 8 | *let* | | | | |
| 9 | *gu* | | | | |
| 10 | *kodium* | | | | |

The base-10 system is conquering the world, expanding its territory while crowding out unusual base systems and other ways of counting that we have discussed here. We have come to think of base-10 as the norm. We now face an extinction of mathematical ideas and a near-total homogenization of numerical thinking. Many uncommon systems have already vanished, either because the languages they occur in are nearing extinction or because people have switched to a base-10 system.

Linguist Bernard Comrie, who published a survey of counting systems in over 200 languages, concludes: "As far as numeral systems are concerned, we live in a decimal world, with the decimal type dominant in nearly every part of the world. Some of the other types are highly restricted geographically, in particular the extended body-part type, essentially confined to Australia and Amazonia. Bases other than 10 or 20 are extremely rare in the modern world." Comrie discerns "a worldwide historical trend for the dominant decimal system to encroach on and replace other systems."[60]

Traditional philosophies of mathematics can vanish within a single generation. Supyire speakers in Mali, under pressure from the locally dominant base-10 language Bambara, are currently in the process of switching to a decimal system. Younger speakers have reinterpreted the traditional Supyire word for their base-80 to mean '100'.[61] Owing to such encroachments, Comrie concludes, "non-decimal systems are even more endangered than the languages in which they occur."[62] As New Guinea tribes become more westernized, body-part counting gets used less and less. Anthropologist Jadran Mimica laments: "The Iqwaye are beginning to melt into that developing mass of the Third World humanity which is acquiring the stamp of Western civilization, but at the price of their own cultural impoverishment and amnesia . . . the result is the loss of indigenous cultural diversity and creativity."[63]

## Counting and Cognition

What exactly is being lost as the world moves to a decimal counting system? Will we come to see our modern math as a complete, perfect, and inevitable system rather than as a slow, laborious, and creative adaptation by human minds to specific environments and needs? Based on studies among the Iqwaye tribe, Mimica shows how our insights into human creativity and thinking become impoverished as we come to accept the Western decimal system as our sole norm.

> An indigenous Melanesian mathematical system can be used for the exploration and explication of all basic mathematical structures developed in Western mathematics . . . this (indigenous) mathematics became abstract and elaborated into an efficient science in the course of its long cultural history . . . Worldwide, mathematics is naïvely appreciated as a virtual symbol of Western and, in general, human rationality. What is less commonly considered . . . is the intrinsic ambiguities, paradoxes and contradictions of mathematical knowledge as a human creation.[64]

Number systems of the world's languages provide an important window into human cognition, problem-solving, and adaptation. Even though numbers may be a universal property of the universe, human minds have a degree of freedom in how we conceptualize numbers as mathematical systems. Languages that count with different bases provide an elegant example of mathematical creativity. We have also seen how some languages privilege certain mathematical concepts over others, for example, introducing multiplication before addition in their counting systems. Some contain concepts (such as overcounting) that do not fit well into what we think of as formal mathematical operations, relying instead on spatial metaphors to visualize numbers. We have also seen that languages differ enormously in their notion of what constitutes high numbers and whether or not counting to infinity—or even counting to three—is a sensible mental endeavor.

While our rational mathematics certainly builds upon our modest innate number sense, the details of it *do not* seem to be strictly determined, either by the physiology of the brain or by the nature of the universe. Surprisingly little of the linguistic counting systems we have explored in this chapter are dictated by our innate number sense. And a great deal may be shaped by culture.

In surveying small and endangered languages, we find that intelligent people in different cultures arrive at very different conceptualizations of mathematical systems, even though they could probably still all agree that one plus two equals three. We have much more to learn, not only about the mathematics of our universe (which we gladly leave to the mathematicians) but also about the mathematics of our inner universe, the mind. Human languages, with their startling diversity of mathematical thought and myriad ways of counting, surely hold some of the keys to this universe.

Many unique counting systems remain to be explored in little-studied languages. Any of them could provide us with totally new ways of looking at numbers, fractions, proportions, counting, and the role of the human body in cognition. Nearly all of them are now endangered and may soon disappear without being documented. With a dearth of languages to study, how can we do the math?

## The Leaf-Cup People, India's Modern 'Primitives'

India celebrated the birth of its billionth citizen in May 2000. Amidst this sea of humanity are peoples belonging to many dozens of small cultures. They find themselves under great pressure to assimilate to one of India's big official languages, each boasting tens of millions of speakers.[1] Even a language like Ho, with over a million speakers in northeastern India, finds itself outnumbered and in jeopardy. The tiny Gorum language, with under 300 speakers, is less than a teardrop in the ocean. As India advances on the world stage, developing nuclear weapons and a high-tech sector rivaling America's, it still harbors micro-societies that forage in remote hills and some that until recently wore only clothing made of leaves and hunted with bow and arrow. These small ethnic groups of India, with their sometimes simple material possessions and rudimentary technologies for survival, communicate in complex languages that have not yet been well documented, speaking traditions rich in myth.

In September 2005 I journeyed to India to meet peoples popularly known as 'tribals' and residing below the bottom of India's socially rigid caste system. In Orissa state, I met with members of seven different peoples who all speak different languages of the Munda language family. Munda-speaking groups, like the Ho, the Remo, the Juang, and the Gutob, are the original tribal peoples of eastern India. Their ancestors settled here long before the arrival of the Aryan and Dravidian populations who now dominate them. To this day, Munda are referred to as *adivasi*, or 'first' peoples.

In stark contrast to Hinduism practiced by 81 percent of India's citizens, Munda people eschew the worship of gods in temples. They worship outdoors, in nature, some venerating stone megaliths built by their ancestors, others maintaining sacred groves, and some ritually sacrificing water-buffalo. The Munda once drank home-brewed liquor from cups made of leaves. They still have a word—*pu*—for this culturally important object. Of dozens of Munda languages still spoken, all are poorly documented and most are endangered, ranging from Ho down to tiny Gorum.

I met many Munda people during my trip to India and heard many stories that stuck in my mind. One self-taught scholar, Mr. K. C. Naik Biruli of the Ho people, did not fit the image popular in India's press of an uncivilized 'tribal'. Neatly dressed and speaking fluent English, Naik narrated for me an ancient Ho creation story, then expertly translated it into English. He also showed off the nascent Ho alphabet, a writing system that has not yet gained wide use among his people, nor been accepted into worldwide technology for writing on computers.[2] Ho stories are passed on almost exclusively by word of mouth, and even when the Ho language is written down, it must be written by hand.

Sipping tea, Naik narrated a radically alternative creation myth. As the Ho tell it, drunkenness, sexuality, and shame are a gift of the gods, intended to make humans reproduce and populate the earth. The Ho god's caprices lead, in the end, to a near-paradise on earth. Here is the story Naik told:

*The story of past times.*[3]
*Once there was old man Luku and old woman Lukumi.*
*They two were alone on this Earth.*
*There were forests and mountains everywhere.*
*There were very beautiful springs, with fruits, flowers, leaves, trees and stones.*

*Old man Luku and old woman Lukumi were very happy eating fruits that were in the trees.*
*They two had no sinful thoughts in their minds.*
*As for clothes, they didn't have any on their bodies.*

*God thought, "If they stay like this, there will be no more generations."*
*So God came down, and taught them how to make liquor from grass seeds.*
*They drank the liquor in a cup made from leaves of the sar–fruit tree, and they got drunk.*

*In their minds they felt another type of joyful thoughts; they thought about coming together as man and woman.*
*Then they started copulating, and shame and arousal came to them.*

*So they covered each other up at the waist with tree bark.*
*Ten months later from Lukumi's body, a boy child was born.*
*In this manner, they bore seven boys and seven girls.*

*Thus they spread us humans on this earth.*
*It was a Golden Age at that time*
*There was no cheating, quarreling, cruelty, nothing bad.*
*There was no cold or starvation, fever or sadness.*
*The people remained in joy, happiness and peace; This is called paradise.*

As Naik told this story, a local group of Ho schoolchildren clustered around, wide-eyed at this racy creation myth. Most of them could not read and write the Ho language, and rarely heard it spoken during their boarding school education. Raised to be modern citizens of India, speakers of Hindi, they nonetheless listened eagerly, proud of their Ho heritage, and heartened to hear that their ancestral culture could offer a tale as titillating as any Bollywood flick.

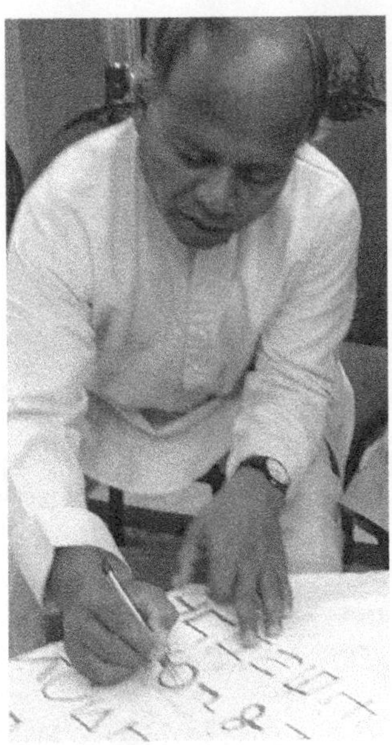

Mr. K. C. Naik Biruli demonstrates the Ho writing system, 2005. Photo courtesy of Living Tongues Institute for Endangered Languages

# 7 Worlds within Words

"Do you find it easy to get drunk on words?"
"So easy that, to tell you the truth, I am seldom perfectly sober. Which accounts for my talking so much."
—Harriet Vane and Lord Peter Wimsey in *Gaudy Night*, by Dorothy Sayers

Studying the form of a linguistic expression without studying the meaning is like sipping a fine wine, swishing it around in your mouth, and spitting it out—it can be fun, but not intoxicating.
—Randall Eggert, Linguist

All linguists share a fascination with words, and we are trained to seek out and describe intricate patterns within human languages. As languages rapidly vanish into the vortex of cultural assimilation, linguists justifiably fear they will never see the full range of complexity and structures human minds can produce.[1]

When Noam Chomsky proclaimed language 'a window on the mind', an entire research program for the discipline of linguistics was launched. In the fifty years since, this research has already yielded many important insights into human cognition. With his famous sentence "Colorless green ideas sleep furiously," Chomsky demonstrated how linguists can explore complex structures (sounds, phrases, sentences, etc.) even when there is no meaningful content at all. The lack of meaning does not hinder linguists in our investigation of mental structures: we have come to focus mainly on the structures themselves, not their cultural meanings. This has been the conventional wisdom in linguistics for at least four decades.

But although languages certainly contain abstract structures, they evolve and exist to convey information within a specific cultural matrix, and that function permeates and influences every level of language. To its critics, including me, the Chomskyan program has been unduly narrow, overly focused on large, globally dominant languages, and preoccupied with structure at the expense of content.[2]

Linguists' preoccupation with these abstract structures (collectively termed 'grammar') has led to a microscopic approach that treats languages like laboratory specimens, utterly divorced from their natural environments, the people who speak them, and the content of those peoples' thoughts. As linguist Mary Haas pointed out, this approach hinders us in seeing the larger picture: "In their search for universal tendencies . . . some scholars have taken an atomistic approach. In other words, they have obtained examples of relative clauses, auxiliary verbs, the copula, and so on, from speakers (or grammars) of as many languages as possible without regard to anything else in the language." Endorsing a sensible alternative, Haas continues, "In the present climate of interest in the problem of language universals, we must not overlook the importance of the holistic approach. . . . A language must be understood and described as a whole. It is not a thing of bits and pieces, haphazardly strung together."[3]

Linguists who do field work on languages find it hard to ignore the rich cultural matrix or to examine things like sentence structure in isolation from the rest of the language. As soon as one looks at the content of language—what people care to talk about—it is obvious that this is also richly structured and a worthy object of study for any science investigating the mind. And it becomes obvious that structure may be grossly misunderstood if meaning is ignored. One example of this is the complexities surrounding how to say 'go' in Tuvan, as discussed in chapter 4. Without awareness of how speakers attend to ground slope underfoot, and to river current, it is hard to imagine even understanding that this system exists, let alone how it works. This small portion of Tuvan grammar depends on the human body's interaction with the local environment, as interpreted through Tuvan cultural norms. Such examples may be found for every language mentioned in this book, if we take care to look deeply enough.

One goal of this book is to advocate a restored balance between studying the structure of language and its meaningful content. We linguists have perhaps only a few decades left to document the lion's share of linguistic diversity before it vanishes forever. Endangered languages stand to play an increasingly central role in the study of the mind.[4] Any language, no matter how obscure or well-known, how large or how small, provides challenging patterns and complexities for linguists to describe. Even English, studied by hundreds of linguists for hundreds of years, has yet to yield all its secrets to science. As with word order in Urarina (discussed in chapter 1), an obscure fact from a language spoken by just a few dozen people can take a well-established scientific theory and turn it completely upside-down. Since we cannot know the goals and tools science will have fifty or one hundred years hence, we must aim for the fullest description possible of each language now.

## Language Change Just Happens

Languages are highly complex, self-organizing systems in constant flux. The English spoken by our great-great-great grandparents, who might have used a word like 'hither', is very different from how we 'conversate' nowadays. Geoffrey Chaucer could not chat with Bill Gates. We all participate in constant change, but no individual speaker controls the speed, trajectory, or character of change. A process of emerging complexity—not yet well understood—gives a language its constantly changing and characteristic shape.

Individual speakers of any language can and do make up new structures on a whim, by slip-of-the-tongue, or through creativity. Rap singers' terms 'b-iz-itch' (or 'biznitch' or 'biznatch') or cartoon character Homer Simpson's 'saxa-ma-phone' and 'platy-ma-pus' are examples of recently invented speech play.[5] These innovations only become part of the language by a mysterious process of social learning and consensus. Other speakers must adopt and use (and perhaps revise or expand upon) these new ways of talking. At first, purists may denounce such changes as 'bad English'. But if the changes endure, dictionary writers and grammar teachers eventually catch up and acknowledge such innovations.

Besides consciously creative innovations, many changes take place of which speakers are unaware. Californians whose grandparents pronounced the words 'cot' and 'caught' differently now pronounce these words the same. Somewhere along the line they lost an entire vowel. Nobody decided to jettison it, it just happened. Eastern U.S. speakers who maintain the 'cot'/'caught' distinction may find this vexing, leading to misunderstandings. (When I listen to people who lack that vowel, I often wonder, did they mean 'sot' or 'sought', 'hottie' or 'haughty', 'body' or 'bawdy'? For me, and speakers who share my set of vowels, these paired words all sound unambiguously distinct.)

People also unconsciously change their own speech habits even over the course of a lifetime. We adopt new words like 'phat', 'metrosexual', 'pizzled', new expressions like 'twenty-four seven', and we may even shift our pronunciation. Queen Elizabeth II's speech has changed noticeably in the fifty years since she ascended the throne. Measurements of her vowels in her annual Christmas radio speeches showed that from the 1950s to the 1980s she shifted noticeably away from the "Queen's English" and towards pronunciations favored by the lower social classes.[6]

Nobody directs this intricate process of language change, on its individual or group levels—it is an orchestra without a conductor or even a musical score. There is no central decision-maker or authority, but orderly change happens nonetheless. Like complex termite mounds that get built with no blueprint, architect, or foreman, language is a self-organizing system. It has many distinct parts that interact in complex and often unpredictable ways, resulting in surprising and unplanned patterns.

No schoolteacher, committee, or lexicographer has authority to decide whether 'biatch'[7] or 'puhleeze'[8] counts as a word of English or not. If English speakers use such words widely enough, they become part of English. This is true of new meanings for old words ('spam' used to mean canned meat, now it means unsolicited e-mail), new coinages ('e-commerce', 'conversate'), borrowings (*jihad* from Arabic, *perestroika* from Russian), and even new grammatical constructions.

## Are All Languages Equally Complex?

It has become almost dogma in linguistics to affirm that "all languages are equally complex." This statement is usually followed by "and capable of expressing any idea."[9] The second idea is logically separate from the first. Any language can indeed express any concept or idea that its speakers care to talk about—this is a testable hypothesis. So while it is uncontroversial that all languages possess equal expressive potential, at the level of structures languages do differ widely. Once the equal complexity model is adopted, a number of further assumptions follow, for example: "A language which appears simple in some respects is likely to be more complex in others."[10] This often popularly construed as the notion that if a language simplifies one part of its grammar it necessarily gains some complexity elsewhere, as if regulated by a thermostat.

Such claims are problematic, if only because they remain hard to test empirically. Most of the world's languages remain undescribed or underdescribed. We lack any agreed-upon unit for measuring complexity,[11] especially *across* distinct domains such as vowel pronunciation and sentence building. And complexity arises from many disparate factors, starting certainly with the innate ability of the human brain, but also including the size of the speech community, the level of contact among speakers, the range of uses of a language, the modality (spoken or signed), and intricate historical processes of language change.

Yet one finds the 'equal' complexity idea in textbooks, blogs, introductory linguistics classes, and the like.[12] As evidence, it is noted that any neurologically normal human child can learn any human language when raised among people speaking that language. An Icelandic child raised by Swahili parents will come to speak flawless Swahili, and vice versa. Studies comparing acquisition rates of children learning different languages show slight differences for certain kinds of structures, but all kids still all turn out to be fluent speakers of their native tongue by age 7 or so.[13]

The sentiment behind this argument is noble: of course, we should not regard any other people or culture as primitive or any more or less intelligent than ourselves. Ultimately, statements about the equal complexity of languages may owe more to political correctness than they do to any empirical evidence. However, a fundamental quantitative problem with the claim remains: we have no established way to measure complexity within a single language or across multiple languages. Further, if the scope of our investigation is narrowed to certain parts of a language (say, only

**Figure 7.1**
Timothy Taureviri, a speaker of Central Rotokas who has worked with linguists like Stuart Robinson for years, transcribing his language. Courtesy of Stuart Robinson

**Figure 7.2**
Rotokas villagers from Togarao taking a rest from performing *singsing kaur,* a traditional song and dance performance with bamboo flutes. Courtesy of Stuart Robinson

sounds or only word-structure), certain languages appear vastly more complex in specific areas than do others.

One example comes from phonology, or the organization of sounds in language. Rotokas (spoken in New Guinea by 4,320 people) reportedly gets by with a mere six consonants: *p, t, k, v, r,* and *g,* while Ingush, a language of the Caucasus (230,000 speakers) boasts a whopping 40 consonants.[14] Besides many common sounds like 'p', 'b', and 'f', Ingush uses a special series of ejective consonants that are produced by closing and raising the vocal chords to compress air inside the pharynx, then releasing the pressure suddenly to create a popping sound to accompany the consonant. Ejectives are moderately rare, occurring in only about 20 percent of the world's languages. To employ *seven* distinct kinds of ejectives, as does Ingush, is exceedingly rare.[15] But even Ingush is not the upper limit: Ubykh, which reportedly had 70 consonants, lost its last speaker in 1992.[16]

Rotokas, which may have as few as six consonants, is by no means a simple language. On the contrary, Rotokas crams entire utterances into single words. The following 13 syllables constitute just a single word, with hyphens inserted here for readability (notice the reduplicated form of the verb form *rugo* 'to think', in boldface).[17]

*ora-**rugorugo**-pie-pa-a-veira*
'They were always thinking back.'

As evidenced in this word, Rotokas has simple syllable structure, allowing only one vowel and a maximum of one consonant per syllable. Ingush appears more complex, allowing multiple consonants to sit next to each other, for example, *bw, hw, ljg,* and *rjg*:

*bwarjg* 'eye'
*hwazaljg* 'bird'[18]

So Rotokas and Ingush show two very different kinds of complexity in their sound systems. Ingush has 40 consonants, somewhat shorter words, and allows multiple consonants per syllable. Rotokas has few consonants, permits only one consonant per syllable, and builds very long words. Each language has complexity of a different type and in a different area of its grammar.[19] These are apples and oranges; we cannot yet sensibly pose or answer the question of which system is more complex. Further, such an egalitarian position would be meaningless.

Setting aside the controversy over equal complexity, professional linguists would probably all agree on the following. If we took a survey of *only* the world's 100 biggest languages, we would not only miss many unique complexities found in smaller languages and thus present in human language in general—but our very notion of what human language is would be severely skewed.

Imagine a zoologist describing mammals by looking only at the top hundred most common ones. It would be easier to examine dogs and cats and cows and rabbits, all of which are composed of the same building blocks as other mammals. But if we did, we would never know that a mammal could swim (whales), fly (bats), lay eggs (echidna), use tools (sea otters and orangutans), or have an inflatable balloon growing from its head (male hooded seal).[20] Ignorance of unusual mammals would impoverish our notion of what mammals can be. It is precisely the weird and wonderful exceptions that afford us a full view of the possibilities.[21]

## Complexity Run Amok

Small languages whose grammars seem otherwise average or run-of-the-mill often contain islands of astonishing complexity. While all languages may look more or less complex from a distant, bird's eye view, upon closer inspection we find particular areas of some languages' grammars that seem to have run amok, stretching the very limits of complexity. This does not demonstrate that some languages are *on the whole* more complex than others, but it certainly opens the door for us to pose the question. Since grammars are shaped by culture and environment, as well as by human brains, and are constantly changing, they might plausibly vary within the limits of what intelligent human brains require of them.

In this chapter, I present some impressively complex sub-systems of the grammars of small and endangered languages. And I argue that, were these systems to vanish undocumented, we might never imagine or suspect their possible existence. We would thus remain ignorant of some types of linguistic complexity that can arise. Because they arose over long periods of time in unique conditions (and owe something to random chance), such systems would not likely reappear in the subsequent future course of linguistic change. Lacking knowledge of tongues like Tabasaran, Rotokas, Sora, Gros Ventre, or Yanyuwa, we are deprived of unique insights into human cognition and the upper bounds of linguistic complexity.

In this chapter, we look at some linguistic complexities rich enough to intoxicate any language lover. For non-linguists, all examples are explained clearly and compared to English or other widely spoken languages. We will consider what they may tell us about human cognition and the self-organizing system known as language that has colonized our brains. How far can it go? What kinds of fantastic structures does it build?

Answering this question has long been the prime directive of linguistics. As Noam Chomsky eloquently put it:

> Language is a mirror of mind in a deep and significant sense. It is a product of human intelligence. . . . By studying the properties of natural languages, their structure, organization, and use, we may hope to learn something about human nature; something significant, if it is true that human cognitive capacity is the truly distinctive and most remarkable characteristic of the species.[22]

Many of Chomsky's intellectual heirs have interpreted the directive narrowly. They investigate some small sub-part of language structure, often paying scant attention to the intellectual and cultural content of what people are actually saying. I have tried to demonstrate in this book that many kinds of linguistic knowledge, such as when to say 'go' in Tuvan (chapter 4), cannot be properly understood or described if divorced from their social and physical environment. In this chapter, I will show that many of the kinds of structures Chomsky and his followers have been interested in are to be found only in small, obscure, and endangered languages.

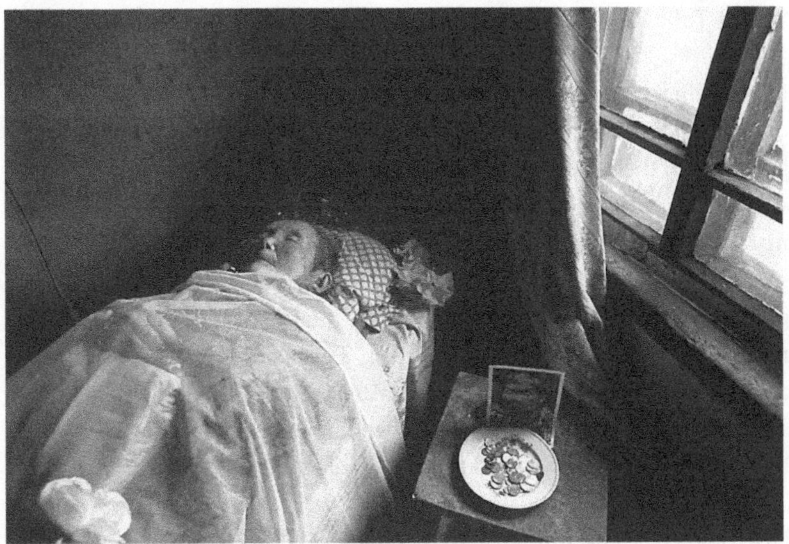

**Figure 7.3**
Galina Innokentovna Adamova (1924–2001), shown here on her funeral bier in June 2001. Among the last fluent speakers of Tofa, she worked with me to record Tofa songs and narratives. Photograph by Thomas Hegenbart, courtesy of Contact Press Images

## Smelly Talk

Starting with a very simple example, we will look at a single morpheme in Tofa, the language of Siberian reindeer herders discussed in chapter 2. A morpheme is the smallest meaningful building block in language that may be used to build a complex word. In English, the word 'sing' is one morpheme, and the suffix '-able' is another kind of morpheme that attaches to it to build the word 'singable'. Many morphemes, like '-able', never stand alone as words, but can be added to other words to change their meaning.

Tofa has a morpheme that speakers can add to any noun. It changes that noun into an adjective meaning 'smelling of' or 'smelling like'. So if we take the word *ivi* 'reindeer' and add the olfactory suffix *-sig*, we get a new word *ivisig* that means 'smelling like a reindeer'. The smell suffix has not been reported for other languages, though it certainly might exist elsewhere. And we can only guess as to why smelliness was regarded as important enough to Tofa culture that their language evolved a unique morpheme to signal it.

## Sound Talk

Moving on to a more complex case, let us take a look at Tuvan, the language of nomadic yak herders discussed in chapters 3, 4, 5, and 7. Tuvans spend a great deal of their time hunting and herding animals in the mountain landscape. They seem to have a heightened sensitivity to sounds, especially animal sounds, nature sounds, and the natural acoustic properties of outdoor spaces (types of echoes). Their sound aesthetic is partly reflected in the art of "throat-singing" or "overtone singing" that has made them world famous.[23] But on a more day-to-day basis, Tuvans who hunt and herd animals show superb abilities to mimic natural sounds. They use this ability to sing to the yaks to calm them, to call wild boars while hunting, to imitate bird and marmot sounds, and to tell playful stories involving animals.

The Tuvan language, not surprisingly, has evolved a very rich vocabulary to describe and imitate natural sounds. Of course, all languages have onomatopoeia: English has words like 'sizzle', 'bang', and 'rustle', all giving an imitative sense of the actual sound. But English speakers cannot really make up a new onomatopoetic word on the fly and be understood. If I want to describe the sound of a cow chewing its cud, I might say 'munching' or 'chomping', but I cannot just invent a whole new word, say, 'flarping', and expect to be understood. Tuvan speakers *can* do this. Their language allows them to describe a very wide range of natural sounds, using both ready-made words and newly coined ones. Tuvan provides means for speakers to creatively make up brand new words to represent sounds and be immediately understood by others.

It works like this. Pairs of consonants in Tuvan represent classes of sounds. For example, a word with a *k* and *ng* (as in English 'king') would represent a metallic ringing or impact sound. The speaker can fill in different vowels: high vowels to represent high-pitched or rapid sounds, low vowels to represent low-pitched or slow sounds, and so on. *Kongur* is the sound of a big bell ringing or a large metal pipe striking an object. *Kingir* or *küngür* would be jangling stirrups or clanging keys, while *kangyr* might be a giant empty metal barrel rolling along. With eight vowels, Tuvan provides many possible combinations, and speakers can use and understand most of these combinations, even if they have never heard them used before.

For example, if you hear someone blowing their nose or the sound of water in a babbling brook, you might use or create a word with the consonants *sh* and *l* combined with various possible vowels:

*šülür* sound of a nearly dried up river, or sound of mucous (snot) being forcefully blown out of the nose.
*šölür* sound of a bundle of wood falling loudly, or sound of loud slurping
*šalyr* sound of dry leaves or grass rustling
*šolur* sound of water in a babbling brook
*šylyr* sound of rustling (e.g., paper in the wind)
*šulur* to chatter or blab
*šilir* (this word does not exist, but when asked, native speakers reliably report it has something to do with water sounds)[23]

Tuvan thus equips its speakers with an unusually complex, combinatory system for expressing and representing sounds.[24]

We do not know the full extent of sound symbolic words in the world's languages. A similarly rich and expressive system was documented by linguist Martha Ratliffe in White Hmong (about 500,000 speakers), where *mis mos* is the "sound of cows or horses pulling up grass," *mig mog* denotes "dogs fighting over a bone," *plij plawj* "pigeons flying or dry husks falling off bamboo," *nphis nphoos* the sound of a "drip from a pipe into a tank," *mlij mloj* the sound of "two separated cats meowing before fight[ing]," and *rhiv rhuav* imitates "people shuffling through dry leaves with force."[25] While onomatopoeia is known to exist in all languages, few documented ones have shown such rich possibilities as Tuvan and White Hmong.

## Willy-nilly Talk

Nearly all known languages have processes for building doubled words like 'flim-flam', 'helter-skelter', or 'money-schmoney'. Often in such paired words, the individual parts have no meaning (what is a 'flim' anyway, much less a 'flam'?), but they take on meaning as part of a whole. Sometimes only one half of a doubled word is a real word, like 'fiddle-faddle', and sometimes both have meaning, as in 'flip-flop'. The words may differ depending on the language, but this process—which linguists dub 'reduplication'—pops up predictably and in subtly different forms in languages all over the world.

Scientists have collected examples of reduplication from over a thousand languages, seeking large-scale patterns and similarities in form or meaning.[26] Many languages use reduplication much more often than English does, but we are far from knowing the full range of possible patterns.

Not surprisingly, reduplication often signals repetition of an action or event. In Tuvan, the verb *halyr* means 'to run'; the doubled form ***halyr**-halyr* means to run repeatedly, over and over. Reduplication can also add emphasis or intensity to a word. The Tuvan word *kyzyl* means 'red' and *borbak* means 'round'. These same words, when partially reduplicated as ***kyp**-kyzyl* and ***bop**-borbak*, mean 'intensely red' and 'completely round'.

Rotokas, the language with so few consonants, takes a simple noun or verb and doubles part of it to express greater quantity or frequency (reduplicated portions of words are boldfaced below).[27]

| | | | | |
|---|---|---|---|---|
| *tapa* | 'to hit' | > | ***tapa**tapa* | 'to hit repeatedly' |
| *kopi* | 'a dot' | > | ***kopi**kopi* | 'spotted' |
| *kavau* | 'to bear a child' | > | ***kava**kavau* | 'to bear many children' |

There are many more ways languages build reduplicated forms, but they tend to add the same kinds of meanings: repetition, intensity and emphasis. But a most unusual and unexpected use of reduplication is found in Eleme, a language spoken by 58,000 people in Nigeria. Eleme speakers double part of a verb in order to *negate* it.[28]

| | | | | |
|---|---|---|---|---|
| *moro* | 'He saw you.' | > | *mo**mo**ro* | 'He didn't see you.' |
| *rekaju* | 'We are coming' | > | *reka**ka**ju* | 'We are **not** coming.' |

Without knowing Eleme, linguists might never have guessed that the fairly common mechanism of reduplication could take on such an unusual function—one in which more quite literally means less.

## Touchy-feely Talk

If asked what clams, buttons, and frisbees had in common, you might say they are all basically flat and round, even though they differ in so many important ways (one is alive, one has holes, one flies, etc.). At some abstract level of thought, it may make sense to lump them together. Many languages—called classifier languages—do just that, by assigning every noun to one of several abstract categories. Of course, millions of substances, colors, smells, and tastes exist, and they combine in infinite ways in natural objects. So how many categories do we sensibly need and what are they?

The Carrier language, spoken by 1,500 people in Canada's British Columbia, employs a classifier system that forces speakers to pay attention to tactile and other qualities of objects. In Carrier, you cannot usually just say 'I gave.' What is the object given? Is it small and granular? Liquid in an open container? Mushy? Fluffy? Two-dimensional and flexible? Long and rigid? Depending on these shape and tactile qualities, which determine how your hand would grasp the object, an entirely different verb form must be used.[29]

Of course, English speakers experience objects in a tactile way, too, and we are aware of their physical properties. But English does not force us to pay attention to these qualities each time we refer to an object. They are there to be described if we choose, but most often we simply say 'give'. Languages can force their speakers to pay attention to certain aspects of the world, thus shaping how people think. Clearly, there is no universal set of categories or ways to divide up the natural world; just try to get people to agree whether a tomato is a more like a vegetable or a fruit, or a dolphin more like a fish or a cow. For speakers of classifier languages, certain

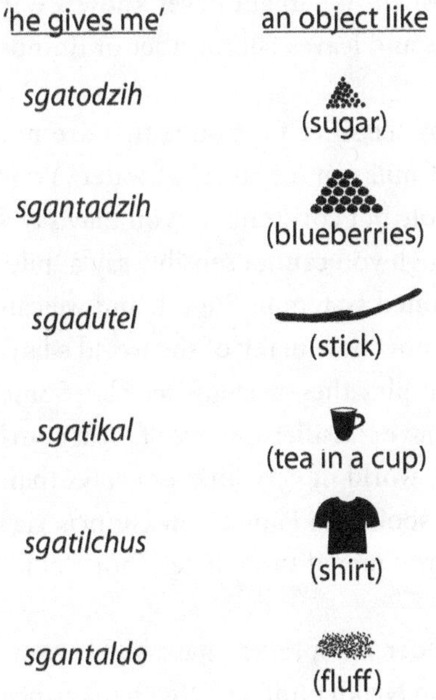

| 'he gives me' | an object like |
|---|---|
| *sgatodzih* | (sugar) |
| *sgantadzih* | (blueberries) |
| *sgadutel* | (stick) |
| *sgatikal* | (tea in a cup) |
| *sgatilchus* | (shirt) |
| *sgantaldo* | (fluff) |

**Figure 7.4**
Speakers of Carrier use very different forms of the word "give" depending on the tactile properties of the object being given.

subtle similarities among objects may be made more readily apparent because they are built into in the very grammar and talked about on a daily basis.

Cantonese, with 52 million speakers, sorts all objects and entities into classes. Native speakers sometimes disagree about what falls into which category. They even debate on Internet discussion boards which classifiers apply to certain objects and proffer examples to clarify usage:

> "Use 塊 faai (with the 3rd tone), for large, flat, sometimes hard objects (cookies, boards, individual leaves)."
>
> "Use 舊 gau (with the 6th tone), for small pieces of edible food and other chunks of smallish things (cake, buns, many of the dim sum foods, rocks and boulders, unidentifiable chunks of things)."[30]

Cantonese classifiers *must* be used whenever you use numbers, for example, you cannot say 'five rocks' in Cantonese without inserting the appropriate classifier word between the number and the object name: 'five *gau* rock' or 'two *faai* leaf'. If the language were to vanish—an unlikely scenario for Cantonese, but a looming threat for almost every other language I've discussed—our understanding of how the human brain can categorize objects would be impoverished. We might never know a way of viewing the world in which cookies and leaves fall together or dumplings group with boulders.

English sometimes uses a type of classifier for nouns that are not countable: a 'pile' of sand, a 'glass' of milk, an 'expanse' of water. Your choice of what classifier to use is flexible but constrained. You may say a 'cup' of sand or a 'pool' of water, though you cannot sensibly say a 'pile' of water. But classifiers make up a limited system in English and we can get by without them. We do not yet know how many of the world's languages employ classifiers and how complex these systems may be. Some very small and endangered languages have classifier systems of great complexity, but that divide up the natural world in very different ways than does Cantonese. Yupno, for example, spoken in Papua New Guinea, rigidly classifies eveything in the world into one of three states: 'hot', 'cold' and 'cool'.[31]

Nivkh, a Siberian language with under 300 speakers, has a highly complex classifier system that applies only in Nivkh numbers. Nivkh may once have resembled Cantonese in that the number word came first, then the classifier word, then the object. But Nivkh classifier words no longer stand alone: they have become a part of the number word itself. In what may be the most elaborate counting system yet known in any language, Nivkh uses 26 distinct number series. Each series is limited to a special object or class of objects. Nineteen of the classifiers apply only to very specific objects, such as boats, sleds, fishing nets, skis, finger widths used to measure the thickness of animal fat, and batches of dried fish. Six other classifiers apply to classes of objects united by some common, abstract property:

| *common quality* | *examples of objects* |
|---|---|
| come in pairs | eyes, ears, hands, legs, boots, mittens |
| small and roundish | nuts, bullets, berries, teeth |
| thin and flat | leaves, blankets, shirts |

The twenty-seventh Nivkh classifier is for odd objects that do not fit into any class.

Another special use of numbers to classify things is found in Native American languages belonging to the Salish family, spoken in the Pacific Northwest. These languages adjust their words in special ways to signal what is being counted. The adjustment involves taking a part of the word and repeating it, using 'reduplication' as discussed earlier in this chapter. By analogy, if I said 'twenty' or 'fifty' while counting objects, imagine that in Salish I would have to say '**twe**-twenty' or '**fi**-fifty' for counting people. Salishan languages have special number forms for animals, so a three-way classification pits objects vs. people vs. animals. Again, we could imagine a special form in English, where 'fifty-**ifty**' and 'twenty-**enty**' might indicate that animals are what is being counted.

Salish languages also adjust the words for 'what?" and 'how many?' so you can always tell if a Salish speaker is asking about numbers of animals, things, or people. Imagine if in English '**ho**-how' meant 'How many people?' while 'how-**ow**' meant 'how many animals'? The chart in table 7.1 shows some counting words from Squamish (15 speakers), a language of the Salish family. We use special phonetic characters to represent some unusual Squamish sounds, but what is important here is to notice the boldfaced parts of the words that have been reduplicated. There are three patterns. For counting objects, just the basic form is used. For people, a rather large chunk (or all) of the basic form is reduplicated, while for animals a smaller chunk is doubled, plus the original word may lose a vowel.[32]

**Figure 7.5**
On the left, a speaker of Nivkh, photographed in Siberia in 1898–1899. On the right, contemporary Nivkh speakers Sergei and Natasha Firun with their two children in the town of Liugi, on the northwest coast of Sakhalin Island, June 1990. Courtesy of the American Museum of Natural History (left), and courtesy of Bruce Grant (right)

Looking at just five languages that classify objects (English, Cantonese, Carrier, Squamish, and Nivkh), we can see how such systems divide up the world in radically different ways. They impose categories of shape, dimensionality, and animacy onto objects and force speakers to attend to these properties of the world, for example, whenever they wish to count. English imposes a minimal burden; we can simply use the number 'two' for any pair of objects. If we want to signal some kind of special unit, we might say 'pair', 'twosome', 'couple', or 'duo', but such uses are rare. And we can always just say 'two shoes'.

Speakers of Nivkh or Squamish, by contrast, must know the proper class of objects in order to count them.[33] Counting is an area where dif-

**Table 7.1**
**Examples of reduplicated numbers in Squamish**

| | *Counting objects* | *Counting people* | *Counting animals* |
|---|---|---|---|
| 9 | c'əs | c'əs-c'əs | c'ɪ-c's |
| 10 | ʔupn | ʔəp-ʔúpn | ʔú-ʔpn |
| How many? | kw'in | kw'ɪn-k$^{w}$in | k$^{w}$'ɪ-k$^{w}$in |

ferent languages can impose complex classification systems and thus increase both the cognitive task (sorting things into categories) and the amount of information hidden in simple counting.

Languages like Carrier, Nivkh, and Squamish each force a speaker to pay attention to some particular aspect of the world around them and then encode this information in the grammar of everyday talk. Scientists still do not know the possible range of such systems, and this limits our understanding of the interface between grammar, the human body, and the environment. To what extent can a language encode and make mandatory in its grammar information about physical objects in the world? Urgent studies of small and endangered languages will be needed to complete the picture.

## Information Packaging

Languages contain and package ideas in a way that few other media can. Of course, you can express lots of ideas without language: ever play charades? See a stone cross in a cemetery? Hear a Chopin sonata? All these symbolic media express ideas without language. But language is so much more efficient. That is why we have textbooks in schools rather than teaching biology through the medium of dance, song, and charades, nor (usually) by sending students out to observe animals (though observation and dissection can complement biology lessons). Humans rely first and foremost on language because it is the most compact and efficient channel for transmitting ideas.

If you think this is just a matter of names or labels for things, you have underestimated the vast efficiency of information packaging that goes on in language. We take this entirely for granted! If I say 'my nephew' in English, what information is encoded? You know I am talking about a male

<table>
<tr><th></th><th>Nivkh</th><th>Squamish</th><th>English</th></tr>
<tr><td>people</td><td>men<br>'two (people)'</td><td>?n?an?us<br>'two people'</td><td rowspan="6">two<br>(of anything)</td></tr>
<tr><td>leaves</td><td>merakh<br>'two thin flat things'</td><td rowspan="4">?an?us<br>'two things'</td></tr>
<tr><td>skis</td><td>mirsh<br>'two skis'</td></tr>
<tr><td>batches of dried fish</td><td>mer<br>'two batches of dried fish'</td></tr>
<tr><td>boats</td><td>mim<br>'boats'</td></tr>
<tr><td>animals including fish</td><td>mor<br>'two (animals)'</td><td>?ann?us<br>'two animals'</td></tr>
</table>

**Figure 7.6**
A comparison of six of Nivkh's twenty-six distinct number categories, all of Squamish's three number categories, and the one English category.

person, but then it gets more vague. Is he related to me by blood or marriage? Unclear. Is he older or younger than me? Unclear. Is he the son of my sister or my brother? Unclear. Is he the son of an older sibling of mine or a younger sibling? Unclear. Is he a boy or a man? Unclear.

The English word 'nephew' reflects a set of tools (kinship terms) we use to define social relations. These tools also reflect our society's decisions about what information to include and what to leave out. These decisions are made not by individuals with executive powers, but by tacit consensus within a speech community about what is worth labeling and noting. Evolving over centuries, and by a mysterious process we do not yet understand, word labels are no less real or effective because of how they came about.

Different societies have traversed very different decision paths in constructing their social reality, and maintaining or changing their kinship terms. It is no surprise then, that corresponding to the single English word 'nephew', many languages have a much larger repertoire of more specific terms. Rotuman (9,000 speakers) has a highly complex set of kinship terms, with unique words, for example, denoting 'elder son of elder brother', 'younger son of elder brother', 'elder son of younger brother', or 'younger son of younger brother'. These terms help reinforce a legal framework for enforcing inheritance and land tenure in Rotuman society.[34] Linguistically, the result is a highly compact, highly efficient system of knowledge that packs multiple bits of information into small spaces. The more information there is in a label, the less inductive reasoning or context-based inference is required.

The less information there is in a label, the more the brain must work to construct general categories. Highly abstract terms can be harder to learn: for example, 'vegetable' in English includes a very wide range of things, ranging from spherical and purple (beets) to long and green (scallions). You might be well into adulthood before you learn that a previously unknown item (okra) falls into this class, or that a long-familiar one (tomato) does not. A large and diverse class of objects grouped under one label can be hard to learn. Similarly, a very narrow and specific label can be hard to learn. Tuvan has a special kinship term that means 'the two wives of my two brothers'. If you have three brothers, or only one brother has a wife, the term never applies. The word applies only to a specific sibling and spouse scenario, but is also quite abstract and rarely used.

Linguistic labeling systems do seem to follow a certain logic. For example, there are no known systems that call all yellow objects 'blue' on Tuesdays but 'yellow' the rest of the week. And there are no known labels that denote an animal and its tail (though many languages use the same word for an animal and its edible meat, or an animal and its pelt, or a tree and its fruit, or younger brothers and sisters collectively). The logic of information packaging in linguistic labels only vaguely mirrors natural categories out there in the world. More often, it imposes socially constructed and culturally specific categories. The possible range of such systems provide important insights into how language mediates and shapes or is itself shaped by human perception of and interaction with the world.

## World Record Languages?

Anyone who has tried to learn classical Greek or Latin will be familiar with the so-called case system as manifested in endings that are added onto nouns, pronouns, or adjectives. Latin has six cases: nominative, genitive, dative, accusative, ablative, and vocative, plus remnants of a locative case. Cases indicate relations among words. Latin *puella* means 'girl', but *puellae* means 'for the girl' or 'of the girl' (the ending *-e* signals the word is in the dative case). We know many languages get by with no case at all, while others have very complex systems. Mandarin has no cases, English has only a residue of earlier cases, apparent in differences in pronouns like 'him' vs. 'he' vs. 'his'. Russian has six cases, while Finnish has at least 14. But it is not yet known how much complexity is possible in a case system, or the full range of word-to-word relationships that may be signaled by case endings.

Two languages spoken in the Caucasus mountains of southern Russia show very rich case systems, perhaps far in excess of other languages. Tabasaran, spoken by 95,000 people, even got listed in the 1997 *Guinness Book of Records* as having the most (52) cases. It turns out this number may have been a bit inflated by enthusiastic linguists. Nonetheless, Tabasaran and the nearby Tsez (spoken by 7,000 people) both have case systems of astonishing complexity.[35]

The question of exactly how many is one we will leave to the experts. Linguist Bernard Comrie points out that a basic distinction needs to be made in Tabasaran between 'core' cases (which can attach directly to a noun) and 'non-core', which can only attach after another case suffix is already present. He notes that while Tabasaran cases have probably been overestimated, there is still a large number of possible combinations of multiple suffixes, each with a unique meaning. A Tabasaran noun may have up to 53 distinct forms, once you add case suffixes specifying location and movement of objects in relation to that noun.

The following examples show a Tabasaran word with multiple possible case suffixes:

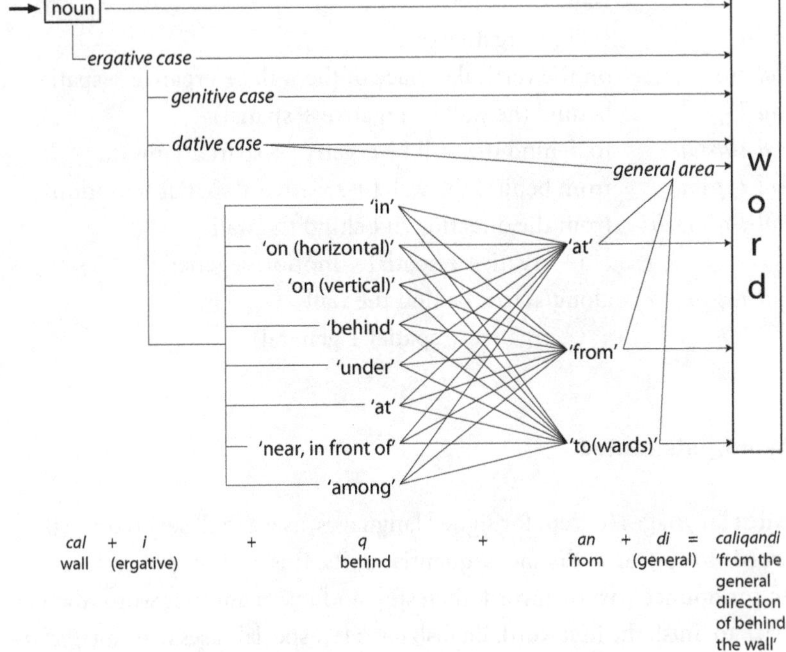


**Figure 7.7**
A flow-chart showing how to build a complex word using the Tabasaran case system. Starting with a noun in the upper left, follow one of many possible paths to add one or more suffixes that encode spatial and other meanings.

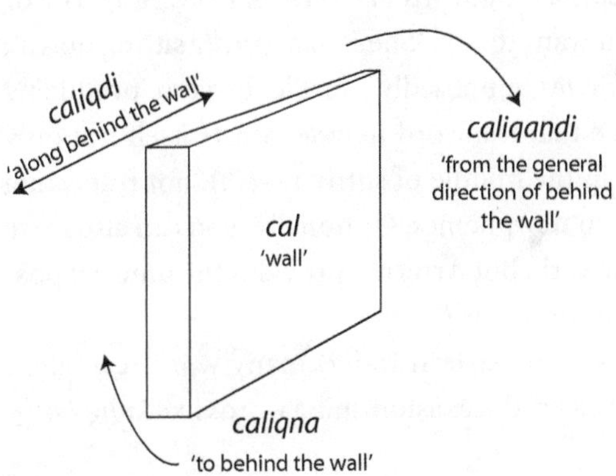


**Figure 7.8**
Location, direction, and motion expressed by complex Tabasaran nouns with case suffixes.

| | |
|---|---|
| *cal* | wall |
| *cal-i* | wall (+ ergative case) |
| *cal-i-k* | on the vertical surface of the wall (+ ergative + spatial) |
| *cal-i-q* | behind the wall (+ ergative + spatial) |
| *cal-i-q-na* | to behind the wall (+ ergative + spatial + motion) |
| *cal-i-q-an* | from behind the wall (+ ergative + spatial + motion) |
| *cal-i-q-an-di* | from the direction of behind the wall (+ ergative + spatial + motion + general) |
| *cal-i-q-di* | along/across behind the wall (+ ergative + spatial + general) |

## Word, Interrupted

Most languages (except for signed languages, as we shall see) require their words to appear as distinct sequential units. It is rare in spoken language to pronounce part of a word, then stop and insert another word, then go back to finish the first word. English has a few special cases like 'fan-*fuckin*-tastic' or 'whoop-dee-*damn*-doo', but speakers cannot just insert any old words wherever they please.

In Eastern Arrernte (2,000 speakers in Australia), many words can appear inside of other words. The Arrernte word for 'sitting down' is made up of three parts, a verb and two suffixes:

| | | |
|---|---|---|
| verb | *arrern* | 'to place' |
| suffix 1 | *-elh* | (indicates an action done to oneself) |
| suffix 2 | *-eme* | (indicates present tense) |

Stinging these together yields a long word *arrernelheme* meaning '(he or she) is sitting down'. If you want to say, 'She is *supposedly* sitting down', you can insert the word *akwele* ('supposedly') inside the verb, producing *arrerneakwelelheme.* Notice that the word *akwele* inserts itself not only inside the word, but right in the middle of suffix 1 (*-elh*), not respecting any neat boundaries between morphemes. Optionally, you can also leave the word *akwele* outside the verb, but Arrernte provides the unusual possibility of nesting words within words.[36]

In Sora (288,000 speakers in eastern India) many words can glom together into a single one. Sora produces astonishing words like *kung-kung-*

*deduu-boob-mar* (this is all one word, with hyphens inserted for readability) meaning 'a man with a clean-shaven head' (notice that by doubling *kung*, the word for 'shave', we get the meaning 'clean-shaven'). Breaking this word into parts we get 'shave + shave + remove hairs + head + man'. This looks at first glance like compounding, a process of stringing words together to form a single word, which happens in many well-known languages. German is famed for unwieldy long words like *Nasenspitzenwurzelentzündung*, meaning an 'inflammation of the root of the tip of the nose'. But Sora is doing something quite different. It is not merely stringing words together. In Sora, verbs literally swallow other words like pythons, sucking them in by a process linguists call incorporation.

English has a limited form of word incorporation, as in 'We bungee-jumped' where a noun 'bungee' becomes part of (but is not inside of) a verb 'jump'. Sora goes much further, allowing verbs to suck in direct objects, indirect objects, and instruments from elsewhere in the same sentence. If an angry Sora speaker says "I will stab you in the belly with a knife," it comes out as *poo-pung-koon-t-am*. The nouns 'belly' and 'knife' both get sucked up inside the verb *poo-t* 'will stab' like so many rats inside a well-fed python. The result is not a string of words, but a single giant verb.

*poo -pung -koon -t -am*
[STAB +belly +knife +will +thee]

But since Sora, unlike German, has no written form, how do we know *poopungkoontam* is actually one word and not just several spoken rapidly or strung together? When a python swallows a rat, both change in appearance. Rat gets balled up inside, python bulges on the outside. Sora words, sucked up inside of verbs, also contract, morphing into smaller versions of themselves. For instance, *koondin*, 'knife', is squished into *koon*. Even *am*, still hanging out of the python's mouth, as it were, is a compressed form of the full pronoun, 'you'. [37]

An even stranger case is found in the Gta' language, spoken by 3,055 hunter-gatherers in the hills of eastern India. Gta', like Sora, allows verbs to swallow multiple nouns. But an adjective modifying a swallowed noun may remain stranded on the outside, modifying from a distance, as the word 'sharp' in the example "I will stab you in the belly with a *sharp* knife" modifies 'knife':

sharp [STAB +belly +knife +will +thee]

Syntacticians who build tree models of languages find it difficult to accommodate such "exotic" structures because they go against common notions of how we think sentences and words are built.[38] As glaring exceptions, Arrernte, Sora, and Gta' are essential in helping scientists formulate universal rules about how words interact. Without these languages, our understanding of fundamental processes of word-building would be limited.

## Man-Talk, Woman-Talk

In some languages, men and women talk very differently, or a speaker of either sex will talk differently depending on the sex of the interlocutor or the person being talked about. Sex matters a great deal in many languages in ways it barely matters (if at all) in English. Of course, we might say 'sir' to a man and 'sister' for female sibling. In colloquial English, a recent study found that the word 'dude' is three times more likely to be uttered in conversations between men than those involving women.[39] But it is hard to find in English any examples of how the sex of the speaker or addressee affects the actual grammar of the language.

Small and endangered languages offer many examples of how sex interacts directly with grammar. In Arapaho (1,038 speakers in Oklahoma), even expressions like 'hello', 'yes', and 'wait' are totally different when said by a man than by a woman.[40] In Arapesh (spoken by 30,000 speakers in three dialects in New Guinea), if I say the word *mehinen* to you and you are a man, I am talking about your sister's son, but if you are a woman, then I am referring to your brother's daughter.[41] In other words, the sex of the person being talked *about* can only be known if the sex of the person being talked *to* is known. If you were eavesdropping on my Arapesh conversation but could not see my addressee, you would not know if I was gossiping about a man or a woman. Also, it is impossible to translate 'nephew' or 'niece' into Arapesh unless you know who the aunt or uncle is.

In Gros Ventre[42] (10 or fewer speakers left in Montana), men and women once used different sounds, words, and exclamations. For 'bread', men say *jatsa* and women *kyatsa*; for 'hello' boys would say *wei* and girls *ao*.[43] The sound 'ch' was spoken only by adult, fluent male speakers, while 'k' was used in its place by women, children, and non-fluent adult males including visiting linguists. Words like 'teepee', 'porcupine', 'buffalo', and 'boy' had distinctly different pronunciations. All these distinctions began to merge as the number of speakers dwindled. But in the past, the community was keenly aware of sex differences in speech. If a male child entering his teen years continued to pronounce 'k', he would be admonished sternly to use 'ch' instead. A linguist from outside the tribe would be told to use 'k' instead.[44]

Yanyuwa (70 speakers in Australia) women and men talk so differently that their speech is really two different dialects.[45] Differences go beyond sounds or words, encompassing grammatical affixes, pronouns, and other parts of speech. Women's talk is reportedly more complex, and men imitate it only imperfectly. The Yanyuwa rigidly enforce speech-sex differences by scolding mistakes, especially those made by newly-initiated adult men expected to adopt fully male speech. One young Yanyuwa man recounted: "When I spoke like a woman my father said to me, 'Where are your breasts and woman's parts [vagina]?' I was really ashamed. I was very careful for a while after that to speak men's words."[46] Use of opposite sex speech is only tolerated in risqué acts, such as a man impersonating a woman in dance, or in myth songs recounting the female creators' voices.

Similar to the gender restrictions discussed above, many languages require speakers to use different words or speech styles or even different grammar rules when talking to people of higher social status. Formality patterns, found in very large languages like Japanese (125 million speakers) or Javanese[47] (75 million speakers), also pop up in smaller languages. Sasak (2.1 million speakers), spoken on Lombok Island in Indonesia, is said to have at least three distinct levels of formality: low, high, and very polite. Depending on your own social status relative to your addressee, you must utter one of three very different sentences to say exactly the same thing.[48]

**Table 7.2**
**The sentence "What did you just say?" at three distinct formality levels in Sasak**

| *Level of formality* | *'What'* | *'say'* | *'you'* | *'now'* | *'this'* |
|---|---|---|---|---|---|
| Very polite | Napi | basen | dekaji | baruq | nike? |
| High | Napi | basen | pelinggih | baruq | nike? |
| Low | Ape | inin | side | baruq | no? |

*Source:* Data from Syahdan (1996:89), cited in Austin 1998.

Of course, we do this in English too. Speaking to a younger brother you might say "gimme a buck!" whereas speaking to the president you might say "Would you be so kind as to lend me a dollar?" The intent is the same, the style and vocabulary radically different. In English, speech register (or formality level) is encoded mostly in word choice and intonation. In other languages, it is encoded not only in words but in sounds, parts of words, syntax, and other grammatical levels. How extreme can sex-based or status-based differences be within a single language? We do not yet know to what extent such social conventions may influence grammar. With the demise of languages like Yanyuwa, Arapaho, and Gros Ventre, we may never know.

## Handy Talk, Talking Hands

Most of the world's signed languages—spoken natively by deaf people—have never been properly counted or documented. A common myth is that these are just versions of English or Spanish or another local language, with a hand sign for each word. Nothing could be further from the truth. American Sign Language (ASL, used by up to 500,000 deaf people as their primary language) is no closer to English in its words, structures, and grammar rules than is Japanese. Another common myth is that signed languages use mostly *iconic* gestures, meaning hand shapes that look like or mimic the things they refer to, and thus signs can be universal to all deaf people. This is also false. A speaker of ASL and a speaker of Japanese Sign Language have no common language. Signed words are overwhelmingly abstract, not imitative, which is why speakers of one sign language cannot understand what speakers of another one are saying.

Debunking these myths has been a major accomplishment of linguistic science.[49] Researchers have demonstrated that sign languages are fully complex, fully functioning human languages, not simplistic gesture systems or in any way inferior to any other human language. But to get a full picture of human language ability, scientists must include in their research all known sign languages. So far, there are 121 identified and named sign languages used in deaf communities around the world, but potentially a great many more remain completely undocumented.[50]

Many sign languages are now rapidly vanishing. This is in part because many deaf communities possessing unique sign languages are small, indigenous, and rural. As countries spend more resources on their deaf citizens, deaf children are sent to urban boarding schools where they are taught only the standard national sign language used in the country. Many original sign languages are now endangered and will vanish before their existence is ever known to science.

Signed communication systems arise spontaneously wherever deaf people live.[51] These may start out as simple systems of gestures with a limited range of uses. But as soon as there is a community of deaf people, and often within just one generation, these systems develop into full-fledged languages, rapidly becoming as complex as spoken languages.

In fact, in some ways sign languages can even be more complex. Because they speak with the hands, signers have a unique possibility not available to spoken languages or even written texts. Many signs require only one hand, so it is possible to use the other hand to make another sign, uttering two words at exactly the same time. Scientists have documented simultaneous use of two one-handed signs in sign languages of Italy, Ireland, and Quebec. But how often do speakers actually make use of this possibility, and what do they use it for?

In Italian Sign Language (number of speakers unknown), a speaker can say something like 'A car stops at a traffic light' or 'A newspaper lies on the table and one of its pages turns over' by using two one-handed signs simultaneously. What is interesting is that each of the two signs seems to affect the other, changing its shape in some basic way, but still allowing it to be recognized as a distinct gesture.[52] CAR, for example, is supposed to be a two-handed sign, imitating both hands gripping a steering wheel. And TRAFFIC LIGHT flexes the fingers of the right hand to denote a blinking light.[53] In combining the two signs, only the right hand makes the sign for 'car', while the left hand signs 'traffic light'. Of course, there is no spoken language in which you can simultaneously say 'car' and 'traffic light'.

## Unusual Hand Shapes as Words

Signed languages are poorly documented and may have many more surprises in store for us. Because they are not written down, they can only be observed in the moment of speech or recorded on videotape for later analysis. Anthropologist Angela Nonaka studies endangered signed languages

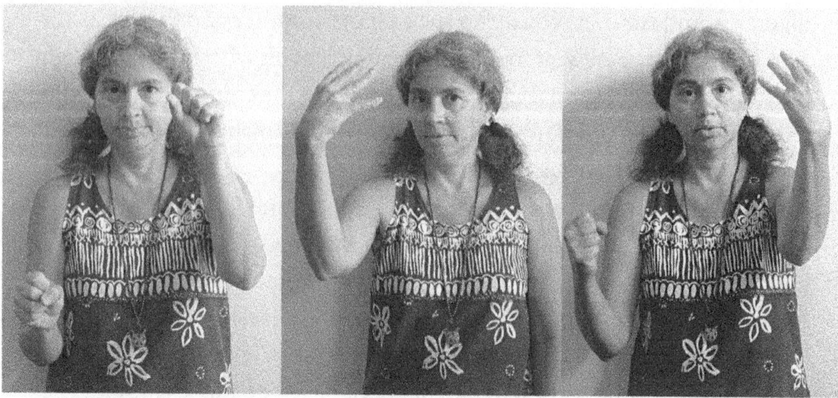

**Figure 7.9**
The two-handed sign in Italian Sign Language (ISL) meaning CAR (left), the right-handed sign TRAFFIC LIGHT (center), and a simultaneous combination of both signs (right), meaning 'A car stops at a traffic light'. Demonstrated here by linguist Donna Jo Napoli, a non-native speaker of ISL and ASL. Courtesy of Robbie Hart

of Thailand and reports that they possess some unusual and scientifically interesting features.

There are at least six signed languages native to Thailand, plus the national standard Thai Sign Language taught to deaf children in schools.[54] The national variety was introduced by educators in the 1950s and is based on American Sign Language (ASL). Two sign languages spoken before ASL arrived, Old Bangkok Sign Language and Old Chiangmai, are now endangered, having no fluent speakers under the age of 45, and no longer being used on a daily basis.

A third, Ban Khor Sign Language, is spoken in a remote village in northern Thailand by fewer than 1,000 deaf people and their relatives. Ban Khor has a hand shape that is one of the most universal ones, found thus far in all known sign languages. In ASL, it is the hand shape used for the letter 'b', of which three variants are shown in figure 7.10.

According to the grammars of signed languages, each hand shape has a number of possible orientations and contact points. For example, once I make the 'b' sign, I can turn my hand in various directions and make contact with various body parts, but all these are strictly limited. Not all possible orientations and hand shapes are allowed by the grammar. This is analogous to spo-

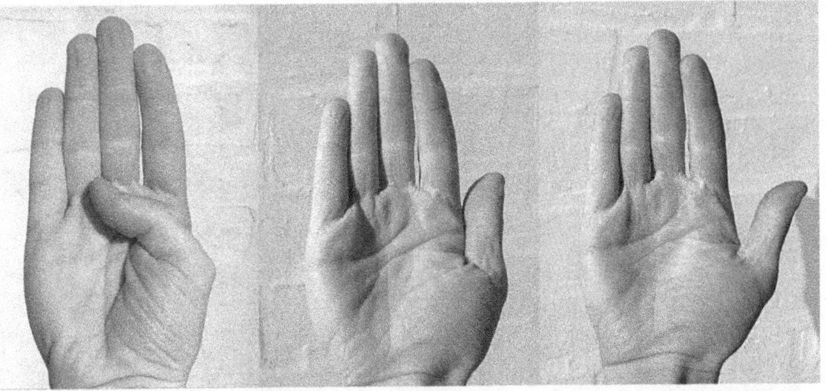

**Figure 7.10**
Three varieties of the 'b' hand sign found in the world's sign languages.

ken languages, where not all sound combinations that can be pronounced by the mouth are allowed. For example, in English, the word *spap* or *smam* are certainly possible combinations of sounds, but to most speakers they sound odd, if not impossible as words. Likewise, English forbids, but Italian allows words to begin with 'sb', such as *sbaffo* ('a smudge'); whereas Italian forbids but English allows words to end with 'sp', such as 'clasp'.

Anthropologist Angela Nonaka has discovered a highly unusual use of the 'b' hand shape in Ban Khor sign language one in which the hand is held vertically in front of the face with the thumb rotated away from the body (fig. 7.11).

So far, no other known sign language takes the 'b' hand shape and places it in this particular turned orientation with respect to the body. It is also unusually (for a stationary sign) positioned so that it obscures the face. Without Ban Khor Sign, we would not know that this placement of the 'b' hand shape was even possible in a signed language. Signed languages are poorly documented and may hold many more surprises in store for us. But many will vanish even before people outside the speech community become aware of their existence.

## Languages and Prehistory

Languages contain buried clues that can help us trace the prehistory of humans and their migrations around the globe. Because language change

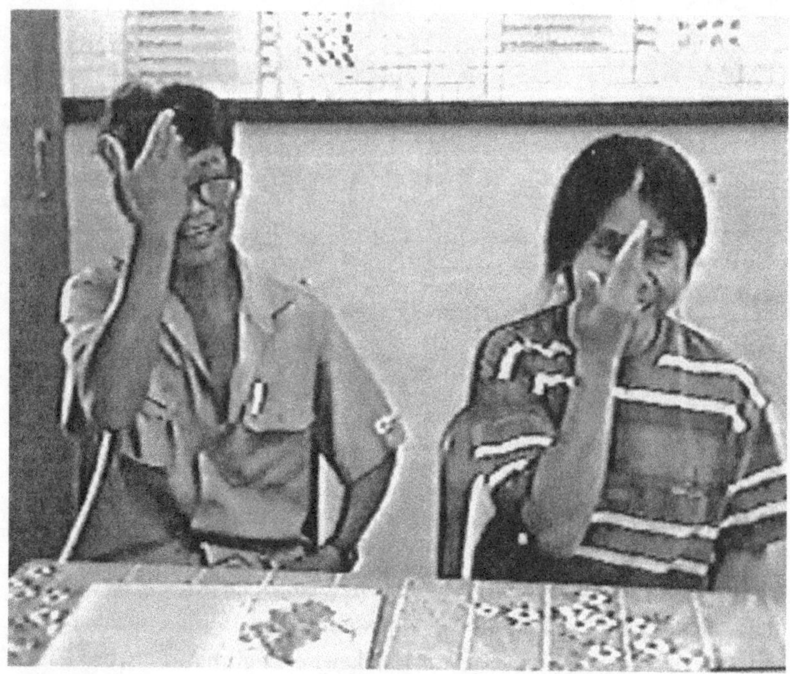

**Figure 7.11**
Signs for "name" and "foreigner" demonstrated by two native speakers of Ban Khor Sign Language. Photograph by Angela Nonaka courtesy of Cambridge University Press

happens so rapidly, when a population splits, the two resulting groups can end up after some time speaking two separate, mutually incomprehensible tongues. Each language is thus one piece in the puzzle to tracing ancient human migrations that led people to the Americas, Polynesia, and so on. Linguistic evidence from shared vocabulary may also reveal prehistoric contacts among unrelated peoples. Two native languages of southern California have in their vocabularies some special words referring to canoes and canoe-making technology. These appear to have been borrowed from ancient Polynesians who must have sailed to California in prehistoric times.[55] Often linguistic evidence is needed to supplement archeological and genetic data in understanding the history of human habitation and contact patterns around the globe.

For example, genetic evidence clearly points to links between natives of Central Siberia and North America, as the two groups share unique traits not found elsewhere.[56] But linguistic links between Siberians and Native

Americans have proved elusive. Languages change so rapidly that after only 1,000 or so years of divergence, what were once close dialects may change beyond recognition, even though the peoples themselves retain cultural or genetic similarities. Linguist Edward Vajda has found intriguing parallels in verb structure and sound correspondences in basic vocabulary that link the Siberian language Ket (990 speakers) to native Alaskan languages like Tlingit (700 speakers) and Eyak (1 speaker), and to the more geographically distant Navajo (148,000 speakers).[57] Though controversial and awaiting further research, Vajda's initial results are tantalizing and may provide elusive clues about the prehistoric peopling of the Americas. They may provide the first solid linguistic link between the populations of North Asia and North America, revealing something about Ice-Age migrations of human populations.

Another intriguing puzzle of human prehistory, and one that linguistics may help solve, is cultural evolution. Humans made the transition from hunting and gathering to agriculture in different places and times. The Mlabri people living in the hills of Thailand and Laos practice a very different way of life than do other peoples in the area, who are all settled agriculturalists. The Mlabri roam the forests, building temporary houses of leaves, and surviving by hunting and gathering. It was assumed that the Mlabri must therefore be descendants of an original hunter-gatherer people who had never adopted agriculture. But when genetic tests were done, the Mlabri showed surprisingly little genetic diversity, indicating that their entire population must have sprung from a common ancestor (perhaps a single woman and from one to four males) as recently as 500 to 1,000 years ago.[58]

Linguistic studies revealed that the Mlabri tongue is related to Tin (46,000 speakers), also spoken in the hills of Thailand. In diverging from Tin, Mlabri underwent a series of well-defined sound and grammar changes over a millennium to bring it to its present form. But since the Tin are known to have been practicing agriculture for well over 1,000 years, the Mlabri would seem to present a rare case of recent *reversion* from a once agriculturalist society to a hunter-gatherer one.

Support for the reversion hypothesis is found in many Mlabri words and myths that refer to agriculture.[59] Scientists do not know what founding event led the Mlabri to go off on their own, abandon agriculture, and become roving forest dwellers. By looking at both genes and languages, it is possible to peer deeper into the past of the Mlabri and thus reconstruct one small part of human prehistory.

## Discoveries Await Us

Throughout this book, I have argued that small and endangered languages will be important to humanity and to science for the kinds of cultural knowledge they contain—technologies for interacting with animals, plants, countable objects, time, and topography. For each of these domains, I also suggested ways in which cultural knowledge is uniquely packaged in any given language and ingeniously encoded in its words and grammatical structures.

In this final chapter, I have departed from cultural knowledge to talk about pure structure of the kind that interests most professional linguists: grammar—the invisible building blocks of cognition. Grammar deservedly preoccupies most linguists, and it is a realm of the mind where many astounding discoveries remain to be made. Any single discovery, even a *eureka* moment, may seem modest or inconsequential on its own. Ban Khor sign language takes a familiar hand shape and places it in an unusual position. Nivkh has a unique classifier for dried fish, Tofa a special morpheme for smell. Mlabri has ancient farming-related words even though its speakers are hunter-gatherers. Rotokas may have as few as six consonants. Eleme doubles part of a word to negate it. Carrier forces its speakers to pay attention to tactile qualities of objects. Sora allows a verb to swallow multiple nouns. Tuvan and White Hmong have unusually rich inventories of words to imitate sounds.

But when we sum up all these discoveries, both across many languages and within a single one, we achieve a clearer insight into the grand realm of human cognition. Language may by its very structure force speakers to attend to certain qualities of the world (shape, size, gender, countability). Languages are self-organizing systems that evolve complex nested structures and rules for how to put the parts of words or sentences together. No two languages do this in the same way. We do not yet have a grasp of what the limits to such complexity are or where the boundaries lie. Endangered languages enormously widen and deepen our view of what is possible within the human mind. As strenuously as I have argued in previous chapters for their importance to humanity and to the planet, I argue here for their deep relevance to pure scientific inquiry. As we delve into languages, many revelatory discoveries await us.

# Notes

## Chapter 1. A World of Many (Fewer) Voices

1. This statement is paraphrased from a similar statement made by Dr. Michael Krauss at a conference on language documentation at Harvard University, July 2005. See also Krauss 1992.
2. Counting languages: Statistics in this and the following paragraph are from Gordon 2005. It is in fact impossible to arrive at any valid and verifiable count of the world's languages (S. Anderson 2004). Many languages exist in a continuum of tongues. Dividing these up into discrete entities remains a purely sociopolitical, not scientific, enterprise. It is also one often deeply biased by the power dynamics of colonialism and outside influence (Mühlhausler 1996, Hill 2002). The remedy to this numbers game is to avoid misplaced faith in numbers or linguistics censuses, and to take seriously the ethnolinguistic nomenclature and classifications used by the people who themselves speak a particular tongue, as I have done, for example in the case of the Ös language of Siberia. Linguist Jane Hill (2002) cautions that counting numbers of speakers of a language can also be a dubious undertaking, especially when those numbers dwindle and become very small. In identifying putative "last speakers," we risk applying outside, normative standards to what counts as a legitimate speaker of a language or member of a speech community. The antidote is to take seriously a speech community's own ideas and standards, and to include in the discussion (and in any eventual documentation project) speakers, rememberers, and community members of all levels of competence.
3. Navajo language shift: Gordon 2005: 305 notes: "First-language speakers among first graders are 30% versus 90% in 1968."
4. Lenape words: Delaware (also spelled Deleware) (Lenape) Tribe of Indians: Homepage (http://www.delawaretribeofindians.nsn.us/), and Lenape Talking Dictionary (http://www.talk-lenape.com/).
5. Delaware (Lenape) tribe population: Delaware (Lenape) Tribe of Indians: Homepage.
6. Biological metaphors for language: For a discussion of "language death," see Crystal 2000. A discussion of metaphors commonly used may be found in Nettle and Romaine's *Vanishing Voices* (2000: 5–7). A critique of such usage may be found in Hill 2002 and Errington 2003. Popular usage of language "death" metaphors is exemplified by Kolbert 2005 and Hitt 2004. The term "endangerment," typically applied to biological species under threat of extinction, may, when applied to languages, suggest a false analogy or similarity between species on the one hand and cultures and languages on the other. Linguist Nora England (2002) suggests that use of such metaphors can contribute to a sense of marginalization or "other"-ness on the part of

a small speech community, and that some people may find it demeaning to be "analogously linked to plants and insects and lower-order animals" (England 2002: 142). Though "endangered languages" is now a widely used and efficiently descriptive term, and one that some small language communities have also embraced, England advocates further reflection about a "way of speaking about disappearing, shrinking or threatened languages that avoids a false biological analogy, and . . . places the discussion in a readily understood context of universal human social action and existence, both individual and collective" (England 2002: 143).

7. Sleeping or dormant languages may be reawakened: Proponents of this view include Rob Amery (1998), Jessie Little Doe Fermino (see Stille 2000), and Wesley Leonard (2004, 2005).
8. Species extinction: Hawksworth and Kaylin-Arroyo 1995. Number of species yet unidentified: Purvis and Hector 2000. See also Heywood 1995. The unexplored biosphere: Wilson 1992: 131–33.
9. Threatened species percentages: Sutherland 2003; Heywood 1995.
10. Tofa comment: Harrison 2001.
11. Children, not parents, may lead the way in a language shift: Fillmore 1999.
12. Some speakers of small languages want their children to speak dominant languages: Ladefoged 1992.
13. *How to Keep Your Language Alive*: Hinton 2002. Green Book: Hinton and Hale 2001.
14. Species documentation in the face of extinction: see Wilson 1992: ch. 8.
15. Chad, Vanuatu populations: CIA World Factbook (Central Intelligence Agency 2005). The factors underlying language diversity go beyond geographical barriers between peoples—see Nettle and Romaine 2000: 85. For a global map of language hotspots, see www.languagehotspots.org.
16. Alaskan native population: Alaska Natives Commission 1994. Alaskan languages: Krauss 1997.
17. Language statistics in this and the following paragraph: Gordon 2005.
18. Population level-off: Brand 2005.
19. Stable bilingualism: A recent mathematical model of language death predicts the stable co-existence of two competing languages to be an unlikely scenario (Abrams and Strogatz 2003).
20. Shamans' medicine: Plotkin 1993.
21. Pharmaceuticals: Posey 1990a.
22. 87% of plant and animal species unidentified: Hawksworth and Kalin-Arroyo 1995. See also Wilson 1992.
23. Marovo fish-schooling knowledge: See chapter 2 of this book; Johannes and Hviding 2000.
24. Seri people's turtle knowledge: Felger, Cliffton, and Regal 1976; Nabhan 2003.
25. Western !Xoon: Kiessling 2005.

26. Creation myths: Found in nearly all cultures, these vary widely in their account of how the universe came to be. But accounts involving ducks seem to be rare. Leeming (1994) lists none, while the classic and enormous *Motif-index of Folk-literature* (Thompson 1932–36) lists only one: the epic story of Finland, called the *Kalevala*, recounts how a mythical duck laid its egg on the lap of a maiden. When the maiden rose to stretch, the egg fell and broke open, and its shell parts became the earth and sky: "From one half the egg, the lower, / Grows the nether vault of Terra: / From the upper half remaining, / Grows the upper vault of Heaven" (trans. Crawford 1888). Finnish is not an endangered language, but since the Reformation and advent of Lutheran Christianity in Finland, the oral epics are confined largely to the small geographical region of Karelia.
27. Urarina: Olawsky 2005.

### Chapter 2. An Extinction of (Ideas about) Species

1. "Berry picking": Marta Kangaraeva, female, born 1930 (Harrison 2001: 98).
2. Gila Pima plant names: Rea 1990.
3. Sorghum: Teshome et al. 1997; Ken Torrance and Awegechew Teshome, personal communications.
4. Spartak Kangaraev, male, born 1930 (Harrison 2001: 90).
5. Todzhu reindeer terms: Harrison 2001; Donahoe, personal communication.
6. Foal and colt vs. 'baby horse': A Google search on January 12, 2006, yielded 1.9 million web pages containing the terms 'horse' and either 'foal' or 'colt' (but lacking the word 'gun'). Some 43,500 pages contained the term 'baby horse' while lacking both 'colt' and 'foal', and a total of 61,000 pages contained the term 'baby horse'.
7. Tuvan horse classification: For a partial description of the system (in Russian and Tuvan) see Darzha 2003.
8. Tuvan folk genetics: Data were collected on field expeditions by me in 1998–2004. Similarly complex systems of classification of livestock according to coat pattern, color, sex, fertility, lactation, and so on have been documented, for example, for cattle among the Bodi people of Ethiopia (Fukui 1996), and the Mursi (or Mun) of Ethiopia (Turton 1980); and for camels among the Bedouins (Ingham 1997).
9. Mendelian genetics: Mendel [1866] 1946.
10. "folksonomy": A contraction of folk taxonomy, the study of how people categorize the natural world, it refers to any emergent, socially constructed classification system. The term itself is widely attributed to blogger Thomas Vander Wal.
11. Tofa word for snake: Rassadin 1995 lists the word [tʃulan] for snake. Tofa consultants interviewed by me during field expeditions in in 2000–2001 lacked knowledge of this word, but were all familiar with 'long worm',

'mountain fish', or 'ground fish'. The apparent disappearance of 'snake' as a lexeme may reflect the end result of a naming taboo.

12. Chehalis creation story: Palmer 1925. *The Ethnologue*, 14th edn. (Grimes 2000) reported seven speakers of Chehalis as of 1990, while *The Ethnologue*, 15th edn. (Gordon 2005) reported that none remained. A similar myth about a great chief who named all the animals (e.g., deer, cougar, grizzly bear, wolf, lynx) and also assigned them chracteristics and habitats was told by the Southern Okanagan people of Washington State (612 speakers) (Cline 1938).
13. Unicorn fish: Foale 1998.
14. Captain Cook's 1776–80 journey: Cook 1785–1787; Kaehr 2000.
15. *kihikihi* appears to be a doubled form of *kihi*, which is listed in an online version of a Hawaiian Dictionary (Pukui and Elbert 2003) as meaning 'edge, tip, extremity, sharp point of a leaf'. A related form, *kikihi*, means 'to be crescent shaped' or 'to dodge or move about quickly, especially with quick turning of sharp corners; canoe sailing, to sail'. The fully doubled form *kihikihi* denotes the Moorish idol fish (*Zanclus cornutus*) and is also applied to objects such as a crescent moon or crescent-shaped gold coin. The fish name *kihikihi* appears thus to denote both the quality of being crescent shaped and the fish's rapid, zig-zagging swimming movements.
16. Taxonomy began in ancient Greece: Godfray 2002: 17.
17. Universal Biological Indexer and Organizer (uBio): Marine Biological Laboratory 2004. As of January 2006, it contained 5,198,016 'scientific' names and 511,326 'vernacular' ones from 442 languages. But so-called 'vernacular' names in uBio appear to come mostly from major world languages. For example, of the 15 'vernacular' names associated with *Agelaius phoeniceus*, 11 are English (including "red-winged blackbird"), 1 French, 1 German, and 1 Spanish. Although certain sectors of life (e.g., tropical fish) have several indigenous names listed in the database, it is clear that non-English and even more so indigenous names are woefully underrepresented in uBio, though we cannot fault biologists for this lacuna. Other large taxonomic database projects appear to provide little room for indigenous, non-Western knowledge, for example, the Integrated Taxonomic Information System (www.itis.usda.gov), the Species 2000 project (www.sp2000.org), and the Global Biodiversity Information Facility (www.gbif.org).
18. Interbreeding is usually considered both a necessary and sufficient criterion to distinguish species, but it turns out not to be in all cases. Mayr (1942) first describes what is now termed a "ring" species, using the example of the Herring Gulls, which live in a habitat that spans the globe. Gulls from any local group can interbreed with neighboring ones on the ring, but where the two ends of the ring come together, the two adjacent varieties of seagull cannot interbreed. Liebers, de Knijff, and Helbig (2004) present DNA evidence that casts doubt on the Herring Gull as a clear example of a ring species. They cite the Asian greenish warbler, which rings

around the Himalayas, as a possible true example of a ring species (Irwin, Bensch, and Price 2001).

19. Tree of life: Hillis, Zwickl, and Gutell (2003) situate 3,000 species in a taxonomic tree. Even this relatively small number, about 0.18% of all species thus far named by modern science, yields a massively complex tree diagram. For a discussion of current and emerging taxonomic models, see Pennisi 2003.
20. 'European kangaroos' and horses: Teichelmann and Schürmann 1840; Cook's kangaroo and its description by analogy: Morrison-Scott and Sawyer 1950, Beaglehole 1968. Of course, the current genetic taxonomy tells us both analyses were way off the mark: horses and hares are closer to humans, genetically, than they are to kangaroos.
21. Plant vs. animal in modern taxonomies: Pennisi 2003
22. Lardil land vs. sea life: McKnight 1999.
23. 'Reptile' definition: *Oxford English Dictionary* online at <html://www.oed.com>. Accessed July 2005.
24. West Nggela fish taxa: Foale (1998) does not give the exact number of scientific taxa for fish known by the West Nggela. But he reports that some single scientific names may correspond to as many as four distinct Nggela names, and that such one-to-many splits are most often found for fish the Nggela commonly use.
25. Thames river fish names: Wheeler 1979.
26. Halkomelem ethnobotany and ethnobiology: See also this page, by the British Columbia Institute of Technology and many Halkomelem elders: <www.sfu.ca/halk-ethnobiology>.
27. Musqueam Halkomelem salmon and trout: Shaw and Grant 2004; Grant personal communication.
28. Genetic taxonomy of salmon and trout: Crespi and Fulton 2004.
29. Toucan chief: This section could not have been written without the painstaking research and inspired analysis conducted by Arpiar Saunders at Swarthmore College in 2005.
30. Wayampi toucans: Jensen 1988, 1990, and personal communication. A fascinating account of Kalam (New Guinea) bird folk classification may be found in Majnep and Bulmer 1977.
31. Wayampi toucans: ibid.
32. Simulations: Wilensky 1999. For online demos of of emergent and self-organizing systems see http://ccl.northwestern.edu/netlogo/.
33. Fish schooling as an emergent, self-organizing system: Parrish, Viscido, and Grünbaum 2002.
34. Marovo: It is not surprising that the Marovo are so interested in observing fish behavior. Johannes and Hviding (2000: 22) write: "Marovo people probably eat or otherwise use a greater variety of species of marine animals than 99% of the world's fishers."
35. Marovo vs. marine biology terms for fish aggregations: Johannes and Hviding 2000.

36. Kayapó bee knowledge: Posey 1990b.
37. Lost words: For an excellent discussion of knowledge loss in language extinction, see Nettle and Romaine 2000: ch. 3 "Lost Words—Lost Worlds."
38. Wayampi knowledge transfer: Jensen 1990 and personal communication.
39. Dog salmon: dog salmon is another name for the chum salmon (*Oncorhyncus keta*), seen in fig. 2.13. In its mating phase, its dark rust-colored 'coat' is striped with light-colored bands. A similarly colored dye was obtained from alder tree bark by the natives of Washington State. In addition to using the color for cedar bark coats, they also dyed fishing nets, making them invisible to fish (Pojar and MacKinnon 1994: 44; Moerman 1998).
40. Folk classification: There is a rich literature on folk taxonomies and their structural and cultural properties. See, for example, seminal works by Conklin (1954, 1980a, b), Berlin, Breedlove, and Raven (1966), Hunn (1975), and successive works by Dwyer (1976), Brandenstein (1977), Brown (1984, 1985), Atran (1990), Medin and Atran (1999), Gurung (2003), and Kakudidi (2004).
41. Barí: Lizarralde 2001. Zent (2001) found similar loss of ecological knowledge corresponding with bilingualism and acculturation in an exploratory study among the Piaroa of Venezuela (12,000 speakers).
42. Rofaifo knowledge erosion tied to change in lifeways: Dwyer (1976: 426) reports that the Rofaifo people of Papua New Guinea have shown a "notable simplification in taxonomic usage" while undergoing cultural change (e.g., dietary, linguistic, hunting-gathering) during their first thirty years of contact with Europeans.
43. Saami folk taxonomy: M. Anderson (1978) cites records from as far back as 1756 to illustrate the erosion of specialized Saami taxonomic knowledge.
44. Michigan and Itza Mayan folk biology: Atran 1998.
45. Sergei Kangaraev, male, born 1959 (Harrison 2001: 98).

### Case Study: Vanishing Herds and Reindeer Words

1. United Nations Environment Program 2001.

### Chapter 3. Many Moons Ago

1. Hunter-gatherer lifestyle practiced by humans until 12,000 years ago: Lee and Daly 1999.
2. Inuit calendar: Thorpe et al. 2001. The remainder of this section reads: "We did not know it was July then. After it disappeared it would return and then it would be August. That is when the caribou furs would get nice. . . . The birds would be flying again. The young birds would have grown then. That is how they knew the seasons."
3. Marshack's discovery: Marshack 1964; , 1972, see also Bayot 2004.

4. English 'fortnight' denotes a unit of two weeks. Curiously, we lack a single English word to exclusively refer to 'one whole day,' '24-hour period', or 'a full day and night'. Russian and Polish have a word for the 24-hour day, as do many other languages.
5. Survival and adaptation of traditional timekeeping: Levinson (2002) offers a compelling account of how and why global timekeeping has invaded the very time-conscious culture of the people of Rossell Island. Schieffelin (2002) recounts how a traditional Papua New Guinea culture, the Bosavi, adapted to foreign (e.g., missionary) notions of timekeeping.
6. I do not mean to suggest that calendar cycles other than the lunar lack meaning for Tuvans. As practicing Buddhists, they also keep track of ritually important dates and may consult a printed religious calendar to determine which days are auspicious for traveling, hair-cutting, weddings, and other activities. This requires literacy and printed calendars, which they purchase, and they do not keep track of such information in their head, nor do they need this information to be successful animal herders.
7. Our modern unit of the seven-day week is essentially meaningless to them. Nothing ever needs doing on a Monday that cannot just as easily happen on Saturday. The fact that the week is a late imposition on their culture is reflected in their utter lack of names for weekdays: Monday through Saturday are simply called 1st day, 2nd day, etc. (or sometimes called by their Russian names). Sunday is called 'big day' though no one can explain why it has any particular significance. Being pastoral animal herders, there is no day of the week that involves any different routine or any less work. The fact that they call Sunday 'big day' simply reflects the influence of the Europeans (Russian) who colonized them, insisting that Sunday was special.
8. Xavante: Maybury-Lewis 1974: 155.
9. The Borôro people, living deep in the interior of Brazil along the Barreiro River, maintain a complex system that uses village architecture and ritual to keep track of moon phases and astronomical cycles. They also use metaphors for moon phases, calling the newly waxing moon 'like the claw of a giant armadillo'. When the moon begins to wane they say the 'moon's eye is getting smaller', and in the third quarter they say it 'dawns over the baldness of the non-Indian people' (Fabian 1992).
10. Carib moons: Ahlbrinck 1931: 327, cited in Magaña 1984: 346.
11. The indigenous people of Russia are not the only ones to name a month after this ubiquitous lily bulb. The calendar of the Ainu, who live in Japan's far north, is now almost forgotten, but Batchelor 1905 records that their name for one spring season was *haprap chup* 'edible-lily-bulb month/moon.'
12. Tofa calendars: Two earlier versions of Tofa calendars were recorded—a 12-month cycle in 1880 (Katanov 1891) and a 13–month cycle in the 1850s (Shtubendorf 1858). Like those remembered by Aunt Marta and the Tofa elders of Gutara, both overlap only partially with each other.

13. Falck's 1785 observations on the Chulym calendar, in the original German, read: "Der erste schneefall ist ihr Neujahr. Von demselben zehlen sie 12 Monathe (Ai), Karakal Ai ist meistens unser Septemb., Garisch Ai Octobr., Kitscha Ai (kurzer Monath) Novem., Ulu Ai (großer Monath) Decembr., Jel Serta (halber Winter) Januar, Tulg Ai (Fuchsmonat) Febr. Kutschugen Ai (Adler Monath) März, Karga Ai (Krähen Monath) April, Koi Ai (Kukuks Monath) May, Kitschi Schilgai (kleiner Sommer) Jun., Ulu Schelgai Ai (großer Sommer) Jul. und Urgai Ai (langer Monath) August, weil er bis sum Schnee dauert." [Translation to English by Steve Holt and Robbie Hart.]
14. Chulym (Ös) calendar terms: 1768: Falck 1785–1786; 2005: K. David Harrison, unpublished field notes and recordings 2003–2005, Anderson and Harrison 2006.
15. Koryak: Alexander King, personal communication. Koryak data originally provided to King by Valentina Romanovna Dedyk in November 2002. Anthropologist John Ziker (2002: 29–30 and personal communication) has described ecological lunar calendars used by native Siberian peoples the Dolgan and Nganasan, including such colorful month names as Dolgan 'chimney pipe month' (February), 'reindeer milking month' (April), and 'ice flow month' (June), or Nganasan 'frosted [trees] month' (February/March) and 'goose mo(u)lting month' (July/August). Comparable northern peoples' calendars include Okanagan (Shaw 2001: 50), with month names like 'whiteout time' (January), 'drifting time' (February), and 'buttercup time' (March).
16. Tlingit months: Emmons 1991.
17. Ainu months: Batchelor 1905 lists thirteen, Watanabe 1973 lists twelve.
18. Natchez months and foods: Le Page du Pratz [1774] 1975: 342, 368. 'Cold-meal month' (named for corn meal) in January possibly reflected a lack of dietary alternatives.
19. Brown (1999: 141) cites Swanton (1946) who cites Le Page du Pratz [1774] (1975).
20. Lenape months: Nilsson 1920: 190–91 (spelled 'Lenope' in this source).
21. Actual length of the year: Online at <http://webexhibits.org/calendars/year-astronomy.html#Anchor-33420>. Accessed January 2005.
22. Chukchee calendar: Sverdrup 1938.
23. Nggela: Foale 1998. By adopting this method of reproduction, the worm reduces the problem of finding a mate from three dimensions (the entire vast ocean) to two dimensions (just the surface). Rachel Merz, personal communication.
24. Yurok: Kroeber 1925.
25. *Wokas*: Barker 1963, Gatschet 1890.
26. Klamath calendar: Kroeber 1925: 322–23. Kroeber may be right that the Klamath system is useless for the practical purposes of our calendar, but he ignores the fact that is quite useful for the purposes of theirs.
27. A month often begins the year: many cultures do not have such a simple designation—the Nganasan divided their 13 lunar months into a 'summer

year' and a 'winter year', but one simply had to know which was which, it was not encoded in the actual names of the months that made up the two half-year periods.

28. O'odham month: Saxton and Saxton 1969.
29. Ifugao: Newell and Poligon 1993.
30. Chukchee body counting of moons: Sverdrup 1938.
31. Yukaghir calendar: Jochelson 1926: 41, also Kreynovich 1979: 203.
32. Ifugao 'sitting period': Newell and Poligon 1993.
33. The Yakut people of Siberia (363,000 speakers) used a traditional time/distance unit *köss*, which simply meant 'kettle'.
34. Yakut *köss* and Yukaghir *'kettle boiled'*: Jochelson 1926: 40.
35. Borôro (also spelled Bororo) body time: Fabian 1992: 87–92.
36. Hanunóo time units longer than a year: Conklin [1957] 1975: 57.
37. *Yamaricura* festival may mark a Metonic cycle: Magaña 1984: 347.
38. Online astronomical tools: www.yoursky.com.
39. 12 or 13 months: This 12/13 alternation may account in part for conflicting reports by many early observers of indigenous cultures as to whether 12 or 13 lunar months were observed.
40. Kewa pig-kill cycle: Franklin and Franklin 1962.
41. Kewa pig-kill festival: Pumuye (1978: 46–47) notes that the Kewa had no year, but the concept is beginning to replace the body-count calendar: "Generally, there was no such period in the old days and a year is therefore an introduced term among the Kewa. . . . Nowadays some of the people are beginning to use the year system in long term planning for many of their traditional activities, such as a pig killing festival which takes place once every five to seven years."
42. Kaluli seasons: Feld (1990: 60–61) quotes E. Schiefflin (1976: 141). The actual name of the calendric period is transcribed as [*tɛn*]. The Rainbow Beeeater [*merops ornatus*] and many other birds also serve as seasonal markers for the Kalam people of New Guinea (Majnep and Bulmer 1977: 126).
43. Yanyuwa: Richard Baker 1993: 136 (italics added). The Australian Bureau of Meteorology, recognizing the value of traditional weather knowledge, is now cooperating with Monash University and various elders to research Yanyuwa and other indigenous weather knowledge.
44. Marovo: Johannes and Hviding 2000.
45. Basis of the week: Some scholars have suggested that early man may have tracked the moon's progress from new to half, full and half, and noticed that each phase lasted about seven days (see Duncan 1998: 46). If true, this suggests a possible basis for a seven-day week, but such a unit was not widely recognized. Given what we have noticed about the irregularity of moon phases and the way they form a continuum, the shapes cannot easily be grouped into seven-day units. Since the week as a unit is only weakly suggested by cosmological or biological rhythms, various cultures that needed a standardized week-unit arrived at different solutions. The seven-day week

first came into use in ancient Babylon, but a ten-day week was adopted by the Mayan Empire, and some Bantu civilizations in Africa adopted a six-day week.

46. The week as a concept requires linguistic anchoring: Jackendoff 1996: 24.
47. Yukaghir weekdays: Jochelson 1926: 42.
48. Saami weekdays: Itkonen 1948.
49. O'odham weekdays: Saxton and Saxton 1969.
50. Yuki weekdays: Foster 1944. Mon. *witpa'* 'work get up', Tues. *wit opi* 'work two', Wed. *wit mólmi* 'work three', Thurs. *wit omahá*$^{n}$*t* 'work four', Fri. *wit huik'ó* 'work five', Sat. *wit powiwístik* 'work one day remaining', Sun. *wit kasnó* 'work rest'.
51. Aneityum days: Lynch and Tepahae 2001. Yesterday (*iyenev*) and tomorrow (*imrañ*) lack symmetry.
52. Sie days: Crowley 2000. The eleven-day unit is named as follows: *no-wisas* 'five days ago', *no-wimpe* 'four days ago', *no-winag* 'three days ago', *marima* 'today', *winag* 'three days from now', *wimpe* 'four days from now', *wisas* 'five days from now'.
53. For extensive coverage of these systems, formally called 'deictic day naming', see Tent 1998.
54. Star lore: Excellent examples of ethno-astronomy are Fabian's 1992 monograph on the Borôro of Brazil and Magaña's 1984 study of the Carib of Guiana.
55. Ecosystem changes can lead to calendar changes: Another scenario, pointed out by Suzanne Romaine, is that new birds have reportedly arrived in arctic ecosystems due to climate change. This could lead to changes in ecological calendars.

## Case Study: Nomads of Western Mongolia

1. Mongolian space: Compare the United States' 4 million miles of paved highways. Data from the CIA World Factbook: Central Intelligence Agency 2005.
2. Monchaks are now shifting to speaking Mongolian, a language also spoken by many nomadic herders who know the same lands and raise the same animals. So the loss of knowledge specific to animal husbandry may be less severe. However, Monchak differs deeply from Mongolian, and so a great deal of cultural content will still be lost.

## Chapter 4. An Atlas in the Mind

1. Peter Bolkhoyev's comment in Tofa was [*dyžymde deg*] 'as if in my dream'. Linguists Gregory Anderson and Sven Grawunder were present.
2. Tofa clan hunting territories and animism are briefly described in Sergeyev 1964. Tofa hunting technologies and ethnogeography are discussed in Mel'nikova 1994.

3. *Kastarma*: Symmetrically shaped stones formed when extreme underground hydrological pressures mold soft clay into curious shapes. Geologists might call them 'concretions'.
4. Tofa distance units: 1 *kösh* = approx. 25 kilometers. Rassadin 1995: 27.
5. Sherpa distance: Fisher 1990.
6. Map sewn into shaman's coat: Okladnikova (1998) cites Chaussonnet and Driscoll (1994).
7. Tofa mythical world: This belief system is schematically reported in Mel'nikova 1994: 196–97 and was discussed in detail by me with native Tofa consultants in 2000 and 2001. It has largely been forgotten.
8. Yukaghir river songs: Nikolaeva and Mayer 2004. These songs were recorded by Nikolaj Lixachev in 1986. Quoted here are lines 1–4 from Lixachev's song 'On the Kolyma'; followed by lines 3–5 from his song 'Oroek'. Transcribed and translated soundfiles of the songs may be found in Nikolaeva and Mayer 2004. On interpreting Yukaghir pictographic writing and maps, see Zhukova 1986. Map (or navigational) songs have been documented for many other cultures, e.g., Pacific Islanders (Stimson 1932, Davenport 1960).
9. Tungus lakes are detached from their effluent rivers: Adler 1910: 121–22. Yakut lakes are bisected by their rivers: Adler 1910: 127.
10. Adler (1910: 106) notes: "maps sketched by different individuals show a great degree of convergence."
11. Yenisei Ostyak (now called Ket): de Hutorowicz 1911: 672.
12. Makonde and Kinyamwesi (Nyamwesi) topographic instinct: Weule [1909] 1970: 372–73, italics added. Also cited in slightly different translation in de Hutorowicz 1911: 674.
13. Yukaghir river mapping: Shirina 1993, cited in Okladnikova 1998: 340. A *verst* is an archaic unit of measurement equal to 1.067 km or 0.66 mile.
14. Sherpa children's maps: James Fisher 1990: 85. A quantitative study of Nepalese children's use of spatial terms (Niraula, Mishra, and Dasen 2004: 117) showed their strong preference for geocentric (not egocentric) terms, applying an orientation system privileging the up/down dimension.
15. Bantawa language notes: Hart 2003 and unpublished field notes. Many Kiranti languages spoken in Nepal share this attention to the vertical dimension. Ebert (1999) discusses this phenomenon across the Kiranti language family and writes that there are also non-spatial connotations: 'up' indicates purity and austerity, while 'down' connotes wealth, abundance, and foreigners. Above (north and uphill) from the Kiranti territory lie the icy, barren slopes of the highest mountains in the world, virtually impassable, and below (south and downhill) are roads, larger towns, and India's fertile Ganges delta. But these concepts that make sense in the local Himalayan terrain can cause confusion when applied to the wider world: Allen (1972) reported that Thulung speakers greeted with considerable skepticism his assertion that England was far to the north of Nepal but still able to have farmland and a mild climate. For them, "north" necessarily meant uphill and much colder.

See Bickel and Gaenszle 1999 for more about Himalayan systems of altitude. For a counter-example of a language (Chantyal) of Nepal that does not seem to have developed verbs encoding vertical paths see Noonan 2005.

16. Hanunóo trails: Conklin [1957] 1975: 56.
17. Hanunóo winds, quotes, and diagram: Conklin [1957] 1975: 35.
18. Bedouin wind names: Young 2005. In phonetic transcription, the Jordanian terms would be [*jiʃarrig*] and [*jiɣarrib*].
19. Malakula: If a specific destination on Malakula is mentioned, however, not just the island in general, then Lolovoli speakers will fall back on the *hage/hivo* distinction. They say *hivo* for intended destinations in the northwest of Malakula and *hage* for destinations in the southeast part of the island.
20. Lolovoli Ambae data: Hyslop 1999 is the source of the data presented here. There is a copious scientific literature on oceanic and island directional and geocentric systems: see, for example, Senft 1997, Bennardo 2003, François 2003, 2004. For more on indigenous navigation technologies, see Gladwin 1958, Hutchins 1983. Arpiar Saunders assisted me in this research.
21. Tuvan is not alone in this metaphorical mapping—the Yupno of Papua New Guinea visualize (and verbalize) the entire river valley they inhabit as the body of a giant mythological man (Wassman 1997) as do the Tiv people of Ghana (Abraham 1933).
22. Animistic mapping was also practiced among Australia's aboriginal Kaurna (no fluent speakers remain). Kaurna people once named places spread over an area of 1,500 square miles on the coast of South Australia, near Adelaide. Each place name corresponded to a body part of an imagined giant kangaroo. In this giant kangaroo landscape, two mountain peaks represented ears, a peninsula the 'nose', two hills eyebrows, one river the 'tail' while a nearby river was 'excrement' and a river delta the 'throat'. Other landscape features represented the brain, feet, etc. (Webb 1936–1937, also see Hercus, Hodges, and Simpson 2002).

    Kaurna is now an extinct language, the last speaker having died in the 1930s. Kaurna youth have grown up with a sense of being aboriginal, but vastly outnumbered by their fellow Australians and lacking any knowledge of their ancestral language. The Kaurna community has recently begun a heroic effort to 'reawaken' this ancient, sleeping tongue. Not surprisingly, they have focused first on geographic place names, re-creating and remembering them, and posting bilingual signs to identify them. Kaurna place names like Yerltowarti 'land's tail' and Warripari 'river throat' reflect the natural world as viewed through the prism of Kaurna culture. And they provide a direct mechanism to re-link the Kaurna people to their ancestral land, now populated mostly by European immigrants. The land has provided inspiration for a new generation of Kaurna working to reawaken their language. As one young Kaurna learner—Dennis Kammamurty O'Brien—has remarked: "I can see a bright future for Kaurna." Perhaps the giant kangaroo, and the traditional Kaurna place names, will inspire more Kaurna to revisit their ancestral knowledge.

23. Tuvan sound symbolism: Harrison 2004.
24. Tuvan sound sensitivity: Levin 2006. Feld 1996: 108 makes similar claims about the Kaluli language of Papua New Guinea, which has a large repertoire of words for water sound and motion. Gell (1995) discusses how phonological iconism shapes and encodes perception of landscapes for other Papua New Guinea peoples.
25. Tabulahan: There are 8,000 speakers total of the Aralle-Tabulahan language. The dialect of Tabulahan village is discussed here.
26. Aralle-Tabulahan directions: McKenzie 1997.
27. Place naming: For an excellent discussion of how indigenous people can encode place names in stories and conversation, see Basso 1996.
28. British orientation: Robin Baker (1989) describes experiments conducted over seven years where 554 subjects were led through unfamiliar woodlands 2–4 km, ending 0.3 to 1.75 km from their (familiar) starting point. They were then asked to point the direction back to their starting point and had an average 17° error (± 10°). They were then asked what cardinal direction they were pointing and had an average 50° error (± 22°). Note that this was a much simpler task than that the Haillom were set. The bushmen were led through what must have been at least semi-familiar bush 15–40 km (ten times as far as the British subjects) and asked to point to numerous *other* familiar locations (*not* just their starting point), some up to 200 km away.

    Levinson (1997: 128 n. 20) interprets the Baker (1989) results to show that "less than half the British subjects judged locations to be in the correct 90° quadrant," a result not directly supported by Baker's 1989 book. An in-depth study of wayfinding behavior in urban humans may be found in Golledge (1999).
29. Topographic gossip: Widlok 1997: 325, and personal communication.

### Case Study: Wheel of Fortune and a Blessing

1. I wish to thank Halina Kobeckaite for her personal assistance in this research. In the December 2001 issue of the Karaim periodical *Awazymyz* ('Our voice') editor Mariola Abkowicz reported that one Józef Firkowicz had been chosen as the *hazzan* to succeed Mykolas Firkovičius: Abkowicz 2001.
2. Linguists Eva Csato and David Nathan have assisted the Karaim community in preserving and revitalizing the language by creating multimedia materials and recordings on an interactive DVD. Karaim people can now play a video clip of Mr. Firkovičius chanting prayers for religious ceremonies. See also <http://www.karaimi.home.pl/index.php?p=4> and <http://daugenis.mch.mii.lt/karaimai/literature1.htm>.

## Chapter 5. Silent Storytellers, Lost Legends

1. Tuvan epic tale: As told by Mr. Shoydak-ool Khapylakovich Khovalyg (born 1929) in 1998, recorded, transcribed and translated by me with assistance from native Tuvan speakers. For the complete tale, entitled Boktu-Kiriš, Bora-Šeelei, with translation and annotation, see Harrison 2005. A streaming video clip of the tale may be viewed at http://tuvan.swarthmore.edu.
2. Tuvan traditional stories: For excellent examples and discussion (in Russian), see Samdan 1994. For a collection of Tuvan folk tales translated from Tuvan into German, see Taube 1978. For a collection of Tuvan folk tales translated from the Russian and retold in English, see Van Deusen 1996. On ritual aspects of other Turkic oral epic traditions, see Reichl 2003.
3. Tuvan epic tales in books: Orus-ool 1997.
4. Oral literature as a petrified form: Dauenhauer and Dauenhauer 1995: section 4, page numbers missing in original. For an excellent collection of Tlingit oral literature, see Dauenhauer and Dauenhauer 1990.
5. Oral performance genres and the feats of memory enabling them have also, of course, existed in literate societies. For an account of these in Roman, medieval, and renaissance cultures, see Yates 1966.
6. Number of languages that have writing: Ong 1982; Edmondson 1971.
7. Assumptions of writing: Buck 1993: 122 (italics added).
8. 'Primary oral' cultures: Ong 1982.
9. Batangan culture of the Philippines: Kikuchi 1984: 29.
10. Worldwide literacy: World Bank 2004.
11. Indian literacy: National Informatics Center 2005.
12. "Literacy is freedom" is the slogan of UNESCO's United Nations Literacy Decade: UNESCO 2005.
13. Ös writing: For additional technical details, texts, and writing samples see Harrison and Anderson 2003, Anderson and Harrison 2006. For an excellent discussion of the ramifications of literacy and orthography for language endangerment and revitalization, see Grenoble and Whaley 2006 (chapters 5 and 6), and also Hinton 2001b.
14. Chulym Christianity: Falck 1785–1786: 557. Translation by Robbie Hart and Stephen Holt, 2004.
15. Ös shaman story: Anderson and Harrison 2004. Original text is from the archives of the Laboratory of the Languages of Siberian Peoples, Tomsk State Pedagogical University. It was collected and written down in 1972 and appears in notebooks compiled by R. A. Pechjorskaja, R. A. Boni, R. M. Birjukovich, and A. P. Dul'zon. I, along with Gregory Anderson, interviewed V. Budeyeva in July 2003 while filmmakers Seth Kramer and Daniel Miller shot video footage. We were not able to re-elicit the shaman story, due to the advanced age and poor health of the subject. We redacted and translated into English the archived 1972 version of the story with the help of members of the Ös community. Copyright herein pertains solely to our English translation. The original Ös text is to be considered the intellectual

property of V. Budeyeva herself and of the Ös community, and it is reproduced with their consent.

16. "Why make books for people who don't read?" This question was first posed by Terrill (2002).
17. For a discussion of the introduction of new writing systems (often designed by linguists) into endangered languages, see Hinton 2001b.
18. Memorization: For an excellent discussion of how memory serves oral traditions, (including the 'polished rock' metaphor), see Rubin 1995.
19. Oral genres elaborately adapted: Shore 1996: 140; cf. Havelock 1982 on Homeric verse.
20. 'Rain in Spain': From Lerner and Loewe's *My Fair Lady* (Lerner 1956).
21. Genres finely tuned: Shore 1996: 140.

### Case Study: New Rice versus Old Knowledge

1. Conklin's renowned studies of Philippine cultures include: Conklin 1954, 1957, 1980a, see also (Jean) Conklin 2003. Selected notable works on Ifugao culture and ethnography include: Barton 1955, 1963, Dulawan 2001. The Ifugao orthography is explained in Conklin 1991.
2. Rice technology words: Newell and Poligon 1993. Names for rice wine containers: p. 492; baskets: p. 586; rice pond field payment terms: pp. 572–76, *tiwātiw*: p. 494.
3. Seed industry: Hurtado 1989: 95.
4. 'Freed from Superstitions': Kindipan 2005: 10.
5. Ramos: Pesticide Action Network Asia-Pacific 2004.
6. Many Filipinos I have interviewed seem to share a national language ideology that relegates all smaller (non-national) languages to being considered merely 'dialects' and advocates switching to larger, national languages like Tagalog or Illocano. If small languages and the knowledge systems in them continue to be devalued, people will not hold onto them.

### Chapter 6. Endangered Number Systems

1. Parry 1824: 556
2. Stone age tallying: Henshilwood et al. 2002.
3. Eagle bone lunar calendar: Marshack [1972] 1991.
4. Extensive study on Kpelle counting and education: Gay and Cole 1967 .
5. Pomo is a family of seven languages: three are recently extinct, three have only a few speakers left, and one, Kashaya or Southwestern Pomo, still has 45 speakers. Revitalization efforts include the number system: Leanne Hinton writes "Cynthia Daniels, the Central Pomo speaker, who never knew how to count above 20 has now learned the numbers up into the hundreds, thanks to a publication by anthropologist Barrett" (Hinton 2001a: 422).
6. Pomo were great counters: Kroeber 1953a.
7. Counting objects in Africa: Zaslavsky 1999: 7.

8. Counting higher: Menninger 1969: 34. The Wiyot of California seem to have stopped at 1,000, which they expressed as "the counting runs out entirely once" (in their tongue *kucerawagatoril piswak*). Presumably clever Wiyot speakers might also have been able to say "the counting runs out entirely twice" to mean "2000." But we shall never know, since the last Wiyot speaker died in 1962: Teeter 1964.
9. Bororo counting: Lounsbury 1978: 761.
10. Inuit counting: Denny 1988:133–134.
11. Yakkha numbers in 1850: Hodgson 1880.
12. Yakkha numbers in 1980s: Gvozdanović 1985.
13. Kaluli: The counting to 20 limit would seem to be imposed by the decimal system of Tok Pisin, not by Kaluli body-counting, 20 for them is "other eye"—an anticlimactic way to end a body-count. Kaluli body-counting system is detailed in B. Schieffelin and Feld 1998. I have simplified some number names in figure 6.3—in Schieffelin and Feld's original orthography these are written *ka:la:n*, *do:*, *de:go:fe*, and *fa:la:lamel.*
14. Davies (1989) tags the complex Kobon expression as (hand pull out-SIM back give\IMP2S). For a grammatical analysis of the morphology involved and a general overview of the Kobon counting system, see Davies 1989. Another fine example of an extended body-counting system is found in the Oksapmin language: Saxe 1981.
15. The Huli like to count: Cheetham 1978. The Loboda rarely count: Thune 1978. The Yupno count certain objects only: Wassmann and Dasen 1994.
16. Iqwaye: Infrequent use of calculations may lead to errors, as when one Iqwaye speaker when queried confidently replied that one thousand would be 'three men', when actually counting a full set digits for all the fingers and toes of three men (20 x 20 x 3) would yield 1,200. Jadran Mimica, the anthropologist posing the question, noted the error but also remarked that this was the highest number he had successfully elicited. Iqwaye counting seems to have no absolute limit. If a counter has time and patience and has enough people, fingers, and toes to refer to, he can approach infinity.
17. Lengua counting system and dice game: Hawtrey 1901: 297.
18. Infants possess numerical concepts: Wynn 1992: 750. She also found that babies gazed longer at a final *expected* number of three puppets as opposed to two. One could interprete these results as evidence that the babies were not merely noticing a difference or recognizing a pattern but counting the puppets, at least as high as three, and also performing addition and subtraction. Further research by Simon, Hespos, and Rochat 1994 replicated Wynn's results and further supported the notion that infants are thinking in an arithmetical mode, and not simply responding to novelty or unexpected outcomes. Research by Xu and Spelke (2000) indicates infants possess a pre-linguistic sense of 'numerosity' (sensitivity to approximate quantity in larger numbers of objects).
19. Rhesus monkeys may have numerical concepts: Hauser, MacNeilage, and Ware 1996.

20. Sheba the chimpanzee: Boysen and Berntson 1989; Davis and Pérusse 1988. Interestingly, though the number of objects did not exceed four in this experiment, her trainers claim Sheba grasped the concept of zero. She learned to select the number zero when all objects had been removed from the box.
21. One example of limited animal numerical competence is Rocky the raccoon: Davis and Pérusse 1988. A more impressive example is that of Alex, an African gray parrot: Pepperberg 1994.
22. Rhesus monkeys may have numerical concepts: Hauser, MacNeilage, and Ware 1996: 1514.
23. Infant's image schemas: Hirsch 1997.
24. Arithmetic is motion metaphor: Lakoff and Núñez 1992: 72–73.
25. Overcounting in Vogul: Riese 2001. Overcounting has been reported to still exist in the highly endangered language Khanty language of Siberia. Andrei Filtchenko, a linguist working among the Khanty people, reports (personal communication) that Khanty overcounting is remembered only in some dialects by elderly speakers. The rest have switched over fully to decimal addition counting, the same type that has come to dominate world counting systems.
26. Gender: For a discussion of some connotations of gender categories within and across languages, see Romaine 1997 and Ervin-Tripp 1962. Grammatical aspects of gender in the world's languages are discussed in depth in Corbett 1991.
27. Culture: A succinct definition is proffered by Richerson and Boyd 2005: 5: "Culture is information capable of affecting individuals' behavior that they acquire from other members of their species through teaching, imitation, and other forms of social transmission."
28. Linguistic gender influences thought: Phillips and Boroditsky 2003.
29. Everett: His controversial findings have been cited by some as strong evidence of linguistic relativity. Yet Everett critiques the classical Sapir-Whorfian view as being too "narrow and unidirectional" (language shapes thought, end of story) while failing to provide for a more fundamental role for culture in shaping language. He notes: "I also argue against the simple Whorfian idea that linguistic relativity or determinism alone can account for the facts under consideration. In fact, I also argue that the unidirectionality inherent in linguistic relativity offers an insufficient tool for language-cognition connections more generally in that it fails to recognize the fundamental role of culture in shaping language" (Everett 2005: 623).
30. Pirahã: Everett 2005 and forthcoming. Everett also notes that the Pirahã lack even a pointing gesture and a word for finger, and also lack words for ordinals ('first,' 'second,' 'third'). Simply put, they lack numbers completely.
31. Gordon's Pirahã experiments: Gordon 2004.
32. Gordon: I note that the very premise of performing Western-style laboratory psychology experiments in an indigenous, Amazonian setting, and without deep knowledge on the part of the scientist of the language and cultural norms, remains extremely problematic.

33. Munduruku counting and critique of Gordon: Pica et al. 2004. For commentary on both the Munduruku and Pirahã studies, see Gelman and Gallistel 2004.
34. Yanoama: Becher 1960.
35. Bases: The term "base" has several meanings in mathematics. For a definition of these, including the sense in which I use the term in this chapter, see Weisstein 2005.
36. Base-2 counting in Aiome (also spelled Ayom): Aufenanger 1960. In addition to this system, Aiome also has a body -counting system similar to that of Kobon. Another example of a base-2 language is Siagha (spoken in Irian Jaya): Drabbe 1959.
37. Loboda rarely count: Thune 1978.
38. Base-15 in Huli: Cheetham 1978.
39. Ös: Written documentation of some varieties and some speakers of Ös, sometimes referred to as "Middle Chulym," was produced between 1950 and 1972 by A. Dul'son, R. Biriukovich and others. Their field notebooks are housed at Tomsk State Pedagogical University. Analog audio recordings were reportedly made in the 1970s but cannot be located. The Ös language is now moribund, is highly endangered, and has not been adequately recorded, described, or documented in a manner that approaches current scientific standards. With funding from the Hans Rausing Endangered Languages Project at SOAS, I am currently undertaking a full, digital audio and video documentation of Ös by recording all of the remaining speakers (see Harrison and Anderson 2003, Anderson and Harrison 2004, 2006).
40. Ainu counting system: Batchelor 1905.
41. Chinese-speaking children grasp math combinatorics more quickly than do English-speaking children: Ho and Fuson 1998.
42. Welsh children grasp bases more easily: Jones, Dowker, and Lloyd 2005.
43. Supyire numbers: Carlson 1994.
44. Bukiyip (Mountain Arapesh) counting: Fortune 1942: 59–60. He writes: "The Arapesh are an example of people speaking a language poor in numeral roots. . . . This is a linguistic phenomenon only, and does not interfere with effective counting. . . . Counting is done with great facility and ease with . . . very few special roots. To suppose that the paucity of the Papuan languages in root words for numerals makes counting difficult to the Papuan is quite incorrect. The Arapesh people count rather more quickly and better than the Melanesian Dobuans, who use a decimal system [like English] with many more root terms."
45. Counting universals: Greenberg 1978. I assign letters here to Greenberg's numbered universals: A = #1, B = #3, C = #11, D = #21, E = #36.
46. Ventureño counting system: Data based on Beeler 1964, 1998. The earlier source is in the original Spanish orthography and differs slightly from 1998 version. I have removed the accents as a probable Spanish orthography bias. Numbers that do not need to be spoken to be understood as bases are boldfaced in the right-most column below. The linguist who recorded this noted with some perplexity that because of these implicit bases, 'seven' and 'twenty-

eight' were pronounced the same and could only be distinguished by the context. Ndom numbers: Lean 1992.

| | *Ventureño number* | *implicit math formula* |
|---|---|---|
| 4 | **scumu** | 4 |
| 5 | *itipaques* | |
| | 'one comes again' | 4 + 1 |
| 6 | *yetishcom* | |
| | 'two comes again' | 4 + 2 |
| 7 | *itimaseg* | |
| | 'three comes again' | 4 + 3 |
| 15 | *paqueet cihue* | |
| | 'one less' | 16 – 1 |
| 16 | **chigipish** | 16 |
| 28 | *itimaseg* | |
| | 'three comes again' | 4 x (4 + 3) |

47. Tongan: Shumway 1971. Tongan (103,200 speakers) may be an exception to Greenberg's universal B. The formal Tongan system is much like that of English. However, in their everyday speech, Tongans reportedly express almost all numbers (except perhaps 10) using a zero-place system, as if they were reading the digits of written numerals. That is, twenty is 'two zero', ninty-nine 'nine nine'. This comes close to violating Greenberg's first universal of numeral systems: namely that "no natural language has a place system with the zero principle, such as found in the written system of Arabic numerals." It is unclear whether in Tongan multiples of ten are really expressed as '[first digit] zero'—it is possible they are usually expressed as bases, instead, as in English. It is also unclear whether this spoken system may be a recent invention influenced by the written numeral system of highly literate Tongans.
48. Lean 1992. The exact gloss for Wampar 'five' is not clear, though Lean says that the morpheme for 'five' contains the word for 'hand', but does not say what the second morpheme *ongan* means (Lean 1992: 37–39). Lean also states (p. 42) that at least 109 non-Austronesian and 30 Austronesian languages of New Guinea use both base-2 and base-5.
49. Kayardild lacks number words past three: Evans 1995.
50. Kayardild approximate terms: Harris 1990: 35.
51. Damara counting: Galton 1891: 81.
52. Micronesian navigation: Hutchins 1983.
53. Innate vs. cultural components of math: The research agenda is nicely summarized by Susan Carey (1998: 642) as follows: "We must specify the nature of nonlinguistic representations of number (there may be many) and characterize the process by which explicit symbolic representations are constructed in the history of each culture and again by each child."
54. Different number systems for different peoples: Hinton 1994: 121.
55. Yuki counting by fours and eights: Kroeber 1925 (qtd. in Hinton 1994: 118).
56. Pomo: Loss of the Pomo word for 100: Loeb 1926 elicits the base-20 term.

Seventy years later, McLendon 1996 can only find the borrowed Spanish version in use.

57. Ventureño Chumash: Beeler 1964, 1967, 1988. Additional Ventureño data may be found in Harrington 1981. A survey of native Californian numeral-base systems is found in R. B. Dixon and Kroeber 1907.
58. Ainu: Batchelor (1905: 96) comments on the 'cumbrous' nature of the Ainu system. There are some very recent efforts at cultural and language revitalization among the Ainu, but very few, if any, speakers remain.
59. The Thulung numbers of 1944 come from Rai 1944 qtd. in Allen 1975, and although whether they were still widely used at that time is in question, they are closer to the Tibeto-Burman proto-forms of the numbers. Thulung numbers of 2000 come from Lahaussois 2003. The orthography has been slightly simplified in this data set.
60. Comrie 2005. This chapter was inspired Prof. Bernard Comrie's lecture entitled "Endangered Numeral Systems," presented in January 2004 at the annual meeting of the Linguistic Society of America, in Oakland, CA.
61. Supyire: data from Carlson 1994.
62. Endangered non-decimal systems: Comrie 2005.
63. Iqwaye losing their numbers: Mimica 1988: 11.
64. Mimica 1988: 11–12.

### Case Study: The Leaf-Cup People, India's Modern 'Primitives'

1. Of India's 17 official languages, only the smallest, Kashmiri, has less than 10 million speakers, and even then, it is many times the size of Ho, the largest of the Munda languages. *The Ethnologue* has population estimates for many of the languages of India: Gordon 2005.
2. Small languages, and even not so small ones like Ho, can find it difficult to break into the computer age if they use a non-latin alphabet or writing system that differs from those used by economically important world languages. For the sake of language revitalization and access to computers by speakers of endangered languages, we hope to see greater progress in ushering the writing systems of small and endangered languages into the worldwide Unicode standard.
3. The Ho origin myth by Mr. K. C. Naik Biruli (born 1957), resident Mayurbanj district, was told in Bhubaneshwar, India, on September 13, 2005. It was recorded in audio and video by Gregory D. S. Anderson and me. This is an abridged version of a yet unpublished translation by Biruli and Anderson. The 'ten months' of pregnancy are lunar months (see chapter 3). To the best of my knowledge, this Ho origin story has not been previously published.

### Chapter 7. Worlds within Words

1. Valuing small languages: Linguist and endangered language expert Nancy Dorian (2002) points out that scientists who valorize the diversity of lan-

guages for the sake of advancing a scientific research agenda are indulging a highly culture-specific (e.g., Western) set of values. Linguists are typically "outside experts" on language loss rather than experiencers of it, so there is a danger that we may be setting our own values ahead of those of the speech communities themselves. For example, Dorian notes linguists tend to "dote upon structural rarity and overemphasize it to the exclusion of other significant matters" (Dorian 2002: 136). I agree with Dorian's assessment and have thus placed this chapter about language structures, traditionally an object of great concern to linguists, at the very end of this book. I also heartily endorse Dorian's challenge that "the rhetoric of advocacy needs to broaden for all audiences so as to acknowledge the vastness of the research challenge, while the investigations need to widen so as to encompass more of the social and cultural as well as the structural range that each language represents" (Dorian 2002: 139). The choice and ordering of the chapter topics in this book, as well as the inclusion of native speakers' points of view are intended as part of such a broadening effort.

2. Chomskyan preference for innate structures over culturally shaped content: As Eve Danziger notes, "In the view of Chomsky (1975) and his followers, all significant linguistic categories exist independently of the situation of their users—including the particular language learned. The categories are present from birth, encoded in human DNA in a form that is autonomous of any subsequent experience. . . . But linguistic and cultural categories are collective conventions that themselves can inspire and construct, as well as reflect, aspects of the individual's experience" (Danziger 2005:66–67).
3. Holistic approach to language: Haas 1976: 43.
4. Panels at recent meetings of the Linguistic Society of America have showcased the importance of endangered languages to linguistic theory.
5. Homer Simpson's speech: For a linguistic analysis, see Yu 2004.
6. Queen's English: Harrington, Palethorpe, and Watson 2000.
7. Biatch: The most popular spelling by far for this recently coined, two-syllable version of the word 'bitch' is 'biatch' with 640,000 Google hits, while 'biotch' has 74,300; 'beyotch' 17,400; 'bioootch' 4,490; and 'biooootch' 1,270. Even exaggerated spellings like 'beeeeatch' get 1,130 hits; 'beeeeeatch' 184; 'beeeeeeatch' 213; and 'beeeeeeeatch' 80 (as of August 2005). No matter how it is spelled, this word appears to be solidly part of the English spoken and written lexicon, though not yet acknowledged in mainstream dictionaries.
8. Puhleeze: An alternative two-syllable form of 'please' indicating exasperation gets 24,500 Google hits. However, this spelling is not winning by such a landslide as 'biatch'. Google also yielded 18,200 hits for alternate spelling 'puhlease', 12,700 for 'puleeze' and solid numbers for longer spellings including 3,130 for 'puhleeeeeze' (as of August 2005).
9. Equal complexity: Fromkin, Rodman, and Hyams 1998.
10. Equal complexity: Fromkin, Rodman, and Hyams 1998. For an interesting counter-argument, see Dixon 1997.

11. Nichols 1992 proposes one method for assessing complexity based on available inflection sites within a typical sentence. Many more such models are needed before linguistic complexity becomes truly quantifiable.
12. Fromkin, Rodman, and Hyams (1998) set forth equal complexity as a fundamental principle: "There are no 'primitive' languages—all languages are equally complex and equally capable of expressing any idea." These ideas are widely repeated, for example, in this statement from a Gallaudet College website (Gallaudet College 1977, 1978): "All languages are equally complex and capable of expressing any idea. A language which appears simple in some respects is likely to be more complex in others."
13. Child language acquisition: Stromswold 2000: 910, notes that "Children who are acquiring languages like Turkish, which have rich, regular, and perceptually salient morphological systems, generally begin to use functional category morphemes at a younger age than children acquiring morphologically poor languages . . . For example, in striking contrast to . . . English-speaking children, Turkish-speaking children often begin to produce morphologically complex words before they begin to use multiword utterances (Aksu-Koc and Slobin 1985)."
14. Rotokas: The reported phonetic consonant inventory is [p], [t], [k], [β], [ɾ], and [g], with allophonic variation; for example, /r/ may be pronounced as [ɾ], [d], [n], or [l]. In the proposed orthography for Rotokas, six consonant symbols are used: {*p, t, k, v, r, g*} (Firchow and Firchow 1969). Robinson 2006 and Robinson, in communication with me in 2005, states that his research shows the Rotokas phoneme inventory now includes [m], [n], and [s], and was either originally misanalyzed or may have recently acquired phonemes from contact with Tok Pisin or English.

    Ingush consonants: University of California, Berkeley Ingush Project under the direction of Prof. Johanna Nichols (website in bibliography) and Johanna Nichols, "A brief overview of Ingush phonology," at http://ingush.berkeley.edu:7012/orthography.html#Phonology (accessed August 2006).
15. Ejectives: Ladefoged 2001: 131–33. Notes that the trade-off between ease of articulation and acoustic distinctness disfavors bilabial ejectives, which differ only slightly in their acoustics from regular bilabial plosives but require more effort. Ladefoged further notes that if a language does adopt ejectives, it tends to have them at places of articulation where it already has other plosives.
16. Ubykh: Dumézil 1959, Vogt 1963.
17. Rotokas: Stuart Robinson 2006, and Robinson personal communication. The full glossed form is:

    ora-rugorugo-pie-pa-a-veira
    REF/REC-think.REDUP-CAUS-PROG-3.PL-HABITUAL
    "They were always thinking back."
18. Ingush words: Nichols 2004.
19. Equal complexity: For a brief, general discussion of equal complexity, see

Dixon 1997: ch. 3. Attempts to assess complexity across languages include Nichols 1992, Juola 1998, Shosted 2005. A discussion of language-specific loci of complexity (and clustering of speakers' errors therein) is found in Wells-Jensen 1999.

20. Biological analogy: In fact, the study of biology offers much the same dichotomy. Some critics decry the modern emphasis on genetic studies, arguing that an understanding of an organism's DNA is useless if we ignore the actual organism: its morphology, behavior, ecological adaptivity, etc. For more on the hooded seal see Lavigne and Kovacs 1988.
21. For a cogent statement on why linguists need a diversity of languages in order to recognize the "strange phenomena," see Corbett 2001.
22. "Language is a mirror of mind": Chomsky 1975: 4.
23. Tuvan acoustic sensibility and throat-singing: Levin 2006 and personal communication; van Tongeren 2002 and personal communication.
24. Tuvan reduplication and sound symbolism: Harrison 2000, 2004.
25. White Hmong: Ratliff 1992: 136–63 and personal communication.
26. Reduplication patterns from many languages: Raimy 2000 and personal communication; Rubino 2005.
27. Rotokas reduplication: Firchow 1987: 13, 54.
28. Eleme reduplicative negation: Data from Gregory Anderson (personal communication); data collected in collaboration with Oliver Bond (Bond 2006). The orthography has been simplified above; the full phonetic forms are: *[mɔ̀-rɔ̃], [mɔ́-mɔ̀-rɔ̃]; [(ɛbai) rɛ̃-ka-dʒu], [(ɛbai) rɛ̃-ka-ka-dʒu].*
29. Carrier: Poser 2005.
30. Cantonese classifiers: Disagreement among speakers about which classifiers to use for novel objects is not surprising, since unless they know the classifier in advance, they have to make a decision based on how they perceive the object. For example, the choice of classifier for glue will depend on the glue's current form. If the 'glue' has congealed and solidified, then even classifiers for solid things might be applicable, e.g., *yat1 juen1 gaau1* ('one brick glue; a brick of gelatin stuff'); a bottle of glue = *yat1 joen1 gaau1 seui2* ('one bottle glue water'); a stick of glue = *yat1 ji1 gaau1 seui2* ('one stick glue water'); a drop of glue = *yat1 dik6 gaau1 seui2* ('one drop glue water'). Thanks to linguist Alan C. L. Yu (personal communication).
31. Yupno 'hot', "cold" and "cool": Wassmann and Dasen 1994b.
32. Salish reduplication: Anderson 1999, Kuipers 1967.
33. Nivkh and Squamish: These languages also each provide a generic class for novel or hard-to-classify objects.
34. Rotuman kinship terms and inheritance: Churchward 1940; Rensel 1991.
35. Tabasaran (also spelled Tabassaran) and Tsez: Comrie and Polinsky 1998. The authors conclude (pp. 105–106): "in both Tabasaran and Tsez, we have a moderately rich number of cases: 14 or 15 in Tabasaran, depending on dialect, and 18 in Tsez. The richness that gives rise to claims such as Tabasaran having 48, 47, or 53 cases, or Tsez having 126 cases, derives from the possi-

bilities of combining these cases with one another" (*Guinness Book of Records* by Young 1997).

36. Arrernte: Henderson 2002: 108. Thanks to Alice C. Harris for bringing this example to my attention.
37. Sora incorporation: Ramamurti 1931. Some data simplified in the text for legibility. Sora also makes incorporated words like *e-jir-ten-e-mandra* 'the man that is going' and *jeruu-lunger-kid-en* 'a tiger that dwells in a deep cave'. Actual phonemic transcriptions given as: [ɹəru-'luŋər-'kid-ən] 'deep+cave +dwells+tiger' (p. 48 ex. 6); [kuŋ-kuŋ-'ded-u:-'bo:b-'mɑr] 'shave+shave +remove hairs+head+man' (p. 49 para. 169 and footnote 2); [ə̱-'jɪr-t-e-ṉ-ə̱-'mɑn(d)rɑ:], lit. 'that+goes+that+man' (p. 49 para. 170 ex. 1). The 'belly stab' example is ['po:-'puŋ-'kun -t-ɑm] 'stab-belly-knife-[will]-thee', i.e. 'I will stab you with a knife in your belly' (p. 44, para. 139). Thanks to Gregory Anderson for pointing out this phenomenon.
38. Gta': externally modified incorporated arguments are briefly mentioned in Sadock 1991 and discussed in greater detail in Anderson (2007). Gregory Anderson (personal communication) notes that the syntactic interpretation of these structures remains controversial, and that theories of incorporation other than Sadock 1991, e.g., M. Baker 1988, disallow (and fail to account for) such 'syntactic transparency' of an incorporated noun. Clearly, further study needs to be done of Gta' and other little-documented Munda languages. A linguistic field expedition to India in September 2005 by Gregory Anderson and me yielded some promising new data on Munda incorporation patterns.
39. "Dude": Kiesling 2004.
40. Arapaho gendered words: Conathan 2006 and personal communication.
41. Arapesh kin terms: Fortune 1942: 24. See also Dobrin 2001: 35.
42. Gros Ventre: Driver 1961: 353–54.
43. Gros Ventre words: Spellings adapted here for the general reader. Flannery (1946) spells Gros Ventre 'bread' phonetically as [dja'tsa] and [kya'tsa]; for 'answer to a hail' she writes [wei'] (male) and [ao'] (female).
44. Gros Ventre: Taylor 1982. Sound samples of Gros Ventre, including male and female speech (though these do not always sound distinctly different where differences are expected), may be downloaded from a Gros Ventre language website (Fort Belknap College 2005). Similar cases of striking differences between men's and women's speech are reported for Chuckchee (10,000 speakers in Siberia) by Dunn 2000 and citations therein, and for 19th century "Esquimaux" (Inuit) of Alaska by Parry 1824:553.
45. Yanyuwa: Kirton 1988.
46. Yanyuwa: Data from Bradley 1998. The young man's quote is attributed to Yanyuwa consultant "J.T."
47. Javanese: For an excellent discussion of formality levels and the linguistic differences they entail, see Errington 1998.

48. Sasak: According to linguist Peter Austin (personal communication), you cannot just say 'sit' in Sasak (2.1 million speakers). Instead, you must use special forms to specify who is doing the sitting, in what part of the house, and with what particular body posture. The Sasak verb system thus encodes physical, topographic, and social information about the sitter. See also Syahdan 2000: 89.
49. Sign languages: For general discussions of sign languages vis-à-vis spoken ones, see Jackendoff 1994: ch. 7; Napoli 2003: ch. 4; and S. Anderson 2004: ch. 9. For a recent typological study of sign languages see Zeshan 2006.
50. Number of sign languages worldwide is unknown: Linguist and sign language expert Ulrike Zeshan (personal communication) writes: "Currently, nobody knows how many sign languages exist in the world. My personal estimate is that there are probably several hundred sign languages, most of which are undocumented. This also includes small village-based sign languages in village communities with a high percentage and long history of hereditary deafness. . . . Leaving a good margin to cover the many white areas on our world map of sign languages, I doubt we would go beyond, say, about 700 sign languages in the final count, if indeed we ever reach that stage."
51. Spontaneous sign: A recent example is Al-Sayyid Bedouin Sign Language, which arose spontaneously over the past 70 years with no apparent outside influence and has evolved the full range of complex structures expected in any human language (Sandler et al. 2005).
52. Italian Sign language simultaneous signs: Russo 2004. For a discussion of sign simultaneity see Zeshan 2002; in Irish sign, Leeson and Saeed 2002; in Quebec sign, Miller 1994.
53. Italian Sign Language signs for CAR and TRAFFIC LIGHT: Radutzky 2001.
54. Thai sign languages: Nonaka 2004: 741 and personal communication.
55. Polynesian canoe words found in Southern California languages Chumashan and Gabrielino: Klar and Jones 2005.
56. Genetic similarities between Native Americans and Native Central Siberians: Schurr 2004; Zegura et al. 2004.
57. Ket (Yeniseic) in relation to Tlingit and Eyak: Vajda 1999, 2005 and personal communication.
58. Mlabri reversion: Oota et al. 2005.
59. Mlabri words: Rischel 1995.

# Bibliography

Abkowicz, Mariola (2001). Od Redakcji. [From the editor] *Awazymyz* 1(5). Online at http://www.karaimi.org/awazymyz/index.php?p=45. Accessed January 2006.

Abraham, Roy Clive (1933). *The Tiv People.* Lagos: Government Printer. [New Haven: Human Relations Area Files, 1998. Computer File]

Abrams, Daniel M., and Steven H. Strogatz (2003). Modelling the dynamics of language death. *Nature* 424: 900.

Adler, Bruno F. (1910). Karty pervobytnykh narodov. [Maps of primitive peoples]. *Izvestiya Imperatorskago Obshchestva Lyubiteley Yestestvoznaniya, Antropologii i Etnografii: Trudy Geograficheskago Otdeleniya* [Proceedings of the Imperial Society of the Devotees of National Sciences, Anthropology and Ethnography: Transactions of the Division of Geography] 119(2).

Ahlbrinck, W. (1931). *Encyclopaedie der Karaïben.* Amsterdam: Koninkliike Akademie van Wetenschappen.

Aksu-Koc, A. A., and D. I. Slobin (1985). The acquisition of Turkish. In D. I. Slobin (ed.), *The Crosslinguistic Study of Language Acquisition,* Vol. 1, pp. 839–880. Hinsdale, N.J.: Erlbaum.

Alaska Natives Commission (1994). *Alaska Natives Commission, Final Report.* Vols. 1–3. Anchorage: Alaska Natives Commission. Online at http://www.alaskool.org/resources/anc_reports.htm. Accessed August 2005.

Allen, N. J. (1972). The vertical dimension in Thulung classification. *Journal of the Anthropological Society of Oxford* 3: 81–94.

——— (1975). *Sketch of Thulung Grammar with Three Texts and a Glossary. Cornell University East Asia Papers* 6. Ithaca, New York: Cornell University.

Amery, Rob (1998). Warrabarna Kaurna!: Reclaiming an Australian Language. Exton, PA: Lisse.

——— (2002). Weeding out spurious etymologies: Toponyms on the Adelaide plains. In Hercus, Hodges, and Simpson (eds.) (2002), pp. 165–180.

Anderson, Gregory D. S. (1999). Reduplicated numerals in Salish. *International Journal of American Linguistics* 65: 407–448.

——— (2007). *The Munda Verb.* Berlin: Mouton de Gruyter.

Anderson, Gregory D. S., and K. David Harrison (2004). Shaman and bear: Siberian prehistory in two Middle Chulym texts. In Edward J. Vajda (ed.), *Languages and Prehistory of Central Siberia,* pp. 179–198. Amsterdam: John Benjamins.

——— (2006). *Ös tili*: Towards a comprehensive documentation of Middle and Upper Chulym dialects. *Turkic Languages* 10(1): 1–26.

——— (forthcoming). A Grammar of Tofa, a Turkic language of Siberia. Amsterdam: Mouton de Gruyter.

Anderson, Myrdene (1978). *Saami Ethnoecology: Resource Management in Norwegian Lapland.* Ann Arbor, Mich.: University Microfilms International. [New Haven: Human Relations Area Files, 1998. Computer File]

Anderson, Stephen R. (2004). *Doctor Dolittle's Delusion: Animals and the Uniqueness of Human Language.* New Haven: Yale University Press.

Anderson, Stephen R. (2004). How Many Languages Are There In The World? http://lsadc.org/info/ling-faqs-howmany.cfm. Accessed December 2007.

Atran, Scott (1990). *Cultural Foundation of Natural History: Towards an Anthropology of Science.* Cambridge: Cambridge University Press.

——— (1998). Folk biology and the anthropology of science: Cognitive universals and cultural particulars. *Brain and Behavioral Sciences* 21: 547–609.

Aufenanger, Heinrich (1960). The Ayom pygmies' myth of origin and their method of counting. *Anthropos* 55: 247–249.

Austin, Peter (1998). Introduction. *Working Papers in Sasak* 1. Online at http://www.linguistics.unimelb.edu.au/research/projects/lombok/sasak.html. Accessed February 2006.

Baker, Mark C. (1988). *Incorporation: A Theory of Grammatical Function Changing.* Chicago: University of Chicago Press.

Baker, Richard (1993). Traditional aboriginal land use in the Borrolola region. In Nancy M. Williams and Graham Baines (eds.), *Traditional Ecological Knowledge: Wisdom for Sustainable Development,* pp. 126–143. Canberra: Australian National University.

Baker, Robin R. (1989). *Human Navigation and Magnetoreception.* Manchester: Manchester University Press.

Barker, Muhammad Abd-al-Rahman (1963). *Klamath Texts.* Berkeley: University of California Press. [New Haven: Human Relations Area Files 1998, Computer File]

Barton, Roy F. (1955). The Mythology of the Ifugaos. New Haven, Conn.: HRAF, 2000. Computer File. Accessed 7.28.2005

——— (1963). *Autobiographies of Three Pagans in the Philippines.* New York: University Books.

Basso, Keith H. (1996). *Wisdom Sits in Places.* Albuquerque: University of New Mexico Press.

Batchelor, John (1905). *An Ainu–English–Japanese Dictionary.* Tokyo: Methodist Publishing House.

Bayot, Jennifer (2004). Alexander Marshack, 86, is dead; studied Stone Age innovations. *New York Times* December 28: 6.

Beaglehole, J. C. (ed.) (1968). *The Journals of Captain James Cook on his Voyages of Discovery: The Voyage of the* Endeavour *1768–1771.* Cambridge: Cambridge University Press.

Becher, Hans (1960). *The Surara and Pakidai, Two Yanoama Tribes in Northwest Brazil.* Hamburg: Kommissionsverlag Cram, De Gruyter & Co. [New Haven: Human Relations Area Files 1995. Computer File]

Beeler, Madison S. (1964). Ventureño numerals. In William Bright (ed.), *Studies in Californian Linguistics*, pp. 13–18. Berkeley: University of California.

——— (1967). The Ventureño confesionario of José Señán, O.F.M. Berkeley: University of California Press.

——— (1988). Chumash numerals. In Closs (ed.), (1988), pp. 109–128.

Bennardo, Giovanni (ed.) (2003). *Representing Space in Oceania: Culture in Language and Mind.* Canberra: Pacific Linguistics.

Berlin, Brent, Dennis E. Breedlove and Peter H. Raven. (1966). Folk taxonomies and biological classification. *Science.* 154: 273–275.

Bickel, Balthasar, and Martin Gaenszle (eds.) (1999). *Himalayan Space: Cultural Horizons and Practices.* Zurich: Völkerkundemuseum Zürich.

Bond, Oliver L. R. (2006). *Aspects of Eleme verbal morphosyntax.* Ph.D. diss., University of Manchester, UK.

Boysen, Sarah T., and Gary G. Berntson (1989). Numerical competence in a chimpanzee (*Pan troglodytes*). *Journal of Comparative Psychology* 103: 23–31.

Bradley, John (1998). Yanyuwa: 'Men speak one way, women speak another'. In Jennifer Coates (ed.), *Language and Gender: A Reader*, pp. 13–20. Oxford: Blackwell.

Brand, Stewart (2005). Environmental heresies. *Technology Review* 108(5): 60–63.

Brandenstein, C. G. von (1977). Aboriginal ecological order in the south-west of Australia: Meaning and examples. *Oceania* 47(3): 169–186.

Brown, Cecil H. (1984). *Languages and Living Things: Uniformities in Folk Classification and Naming.* New Brunswick, N.J.: Rutgers University Press.

——— (1985). Mode of subsistence and folk biological taxonomy. *Current Anthropology* 26(1): 43–64.

——— (1999). *Lexical Acculturation in Native American Languages.* Oxford: Oxford University Press.

Buck, Elizabeth (1993). *Paradise Remade: The Politics of Culture and History in Hawai'i.* Philadelphia: Temple University Press. [New Haven: Human Relations Area Files, 2003. Computer File]

Carey, Susan (1998) Knowledge of number: Its evolution and ontogeny. *Science* 282(5389): 642–642.

Carlson, Robert (1994). *A Grammar of Supyire.* Berlin: Mouton.

Central Intelligence Agency (2005). *The World Factbook.* Online at http://www.cia.gov/cia/publications/factbook/. Accessed January 2006.

Chaussonnet, Valérie, and Bernadette Driscoll (1994). The bleeding coat: The art of north Pacific ritual clothing. In William W. Fitzhugh and Valérie Chaussonnet (eds.), *Anthropology of the North Pacific Rim.* Washington, D.C.: Smithsonian.

Cheetham, Brian. (1978). Counting and number in Huli. *Papua New Guinea Journal of Education* 14: 19–30.

Chomsky, Noam (1975). *Reflections on Language.* New York: Pantheon.

Churchward, C. M. (1940). *Rotuman Grammar and Dictionary.* Sydney: Australian Medical Publishing Company.

Cline, Walter (1938). Tales. In Leslie Spiers (ed.), *The Sinkaietk or Southern Okanagon of Washington*, pp. 1–200. Menasha, Wis.: George Banta.

Closs, Michael P. (ed.) (1988). *Native American Mathematics*. Austin: University of Texas.

Comrie, Bernard (2005). Numeral bases. In Martin Haspelmath, Matthew S. Dryer, David Gil, and Bernard Comrie (eds.), *The World Atlas of Language Structures*, pp. 530–533. New York: Oxford University Press.

Comrie, Bernard, and Maria Polinsky (1998). The great Daghestanian case hoax. In Siewierska and Song (eds.) (1998), pp. 95–114.

Conathan, Lisa (2006). Gendered Language and the Discourse of Language Revitalization among the Northern Arapaho. Poster presented at the Linguistic Society of America annual meeting, Albuquerque, N. Mex., January 2006.

Conklin, Harold C. (1954). The relation of Hanunóo culture to the plant world. Ph.D. diss., Yale University.

——— ([1957] 1975). *Hanunóo Agriculture*. Northford, Conn.: Elliot's Books. [Reprint of 1957 Rome: Food and Agriculture Organization of the United Nations.]

——— (1980a). *Ethnographic Atlas of Ifugao*. New Haven: Yale University Press.

——— (1980b). *Folk Classification: A Topically Arranged Bibliography of Contemporary and Background References through 1971*. [Revised reprinting with author index] New Haven: Yale University Department of Anthropology.

——— (1991). A Systematic Orthography for Writing Ifugao. *Philippine Journal of Linguistics* 22(1–2): 31–35.

Conklin, Jean (2003). *An Ifugao Notebook*. Bloomington, Ind.: AuthorHouse.

Cook, James (1785–1787). *A Voyage to the Pacific Ocean Undertaken by the Command of His Majesty for Making Discoveries in the Northern Hemisphere*. 4 vols. Perth: R. Morison and Son.

Corbett, Greville (1991). *Gender*. Cambridge: Cambridge University Press.

——— (2001). Why Linguists Need Languages. In Luisa Maffi (ed.), *On Biocultural Diversity: Linking language, knowledge and the environment*, pp. 82–94. Washington, D.C.: Smithsonian Institution Press.

Coville, Frederick Vernon (1902). *Wokas: A Primitive Food of the Klamath Indians*. Washington, D.C.: United States National Museum.

Crawford, John Martin (trans.) (1888). *The Kalevala: The Epic Poem of Finland*. New York: Alden.

Crespi, Bernard J., and Michael J. Fulton (2004). Molecular systematics of Salmonidae: Combined nuclear data yields a robust phylogeny. *Molecular Phylogenetics and Evolution* 31: 658–679.

Crowley, Terry (2000). *An Erromangan (Sye) Dictionary*. Canberra: Pacific Linguistics.

Crystal, David (2000). *Language Death*. Cambridge: Cambridge University Press.

Daily, Gretchen C. (2004). Why biodiversity matters. In Bruce Babbit and José Sarukhán (eds.), *Conserving Biodiversity*, pp. 15–24. Washington, D.C.: Aspen Institute. Online at http://www.aspeninstitute.org/site/c.huLWJeMRKpH/b.612689/k.6CBA/Conserving_Biodiversity.htm. Accessed August 2005.

Danziger, Eve (2005). The eye of the beholder: How linguistic categorization affects "natural" experience. In Susan McKinnon and Sydel Silverman (eds.) *Complexities: Beyond Nature and Nurture*, pp. 64–80. Chicago, IL: The University of Chicago Press.

Darzha, Vyacheslav K. (2003). *Loshad' v traditsionnoi praktike tuvintsev kochevnikov.* [The horse in the traditional practice of Tuvan nomads.] Kyzyl, Republic of Tuva, Russian Federation: TuvIKOPR SO RAN.

Dauenhauer, Richard, and Nora Marks Dauenhauer (eds.) (1990). *Classics of Tlingit Oral Literature.* Vols. 1–3. Seattle: University of Washington Press.

——— (1995). Oral literature embodied and disembodied. In Uta M. Quasthoff (ed.), *Aspects of Oral Communication* (no page numbers). Berlin: Walter de Gruyter.

Davenport, William H. (1960) Marshall Islands navigational charts. *Imago Mundi* 15: 19–26.

Davies, John (1989). *Kobon.* London: Routledge.

Davis, Hank, and Rachelle Pérusse (1988). Numerical competence in animals: Definitional issues, current evidence, and a new research agenda. *Behavioral and Brain Sciences* 11: 561–579.

de Hutorowicz, H. (1911). Maps of primitive peoples. *Bulletin of the American Geographical Society* 43(9): 669–679 [abridged translation of Adler 1910].

Delaware (Lenape) Tribe of Indians: Homepage. Online at http://www.delaware tribeofindians.nsn.us/index.html. Accessed January 2006.

Denny, J. Peter (1988). Cultural ecology of mathematics: Ojibway and Inuit hunters. In Closs (ed.), pp. 129–180.

Dixon, R. B., and A. L. Kroeber (1907). Numeral systems of the languages of California. *American Anthropologist* 9: 663–672.

Dixon, R. M. W. (1997). *The Rise and Fall of Languages.* Cambridge: Cambridge University Press.

Dobrin, Lise (2001). Arapesh. In Jane Garry and Carl Rubino (eds.), *Facts About the World's Major Languages: An Encyclopedia of the World's Major Languages, Past and Present*, pp. 33–38. New York, NY: H. W. Wilson.

Dorian, Nancy (2002). Commentary: Broadening the Rhetorical and Descriptive Horizons in Endangered Language Linguistics. *Journal of Linguistic Anthropology* 12(2): 134–140.

Drabbe, P. (1959). *Kafiti en Wambon: Twee awju-dialecten.* 'S-Gravenhage: Martinus Nijhoff.

Driver, Harold E. (1961). *Indians of North America.* 2nd edn., revised. Chicago: University of Chicago.

Dulawan, Lourdes S. (2001). *Ifugao: Culture and History.* Manila: National Commission for Culture and the Arts.

Dumézil, G. (1959). *Etudes oubykhs.* Librairie A. Maisonneuve: Paris.

Duncan, David Ewing (1998). *Calendar.* New York: Avon Books.

Dunn, Michael (2000). Chukchi women's language: A historical-comparative perspective. *Anthropological Linguistics* 42: 305–328.

Dwyer, Peter D. (1976). An analysis of Rofaifo mammal taxonomy. *American Ethnologist* 3(3): 425–445.
Ebert, Karen (1999). The UP–DOWN dimension in Rai grammar and mythology. In Bickel and Gaenszle (eds.) (1999), pp. 105–131.
*Economist* (2001). Kenneth Hale [obituary]. *The Economist* November 3: 89.
Edmonson, Munro S. (1971). *Lore; An Introduction to the Science of Folklore and Literature.* New York: Holt, Rinehart and Winston.
Emmons, George Thornton (1991). *The Tlingit Indians.* Seattle: University of Washington Press.
England, Nora C. (2002). Commentary: Further Rhetorical Concerns. *Journal of Linguistic Anthropology* 12(2): 141–143.
Errington, J. Joseph (1998). *Shifting Languages: Interaction and Identity in Javanese Indonesia.* Cambridge: Cambridge University Press.
——— (2003). Getting language rights: The rhetoric of language endangerment and loss. *American Anthropologist* 105(4): 723–732.
Ervin-Tripp, Susan (1962). The Connotations of Gender. *Word* 18: 249–261.
Evans, Nicholas (1995). *A Grammar of Kayardild.* Berlin: Mouton.
Everett, Daniel L. (2005). Cultural constraints on grammar and cognition in Pirahã: Another look at the design features of human language. *Current Anthropology* 46(4): 621–646.
——— (forthcoming) On the absence of number and numerals in Pirahã. [Online at http://ling.man.ac.uk/Info/staff/DE/pirahanumerals.pdf. Accessed August 2006.]
Fabian, Stephen Michael (1992). *Space-Time of the Bororo of Brazil.* Gainesville: University Press of Florida.
Fabricius, Johan Christian (1778). *Philosophia entomologica.* Hamburg: Carol. Ernest. Bohnius. [Online at http://visualiseur.bnf.fr/Visualiseur?Destination=Gallica&O=NUMM-98943. Bibliotèchque nationale de France, 2006.]
Falck, Johan Peter (1785–1786). *Beyträge zur topographischen Kenntness des russichen Reichs.* Vols. I–III. Johann Gottlieb Georgi (ed.). Online facsimile: http://frontiers.loc.gov/cgi-bin/query/r?intldl/mtfront:@OR(@field(NUMBER+@band(mtfxtx+g335893961c))). Accessed August 2005.
Feld, Steven (1990). *Sound and Sentiment: Birds, Weeping, Poetics, and Song in Kaluli Expression.* 2nd edn. Philadelphia: University of Pennsylvania.
——— (1996). Waterfalls of song: An acoustemology of place resounding in Bosavi, Papua New Guinea. In Steven Feld and Keith H. Basso (eds.), *Senses of Place,* pp. 91–135. Santa Fe, N.M.: School of American Research Press.
Felger, R. S., K. Cliffton, and P. J. Regal. (1976). Winter dormancy in sea turtles: Independent discovery and exploitation in the Gulf of California by two local cultures. *Science* vol. 191, no. 4224 (Jan. 23), 283–285.
Fillmore, Lily Wong. (1999). When learning a second language means losing the first. *Early Childhood Research Quarterly* 6: 323–346.
Firchow, Irwin B. (1987). Form and function of Rotokas words. *Language and Linguistics in Melanesia* 15(1–2): 5–111.

Firchow, Irwin B., and Jacqueline Firchow (1969). An abbreviated phoneme inventory. *Anthropological Linguistics* 11(9): 271–276.

Fisher, James F. (1990). *Sherpas: Reflections on Change in Himalayan Nepal.* Berkeley: University of California Press.

Fishman, Joshua A. (1982). Whorfianism of the Third Kind: Ethnolinguistic Diversity as a Worldwide Societal Asset. *Language in Society* 11: 1–14.

Flannery, Regina (1946). Men's and women's speech in Gros Ventre. *International Journal of American Linguistics* 12: 133–135.

Foale, Simon (1998). What's in a name? An analysis of the West Nggela (Solomon Islands) fish taxonomy. *SPC Traditional Marine Resource Management and Knowledge Information Bulletin* 9: 3–19.

Foning, A. R. (1987). *Lepcha: My Vanishing Tribe.* New Delhi: Sterling Publishers.

Fort Belknap College (2005). *Gros Ventre Language Word Sets.* Harlem, Mont.: Fort Belknap College Website. Online at http://fbcc.edu/library/language/list.html. Accessed August 2005.

Fortune, R. F. (1942). *Arapesh.* New York: J. J. Augustin.

Foster, George McClelland (1944). *A Summary of Yuki Culture.* Los Angeles: University of California Press. [New Haven: Human Relations Area Files, 2003. Computer File]

François, Alexandre (2003). Of Men, hills, and winds: Space directionals in Mwotlap. *Oceanic Linguistics* 42(2): 407–437.

——— (2004). Reconstructing the geocentric system of Proto-Oceanic. *Oceanic Linguistics* 43(1): 1–31.

Franklin, K., and Franklin, J. (1962). The Kewa Counting System. *The Journal of the Polynesian Society* 71: 188–191.

Fromkin, Victoria, Robert Rodman, and Nina Hyams (1998). *An Introduction to Language.* Boston: Thomson Heinle.

Fukui, Katsuyoshi (1996). Co-evolution between humans and domesticates: The cultural selection of animal coat-colour diversity among the Bodi. In Roy Ellen and Katsuyoshi Fukui (eds.), *Redefining Nature,* pp. 319–385. Oxford: Berg.

Gallaudet College (1977, 1978). Myth: Signs are glorified gestures. Online at http://facstaff.gallaudet.edu/harry.markowicz/asl/myth4.html. [html by Harry Markowicz 2001]. Accessed February 2006.

Galton, Francis (1891). *Narrative of an Explorer in Tropical South Africa.* 4th edn. London: Ward, Lock.

Gatschet, Albert Samuel (1890). *The Klamath Indians of Southwestern Oregon.* Washington: Government Printing Office. [New Haven: Human Relations Area Files, 1998. Computer File]

Gay, John, and Michael Cole (1967). *The New Mathematics and an Old Culture.* New York: Holt.

Gell, Alfred (1995). The language of the forest: Landscape and phonological iconism in Umeda. In Eric Hirsch and Michael O'Hanlon (eds.), *The Anthropology of Landscape,* pp. 232–254. Oxford: Oxford University Press.

Gelman, Rochel, and C. R. Gallistel (2004). Language and the origin of numerical concepts. *Science* 306: 441–443.

Gladwin, Thomas (1958). Canoe travel in the Truk area: Technology and its psychological correlates. *American Anthropologist* 60(5): 893–899.

Godfray, H. Charles J. (2002). Challenges for taxonomy. *Nature* 417: 17–19.

Golledge, Reginald G. (1999). Human wayfinding and cognitive maps. In Reginald G. Golledge (ed.), *Wayfinding Behavior: Cognitive Mapping and Other Spatial Processes*, pp. 1–4. Baltimore: Johns Hopkins.

Gordon, Peter (2004). Numerical cognition without words: Evidence from Amazonia. *Science* 306: 496–499.

Gordon, Raymond G. (ed.) (2005). *Ethnologue: Languages of the World*. Dallas: SIL International.

Greenberg, Joseph H. (1978). Generalizations about numeral systems. In Joseph H. Greenberg (ed.), *Universals of Human Language*, Vol. 3, pp. 249–295. Stanford, Calif.: Stanford University Press.

Grenoble, Lenore A., and Lindsay J. Whaley (2006). *Saving Languages: An Introduction to Language Revitalization*. Cambridge: Cambridge University Press.

Grimes, Barbara F. (ed.) (2000). *Ethnologue: Languages of the World*. 14th edn. Dallas: Summer Institute of Linguistics. [Also online: http://www.ethnologue.com]

Gurung, A. B. (2003). Insects—a mistake in God's creation? Tharu farmers' perception and knowledge of insects: A case study of Gobardiha village development committee, Dang-Deukhuri, Nepal. *Agriculture and Human Values* 20: 337–370.

Gvozdanović, Jadranka (1985). *Language System and its Change: On Theory and Testability*. Berlin: Mouton.

Haas, Mary R. (1976). Anthropological linguistics: History. In Anthony F. C. Wallace, J. Lawrence Angel, Richard Fox, Sally McLendon, Rachel Sady, and Robert Sharer (eds.), *Perspectives on Anthropology 1976*, pp. 33–47. Arlington, VA: American Anthropological Association.

Harrington, John Peabody (1981). The Papers of John Peabody Harrington in the Smithsonian 1907–1957: A Guide to the Field Notes: Native American History, Language, and Culture of Southern California/Basin, vol. 3. Elaine L. Mills and Ann J. Brockfield (eds.) Microfilm reels 69, 89, and 94.

Harrington, Jonathan, Sallyanne Palethorpe, and Catherine I. Watson (2000). Does the Queen speak the Queen's English? *Nature* 408: 927–928.

Harris, John (1990). Counting: What we can learn from white myths about aboriginal numbers. *Australian Journal of Early Childhood* 15(1): 30-36.

Harrison, K. David (2000) *Topics in the phonology and morphology of Tuvan*. Ph.D. diss., Yale University.

——— (2001). Unpublished field notes [Tofa].

——— (2004). South Siberian sound symbolism. In Edward J. Vajda (ed.), *Languages and Prehistory of Central Siberia*, pp. 199–214. Amsterdam: John Benjamins.

——— (2005). A Tuvan hero tale with commentary, morphemic analysis and translation. *Journal of the American Oriental Society* 125(1): 1–30.

Harrison, K. David, and Gregory D. S. Anderson (2003). Middle Chulym: Theoretical aspects, recent fieldwork and current state. *Turkic Languages* 7(2): 245–256.

Hart, Robert E. (2003). Up and Down the Mountain. Unpublished undergraduate thesis submitted to Linguistics Department, Swarthmore College, Swarthmore, PA.

Haspelmath, Martin, Matthew Dryer, David Gil, and Bernard Comrie (eds.) (2005). *The World Atlas of Language Structures.* Oxford: Oxford University Press.

Hauser, Marc D., Pogen MacNeilage, and Molly Ware (1996). Numerical representations in primates. *Proceedings of the National Academy of Sciences of the United States of America* 93: 1514–1517.

Havelock, E. A. (1982). *The Literate Revolution in Greece and its Cultural Consequences.* Princeton: Princeton University Press.

Hawksworth, D. L., and M. T. Kalin-Arroyo (eds.) (1995). Magnitude and distribution of biodiversity. In V. H. Heywood (ed.) (1995), pp. 107–192.

Hawtrey, Seymour H. C. (1901). The Lengua indians of the Paraguayan Chaco. *Journal of the Anthropological Institute of Great Britain and Ireland* 31: 280–299.

Henderson, J. (2002). The word in Eastern/Central Arrernte. In R. M. W. Dixon and Alexandra Y. Aikhenvald (eds.), *Word: A Cross-linguistic Typology*, pp. 100–121. Cambridge: Cambridge University Press.

Henshilwood, Christopher S., Francesco d'Errico, Royden Yates, Zenobia Jacobs, Chantal Tribolo, Geoff A. T. Duller, Norbert Mercier, Judith C. Sealy, Helene Valladas, Ian Watts, and Ann G. Wintle (2002). Emergence of modern human behavior: Middle Stone Age engravings from South Africa. *Science* 295: 1278–1280.

Hercus, L., F. Hodges, and J. Simpson (eds.) (2002). *The Land is a Map: Placenames of Indigenous Origin in Australia.* Canberra: Pandanus Books.

Heywood, V. H. (ed.) (1995). *Global Biodiversity Assessment.* Cambridge: Cambridge University Press.

Hill, Jane (2002). "Expert rhetorics" in advocacy for endangered languages: Who is listening and what do they hear? *Journal of Linguistic Anthropology* 12(2): 119–133.

Hillis, David M., Derrick Zwickl, and Robin Gutell (2003). Tree of Life. Online at http://www.zo.utexas.edu/faculty/antisense/Download.html. Accessed January 2006. [As published in *Science* 300: 1692–1697]

Hinton, Leanne (1994). *Flutes of Fire: Essays on California Indian Languages.* Berkeley: Heyday Books.

——— (2001a). The use of linguistic archives in language revitalization. In Hinton and Hale (eds.) (2001), pp. 419–423.

——— (2001b). New writing systems. In Hinton and Hale (eds.) (2001), pp. 239–250.

——— (2002). *How to Keep Your Language Alive.* Berkeley: Heyday Books.

Hinton, Leanne, and Ken Hale (eds.) (2001). *The Green Book of Language Revitalization in Practice.* San Diego: Academic Press.

Hirsch, Eli (1997). Basic objects: A reply to Xu. *Mind and Language* 12: 406–412.

Hitt, Jack (2004). Say no more. *The New York Times Magazine* (February 29), pp. 52–58, 100.

Ho, Connie Suk-Han, and Karen C. Fuson (1998). Children's knowledge of teen quantities as tens and ones: Comparisons of Chinese, British, and American kindergartners. *Journal of Educational Psychology* 90: 536–544.

Hodgson, Brian Houghton (1880). *Miscellaneous Essays Relating to Indian Subjects.* Vol. 1. London: Trübner & Co.

Hunn, Eugene. (1975). A Measure of the degree of correspondence of folk to scientific biological classification. *American Ethnologist* 2(2): 309–327.

Hurtado, Maria Elena (1989). Seeds of Discontent. *South* 15: 95–96.

Hutchins, Edwin (1983). Understanding Micronesian navigation. In D. Genter and A. L. Stevens (eds.), *Mental Models*, pp. 191–225. Hillsdale, N.J.: Lawrence Erlbaum Associates.

Hyslop, Catriona (1999). The linguistics of inhabiting space: Spatial reference in the North-East Ambae language. *Oceania* 70: 25–42.

Ingham, Bruce (1997). Arabian Diversions: Studies on the dialects of Arabia. Reading, UK: Garnet Publishing Ltd.

Irwin, D. E., S. Bensch, and T. D. Price (2001). Speciation in a ring. *Nature* 409: 333–337.

Itkonen, Toivo Immanuel (1948). *The Lapps in Finland up to 1945.* Helsinki: Werner Söderström Osakeyhtiö. [New Haven: Human Relations Area Files, 1996. Computer File]

Jackendoff, Ray (1996). How Language Helps us Think. *Pragmatics and Cognition* 4(1): 1–34.

Jensen, Allen Arthur (1988). *Sistemas indígenas de classificação de aves: aspectos comparativos, ecológicos e evolutivos.* Belém: Museu Paraense Emílio Goeldi.

——— (1990). Biological information transmitted through festival. In Posey et al. (eds.) (1990), pp. 113–123.

Jersletten, Johnny-Leo L., and Konstantin Klokov (2002). Sustainable Reindeer Husbandry. Tromsø: Centre for Saami Studies. [Final Report of the Arctic Council's Sustainable Development Programme's Sustainable Reindeer Husbandry]. Online at http://www.reindeer-husbandry.uit.no/. Accessed January 2006.

Jochelson, Waldemar (1926). *The Yukaghir and the Yukaghirized Tungus.* Leiden: Brill. [*Memoirs of the American Museum of Natural History* 13]

Johannes, R. E., and E. Hviding (2000). Traditional knowledge possessed by the fishers of Marovo Lagoon, Solomon Islands, concerning fish aggregating behaviour. *SPC Traditional Marine Resource Management and Knowledge Information Bulletin* 12: 22–29.

Jones, Dylan V., Ann Dowker, and Delyth Lloyd (2005). *Mathemateg yr Ysgol*

*Gynrad—Mathematics in the Primary School. Trafodion Addysg—Education Transactions* Bangor: University of Wales, Bangor.

Juola, Patrick (1998). Measuring linguistic complexity: The morphological tier. *Journal of Quantitative Linguistics* 5(3): 206–213.

Kaehr, Roland (2000). *Le mûrier et l'épée: Le Cabinet de Charles Daniel de Meuron et l'origine du Musée d'ethnographie à Neu-châtel* [The mulberry tree and the sword: The Cabinet of Charles Daniel de Meuron and the origin of the Ethnographic Museum in Neuchâtel]. Neuchâtel, Switzerland: Musée d'ethnographie.

Kakudidi, E. K. (2004). Folk plant classification by communities around Kibale National Park, Western Uganda. *African Journal of Ecology* 42(1): 57–63.

Katanov, N. F. (1891). Poyezdka k karagasam v 1880 godu. [A journey to the Karagas in the year 1880]. *Zapisy russkogo geograficheskogo obshestva. Otdel geografii.* [Notes of the Russian geographic society. Geography department] 17(2): 131–230. Saint Petersburg.

——— (1903). *Opyt issledovanie uriankhaiskogo yazyka s ukazaniem glavneishykh rodstvennykh otnosheniy ego k drugim yazykam tyurkskogo kornya* [An attempt to research the Uriankhai language demonstrating its primary family relations to other languages of Turkic stock.]. Kazan', Russia.

Kiesling, Scott F. (2004). Dude. *American Speech* 79(3): 281–305.

Kiessling, Roland (2005). Western vs. Eastern !Xoon. Paper presented at DoBeS workshop, Nijmegen, The Netherlands, May 2005.

Kikuchi, Yaksushi (1984). *Mindoro Highlanders.* Quezon City, Philippines: New Day.

Kindipan, Antoinette (2005). Freed from superstitions. *PhilRice* 18(2): 10.

Kirton, J. F. (1988). Men's and women's dialect. *Aboriginal Linguistics* 1: 111–125.

Klar, Kathryn A., and Terry L. Jones (2005). Linguistic evidence for a prehistoric Polynesia–Southern California contact event. *Anthropological Linguistics* 47(4): 369–400.

Kolbert, Elizabeth. (2005). Letter from Alaska. Last words: A language dies. *The New Yorker* (June 6): 46–59.

Krauss, Michael E. (1992). The world's languages in crisis. *Language* 68(1): 4–10.

——— (1997). The indigenous languages of the north: A report on their present state. In Hiroshi Shoji and Juha Janhunen (eds.), *Northern Minority Languages: Problems of Survival,* 1–34 (Senri Ethological Studies 44). Osaka, Japan: National Museum of Ethnology.

Kreynovich, E. A. (1979). The Tundra Yukagirs at the turn of the century. *Arctic Anthropology* 16(1): 187–218.

Kroeber, A. L. (1925). *Handbook of the Indians of California.* Washington, D.C.: Government Printing Office. [Bulletin of the Smithsonian Institution, Bureau of American Ethnology 78]

——— Kroeber, A.L. (1953a). *Pomo Indians.* In Kroeber 1953b.

——— (1953b). *Handbook of the Indians of California.* Berkeley: California Book Company. New Haven, Conn.: HRAF, 2000. Computer File. Accessed 7.28.2005

Kuipers, Aert H. (1967). *The Squamish Language.* The Hague: Mouton.

Ladefoged, Peter (1992). Another view of endangered languages. *Language* 68(4): 809–811.

——— (2001). *Vowels and Consonants: An Introduction to the Sounds of Languages.* Oxford: Blackwell.

Lahaussois, Aimée (2003). Thulung Rai. *Himalayan Linguistics: Archive* 1. Online at http://www.uwm.edu/Dept/CIE/HimalayanLinguistics/adocuments.html. Accessed August 2006.

Lakoff, George, and Rafael E. Núñez (1992). *Where Mathematics Comes From.* New York: Basic Books.

Lavigne, D. M., and K. M. Kovacs (1988). *Harps and Hoods: Ice Breeding Seals of the Northwest Atlantic.* Waterloo, Ontario: University of Waterloo Press.

Lean, Glendon A. (1992). Counting systems of Papua New Guinea and Oceania. Ph.D. diss., Papua New Guinea University of Technology.

Lee, Richard B., and Richard Daly (eds.) (1999). *The Cambridge Encyclopedia of Hunters and Gatherers.* Cambridge: Cambridge University Press.

Leeming, David Adams (1994). *A Dictionary of Creation Myths.* With Margaret Leeming. Oxford: Oxford University Press.

Leeson, Lorraine and John Saeed (2002). Windowing of attention in simultaneous constructions in Irish Sign Language (ISL). Paper presented at the Fifth High Desert Linguistics Conference, 1–2 November, Albuquerque, University of New Mexico.

Lenape Talking Dictionary. Online at http://www.talk-lenape.com/index.php. Accessed January 2006.

Leonard, Wesley Y. (2004). What we can learn from new fieldwork on "sleeping" languages: The case of Miami. Poster presented at the Linguistic Society of America annual meeting, San Jose, CA. January 2004.

——— (2005). *The Social Dynamics of Language Acquisition in a Language Renewal Setting: Findings from a Case Study of Miami Acquisition in the Home.* Manuscript. University of California, Berkeley.

Le Page du Pratz, Antoine-Simon [1774] (1975). *The History of Louisiana*, ed. Joseph G. Tregle, Jr. Baton Rouge: Louisiana State University Press. [Facs. of 1774 London edn.]

Lerner, Alan Jay (1956). *My Fair Lady: A Musical Play in Two Acts, Based on* Pygmalion *by Bernard Shaw.* New York: Coward-McCann. [Music by Frederick Loewe]

Levin, M. G., and L. P. Potapov (eds.) (1964). *The Peoples of Siberia.* Chicago: University of Chicago Press. [Originally (1956). *Narody Sibiri.* Moscow: Russian Academy of Science]

Levin, Theodore (2006). *Where Rivers and Mountains Sing: Sound, Music and Nomadism in Tuva and Beyond.* With Valentina Süzükei. Bloomington: Indiana University Press.

Levinson, Stephen C. (1997). Language and cognition: The cognitive consequences of spatial description in Guugu Yimithirr. *Journal of Linguistic Anthropology* 7: 98–131.

——— (2002). Comments. *Current Anthropology* 43(S): 122–123.

Liebers, Dorit, Peter de Knijff, and Andreas J. Helbig (2004). The herring gull complex is not a ring species. *Proceedings: Biological Sciences* 271(1542): 893–901.

Lizarralde, Manuel (2001). Biodiversity and loss of indigenous languages and knowledge in South America. In L. Maffi (ed.) (2001), pp. 265–281.

Loeb, Edwin Meyer (1926). *Pomo Folkways.* Berkeley: University of California Press. [New Haven: Human Relations Area Files, 2000. Computer File]

Lounsbury, Floyd (1978). Maya numeration, computation and calendrical astronomy. *Dictionary of Scientific Biography.* Vol. 15, supplement 1, pp. 759–818. New York: Scribner.

Lynch, John, and Tepahae, Philip (2001). *Anejom̃ Dictionary.* Canberra: Pacific Linguistics.

Maffi, Luisa (ed.) (2001). *On Biocultural Diversity.* Washington, D.C.: Smithsonian.

Magaña, Edmundo (1984). Carib tribal astronomy. *Sociology of Science* 23: 341–368.

Majnep, Ian Saem, and Ralph N. H. Bulmer (1977). *Birds of My Kalam Country.* Auckland, New Zealand: Auckland University Press and Oxford University Press.

Marine Biological Laboratory (2004). Universal Biological Indexer and Organizer. Online at http://www.ubio.org/. Accessed January 2006.

Marshack, Alexander (1964). Lunar notation on Upper Paleolithic remains. *Science* 146(3645): 743–745.

——— ([1972] 1991). *The Roots of Civilization: The Cognitive Beginnings of Man's First Art, Symbol, and Notation.* 2nd edn. Mount Kisco, N.Y.: Moyer Bell.

Maybury-Lewis, David (1974). *Akwẽ-Shavante Society.* London: Oxford University Press.

Mayr, Ernst (1942). *Systematics and the Origin of Species.* New York: Columbia University Press.

McKenzie, Robin (1997). Downstream to here: Geographically determined spatial deictics in Aralle-Tabulahan (Sulawesi). In Senft (ed.) (1997), pp. 221–249.

McKnight, David (1999). *People, Countries, and the Rainbow Serpent: Systems of Classification among the Lardil of Mornington Island.* Oxford: Oxford University Press.

McLendon, Sally (1996). Sketch of Eastern Pomo, a Pomoan language. In William C. Sturtevant (ed.), *Handbook of North American Indians,* pp. 530–539. Washington, D.C.: Smithsonian Institution.

Medin, Douglas L., and Scott Atran (1999). *Folkbiology.* Cambridge, Mass.: MIT Press.

Mel'nikova, L. V. (1994). *Tofy* [The Tofa]. Irkutsk: Vostochno-Sibirskoe Knizhnoe Izdatel'stvo.

Mendel, Gregor ([1866]1946). *Experiments on Plant Hybridisation.* Cambridge: Cambridge University Press.

Menninger, Karl (1969). *Number Words and Number Symbols: A Cultural History of Numbers.* Trans. Paul Broneer from the rev. German edn. Cambridge, Mass.: MIT.

Miller, Christopher (1994). Simultaneous Constructions and Complex Signs in Quebec Sign Language. In I. Ahlgren, B. Bergman and M. Brennan (eds.), *Perspectives on sign language structure: Papers from the Fifth International Symposium on Sign Language Research*, volume 1, pp. 131–148. Durham, UK: The International Sign Linguistics Association.

Mimica, Jadran (1988). *Intimations of Infinity: The Cultural Meanings of the Iqwaye Counting and Number Systems.* Oxford: Berg Publishers.

Moerman, Daniel E. (1998). *Native American Ethnobotany.* Portland, Ore.: Timber Press.

Morrison-Scott, T. C. S. and F. C. Sawyer. (1950). The identity of Capitan Cook's kangaroo. *Bulletin of the British Museum of Natural History: Zoology* 1(3): 45–50.

Mühlhausler, Peter (1996). *Linguistic Ecology: Language Change and Linguistic Imperialism in the Pacific Region.* London: Routledge.

Nabhan, Gary P. (2003). *Singing the Turtles to Sea: The Comcáac (Seri) Art and Science of Reptiles.* Berkeley: University of California Press.

Napoli, Donna Jo (2003). *Language Matters.* New York: Oxford University Press.

National Informatics Center (2005). Economic Survey 2004–2005. [Information provided by Ministry of Finance, Government of India]. Online at http://indiabudget.nic.in/es2004-05/esmain.htm. Accessed January 2006.

Nettle, Daniel, and Suzanne Romaine (2000). Vanishing Voices: The Extinction of the World's Languages. *New York: Oxford University Press.*

Newell, Leonard E., and Francis Bon'og Poligon (1993). *Batad Ifugao Dictionary.* Manila: Linguistic Society of the Philippines.

Nichols, Johanna (1992). *Linguistic Diversity in Space and Time.* Chicago: University of Chicago Press.

——— (2004). *Ingush–English and English–Ingush Dictionary. Ghalghaai–ingalsii, ingalsii–ghalghaii lughat.* London: Routledge Curzon.

Nikolaeva, Irina, and Thomas Mayer (2004). Online Documentation of Kolyma Yukaghir. Online at http://www.sgr.fi/yukaghir/. Accessed January 2006.

Nilsson, Martin P. (1920). *Primitive Time-Reckoning.* Oxford: Oxford University Press.

Niraula, Shanta, Ramesh C. Mishra, and Pierre R. Dasen (2004). Linguistic relativity and spatial concept development in Nepal. *Psychology and Developing Societies* 16(2): 100–124.

Noonan, Michael (2005). Spatial reference in Chantyal. In Yogendra Yadava (ed.), *Contemporary Issues in Nepalese Linguistics*, pp. 151–188. Kathmandu: Linguistic Society of Nepal.

Nonaka, Angela M. (2004). The forgotten endangered languages: Lessons on the importance of remembering from Thailand's Ban Khor sign language. *Language in Society* 33: 737–767.

Okladnikova, Elena (1998). Traditional cartography in arctic and subarctic eurasia. In Woodward and Lewis (eds.) (1998), pp. 329–345.

Olawsky, Knut J. (2005). Urarina—evidence for OVS constituent order. In Boban Arsenijevic, Noureddine Elouazizi, Frank Landsbergen, and Martin Salzmann (eds.), *Leiden Papers in Linguistics 2(2)*: 43–68.

Ong, Walter (1982). *Orality and Literacy*. London: Methuen.

Oota, Hiroki, Brigitte Pakendorf, Gunter Weiss, Arndt von Haeseler, Surin Pookajorn, Wanapa Settheetham-Ishida, Danai Tiwawech, Takafumi Ishida, and Mark Stoneking (2005). Recent origin and cultural reversion of a hunter-gatherer group. *PLoS Biology* 3(3): e71. Online at http://biology.plosjournals.org/perlserv/?request=get-document&doi=10.1371/journal.pbio.0030071. Accessed August 2005.

Orus-Ool, S. M. (1997). *Tuvinskie geroicheskie skazaniya.* [The Tuvan hero tale] Novosibirsk: VO "Nauka."

Palmer, Katherin van Winkle (1925). *Honné, the Spirit of the Chehalis* (as narrated by George Saunders). Geneva, N.Y.: W. F. Humphrey.

Parrish, Julia K., Steven V. Viscido, and Daniel Grünbaum (2002). Self-organized fish schools: An examination of emergent properties. *Biology Bulletin* 202: 296–305.

Parry, William Edward (1824). *Journal of a Second Voyage for the Discovery of a North-West Passage from the Atlantic to the Pacific; Performed in the Years 1821–22–23, in His Majesty's Ships Fury and Hecla, under the orders of Captain William Edward Parry, R.N., F.R.S., and Commander of the Expedition.* London: John Murray.

Pennisi, Elizabeth (2003). Modernizing the tree of life. *Science* 300: 1692–1697.

Pepperberg, Irene (1994). Numerical competence in an African gray parrot (*Psittacus erithacus*). *Journal of Comparative Psychology* 108(1): 36–44.

Pesticide Action Network Asia-Pacific (2004). Philippine rice farmers denounce rice institute. Online at http://www.panap.net/caravan/news23.cfm. Accessed January 2006.

Phillips, Webb, and Boroditsky, Lera (2003). Can quirks of grammar affect the way you think? Grammatical gender and object concepts. In Richard Alterman and David Kirsh (eds.), *Proceedings of the 25th Annual Meeting of the Cognitive Science Society*, pp. 928–933. Boston, Mass.: Cognitive Science Society.

PhilRice (2005). [Cartoon with speech bubble "Adu ti apitmi ditoy norte."] *PhilRice* 18(2): 3.

Pica, Pierre, Cathy Lemer, Véronique Izard, and Stanislas Dehaene (2004). Exact and approximate arithmetic in an Amazonian indigene group. *Science* 306: 499–503.

Plotkin, Mark (1993). *Tales of a Shaman's Apprentice.* New York: Viking.

Pojar, Jim, and Andy MacKinnon (eds.) (1994). *Plants of the Pacific Northwest Coast.* Vancouver, B.C.: Lone Pine.

Poser, William J. (2005). Noun classification in Carrier. *Anthropological Linguistics* 47(2): 143–168.

Posey, Darrell A. (1990a). Intellectual property rights and just compensation for indigenous knowledge. *Anthropology Today* 6(4): 13–16.

——— (1990b). *Kayapó Ethnoecology and Culture.* London: Routledge.

Posey, Darrel A., William Leslie Overal, Charles R. Clement, Mark J. Plotkin, Elaine Elisabetsky, Clarice Novaes da Mota, and José Flávio Pessôa de Barros (eds.) (1990). *Ethnobiology: Implications and Applications. Proceedings of the First International Congress of Ethnobiology (Belém 1988).* Belém, Brazil: Museu Paraense Emílio Goeldi.

Pukui, Mary Kawena, and Samuel H. Elbert (2003). *Hawaiian Dictionary.* Honolulu: University of Hawai'i Press. Online at http://wehewehe.org/gsdl2.5/cgi-bin/hdict?l=en. Accessed January 2006.

Pumuye, Hilary (1978). The Kewa Calendar. *Papua New Guinea Journal of Education* 14: 47–55.

Purvis, Andy, and Hector, Andy (2000). Getting the measure of biodiversity. *Nature* 405: 212–219.

Radutzky, Elena (2001). *Dizionario bilingue elementare della lingua italiana dei signi.* Edizioni Kappa.

Raimy, Eric (2000). *The Phonology and Morphology of Reduplication.* Berlin: Mouton de Gruyter.

Ramamurti, G. V. (1931). *A Manual of the So:ra (or Savara) Language.* Madras: Government Press.

Rassadin, V. I. (1995). *Tofalarsko–russkij, russko–tofalarskij slovar'* [Tofalar–Russian, Russian–Tofalar dictionary]. Irkutsk: Vostochnoe sibirskoe knizhnoe izdatel'stvo.

Ratliff, M. (1992). *Meaningful Tone: A Study of Tonal Morphology in Compounds, Form Classes, and Expressive Phrases in White Hmong.* Dekalb: Center for Southeast Asian Studies, Northern Illinois University.

Rea, Amadeo M. (1990). Naming as process: Taxonomic adjustments in a changing biotic environment. In Posey et al. (eds.) (1990), pp. 61–79.

Reichl, Karl (2003). The search for origins: Ritual aspects of the performance of epic. *Journal of Historical Pragmatics* 4(2): 249–267.

Rensel, J. P. (1991). Housing and social relationships on Rotuma. In Anselmo Fatiaki et al., *Rotuma: Hanua Pumue*, pp. 185–203. Suva: Institute of Pacific Studies, University of the South Pacific.

Richerson, Peter J., and Robert Boyd (2005). *Not by Genes Alone: How Culture Transformed Human Evolution.* Chicago: University of Chicago Press.

Riese, Timothy (2001). *Vogul.* Munich: Lincom Europa.

Rischel, Jørgen (1995). *Minor Mlabri: A Hunter-Gatherer Language of Northern Indochina.* Copenhagen: Museum Tusculanum Press.

Robinson, Stuart (2006). The phoneme inventory of the Aita Dialect of Rotokas. *Oceanic Linguistics* 45(1): 1–4.

Romaine, Suzanne (1997). Grammar, gender and the space in between. In Helga Kotthoff and Ruth Wodak (eds.), *Communicating Gender in Context*, pp. 51–76. Amsterdam: John Benjamins.

Rubin, David C. (1995). *Memory in Oral Traditions.* Oxford: Oxford University Press.

Rubino, Carl (2005). Reduplication. In Martin Haspelmath, Matthew S. Dryer, David Gil, and Bernard Comrie (eds.), *The World Atlas of Language Structures*, p. 114. New York: Oxford University Press.

Russo, Tomasso (2004). Iconicity and productivity in sign language discourse: An analysis of three LIS discourse registers. *Sign Language Studies* 4(2): 164–197.

Sadock, Jerrold M. (1991). *Autolexical Syntax: A Theory of Parallel Grammatical Representations.* Chicago: University of Chicago Press.

Samdan, Z. B. (compiler) (1994). *Tuvinskie narodnie skazki.* [Tuvan national folktales] Novosibirsk: VO Nauka.

Sand, Natalie (1996). The Akyode calendar. In Tony Naden (ed.), *Time and the Calendar in Some Ghanaian Languages*, pp. 103–107. Ghana Institute of Linguistics, Literacy and Bible Translation.

Sandler, Wendy, Irit Meir, Carol Padden, and Mark Aronoff (2005). The emergence of grammar: Systematic structure in a new language. *Proceedings of the National Academy of Sciences of the United States of America* 102(7): 2661–2665.

Sape, Gilbert (2004). Philippine Rice Farmers Denounce Rice Institute. Pesticide Action Network: Online at http://www.panap.net/caravan/news23.cfm. Accessed January 2006.

Sapir, Edward (1921). *Language.* New York: Harcourt.

Saxe, Geoffrey B. (1981). Body parts as numerals: A developmental analysis of numeration among the Oksapmin in Papua New Guinea. *Child Development* 52: 306–316.

Saxton, Dean, and Lucille Saxton (1969). *Dictionary: Papago/Pima–English, O'odham–Mil-gahn, English–Papago/Pima, Mil-gahn–O'odham.* Tucson: University of Arizona.

Schieffelin, Bambi B. (2002) Marking time: The dichotomizing discourse of multiple temporalities. *Current Anthropology* 43(S): 5–17.

Schieffelin, Bambi B., and Steven Feld (1998). *Bosavi–English–Tok Pisin Dictionary (Papua New Guinea).* Canberra: Pacific Linguistics. [Pacific Linguistics Series C-153]

Schieffelin, Edward L. (1976). *The Sorrow of the Lonely and the Burning of the Dancers.* New York: St. Martin's Press.

Schurr, Theodore G. (2004). The peopling of the new world: Perspectives from molecular anthropology. *Annual Review of Anthropology* 33: 551–583.

Senft, Gunter (ed.) (1997). *Referring to Space: Studies in Austronesian and Papuan Languages.* Oxford: Clarendon.

Sergeyev, M. A. (1964). The Tofalars. In M. G. Levin and L. P. Potapov (eds.) (1964), pp. 474–484.

Shaw, Patricia. (2001). Language and identity, language and the land. *British Columbia Studies* 131: 39–55.

Shaw, Patricia A., and Larry Grant (2004). A delicate balance: Dynamics of collaboration in critically endangered language documentation. [Conference talk and handout at *A World of Many Voices*, Frankfurt. September 2004]

Sheik, Adam (2005). Numerical Classifiers (1)—Cantonese Help sheets. Online at http://www.cantonese.sheik.co.uk/classifiers1.htm. Accessed February 2006.

Shirina, D. A. (1993). *Ekspeditsionnaya deyatel'nost' Akademii Nauk na Severovostoke Azii, 1861–1971 gg* [Expeditionary activity of the Academy of Science in Northeast Asia, 1861–1917]. Novosibirsk: Nauka.

Shore, Bradd (1996). *Culture in Mind: Cognition, Culture and the Problem of Meaning.* New York: Oxford University Press.

Shosted, Ryan K. (2005). Correlating complexity: A typological approach. *UC Berkeley Phonology Lab Annual Report.*

Shtubendorf, Yu. (1858). *O karagasakh.* [On the Karagas] *Etnograficheskiy sbornik.* 1858: 1–18.

Shumway, Eric B. (1971). *Intensive Course in Tongan.* Honolulu: University of Hawaii.

Siewierska, Anna, and Jae Jung Song (eds.) (1998). *Case, Typology and Grammar.* Amsterdam: John Benjamins.

Simon, Tony J., Susan J. Hespos, and Philippe Rochat (1994). Do infants understand simple arithmetic? A replication of Wynn (1992). *Cognitive Development* 10: 253–269.

Stille, Alexander. (2000). Speak, cultural memory: A dead-language debate. *New York Times* (September 30), pp. B9, B11.

Stimson, J. Frank (1932) Songs of the Polynesian voyagers. *Journal of the Polynesian Society* 41(163): 181–201.

Stromswold, K. (2000). The cognitive neuroscience of language acquisition. In M. Gazzaniga (ed.), *The Cognitive Neurosciences*, 2nd edn., pp. 909–932. Cambridge, Mass.: MIT Press.

Sutherland, William J. (2003). Parallel extinction risk and global distribution of languages and species. *Nature* 423: 276–279.

Sverdrup, Harald Ulrich (1938). *With the People of the Tundra.* Oslo, Norway: Gyldendal Norsk Forlag. [New Haven: Human Relations Area Files, 1996. Computer File]

Swanton, John R. (1946). The Indians of the southeastern United States. *Bureau of American Ethnology Bulletin* 137.

Syahdan (2000). Code-switching in the speech of elite Sasaks. In Peter Austin (ed.), *Working Papers in Sasak*, Vol. 2, pp. 99–109. Melbourne: University of Melbourne.

Taube, Erika (1978). *Tuwinische Volksmärchen.* Berlin: Akademie-Verlag.

Taylor, Allan R. (1982). "Male" and "female" speech in Gros Ventre. *Anthropological Linguistics* 24: 301–307.

Teeter, Karl V. (1964). *The Wiyot Language*. University of California Publications in Linguistics No. 37.

Teichelmann, C. G., and C. W. Schürmann (1840). *Outlines of a Grammar, Vocabulary and Phraseology of the Aboriginal Language of South Australia, Spoken by the Natives in and for Some Distance around Adelaide*. Adelaide: Robert Thomas & Co.

Tent, Jan (1998). The structure of deictic day-name systems. *Studia Linguistica* 52.2: 112–148.

Terrill, Angela (2002). Why make books for people who don't read? A perspective on documentation of an endangered language from Solomon Islands. *International Journal of the Sociology of Language* 155/156: 205–219.

Teshome, A., B. R. Baum, L. Fahrig, J. K. Torrance, T. J. Arnason, and J. D. Lambert (1997). Sorghum [*Sorghum bicolor* (L.) Moench] landrace variation and classification in North Shew and South Welo, Ethiopia. *Euphytica* 97: 255–263.

Thompson, Stith (1932–1936). *Motif-index of Folk-literature: A Classification of Narrative Elements in Folk-tales, Ballads, Myths, Fables, Mediaeval Romances, Exempla, Fabliaux, Jest-books, and Local Legends*. Vols. 1–6. Bloomington, Ind.: Indiana University Press.

Thorpe, Natasha, Naikak Hakongak, Andra Eyegetok, and the Kitikmeot Elders (2001). *Thunder on the Tundra: Inuit Quajimajatuqangit of the Bathurst Caribou*. Vancouver, B.C.: Douglas and McIntyre.

Thune, C. E. (1978). Numbers and counting in Loboda; an example of a non-numerically oriented culture. *Papua New Guinea Journal of Education* 14: 69–80.

Turton, David (1980). There's no such beast: Cattle and colour naming among the Mursi. *Man* 15(2): 320-338.

UNESCO (2005). United Nations Literacy Decade (UNLD) and LIFE. United Nations Educational, Scientific and Cultural Organization. Online at http://portal.unesco.org/education/en/ev.php-URL_ID=41139&URL_DO=DO_TOPIC&URL_SECTION=201.html. Accessed January 2006.

United Nations Environment Program (2001). Globalization threat to world's cultural, linguistic and biological diversity. News Release January 18, 2001. Online at http://www.unep.org/Documents.multilingual/Default.asp?DocumentID=192&ArticleID=2765. Accessed August 2005.

University of California, Berkeley Ingush Project. Ingush Phonology and Orthography. Online at http://ingush.berkeley.edu:7012/orthography.html#Phonology. Accessed February 2006.

Vainshtein, Sevyan I. (1961). *Tuvintsy-todzhintsy: Istoriko-etnograficheskie ocherki*. [Tuvans-Todzhans: Historical-ethnographic overview.] Moscow: Izdatel'stvo vostochnoi literatury.

——— (1980). *Nomads of South Siberia*. Cambridge: Cambridge University Press.

Vajda, Edward (1999). Yeniseian and Athabaskan-Eyak-Tlingit: Some grammatical evidence for a genetic relationship. *Sravnitel'no-istoricheskoe i tipologicheskoe izuchenie jazykov i kul'tur*, pp. 22–34. Tomsk, Russia: Tomsk State Pedagogical University.

——— (2005). Yeniseic and Na-Dene. Talk delivered at the Max Planck Institute for Evolutionary Anthropology, Leipzig, Germany. December 8.

Van Deusen, Kira (1996). *Shyaan am! Tuvan Folk Tales*. Bellingham, Wash.: Udagan Books.

van Tongeren, Mark C. (2002). *Overtone Singing: Physics and Metaphysics of Harmonics in East and West*. Amsterdam: Fusica.

Vogt, Hans. (1963). *Dictionnaire de la langue oubykh avec introduction phonologique, index français-oubykh, textes oubykhs*. Oslo: Universitetsforlaget.

Wassmann, Jürg (1997). Finding the right path: The route knowledge of the Yupno of Papua New Guinea. In Senft (ed.) (1997), pp. 143–174.

Wassmann, Jürg, and Pierre R. Dasen (1994a). Yupno number system and counting. *Journal of Cross-Cultural Psychology* 25: 78–94.

——— (1994b). "Hot" and "cold": Classification and sorting among the Yupno of Papua New Guinea. *International Journal of Psychology* 29(1): 19–38.

Watanabe, Hitoshi (1973). *The Ainu Ecosystem*. Seattle: University of Washington Press.

Webb, Noel Augustin (1936–1937). Place names of the Adelaide tribe. In *Municipal Year Book, City of Adelaide*, pp. 302–310. Adelaide: *The Advertiser*.

Weisstein, Eric W. (2005). Base. In *MathWorld—A Wolfram Web Resource*. Online at http://mathworld.wolfram.com/Base.html. Accessed August 2006.

Wells-Jensen, Sheri (1999). *Cognitive correlates of linguistic complexity: A cross-linguistic perspective*. Ph.D. diss. Buffalo, N.Y.: University of New York.

Weule, Karl ([1909] 1970). *Native Life in East Africa*, trans. Alice Werner. Westport, Conn.: Negro Universities Press.

Wheeler, Alwyne (1979). *The Tidal Thames: The History of a River and its Fishes*. London: Routledge.

Widlok, Thomas (1997). Orientation in the wild: The shared cognition of Haillom bush people. *Journal of the Royal Anthropological Institute (N.S.)* 3: 317–332.

Wilensky, Uri (1999). *NetLogo*. http://ccl.northwestern.edu/netlogo/. Center for Connected Learning and Computer-Based Modeling, Northwestern University, Evanston, Ill.

Wilson, Edward O. (1992). *The Diversity of Life*. New York: Norton.

Woodward, David, and G. Malcolm Lewis (eds.) (1998). *Cartography in the Traditional African, American, Arctic, Australian, and Pacific Societies*. Chicago: University of Chicago Press. [The History of Cartography, Vol. 2, Bk. 3]

World Bank (2004). World development indicators online. Online at http://www.worldbank.org/data/onlinedbs/onlinedbases.htm. Accessed August 2005.

Wynn, Karen (1992). Addition and subtraction by human infants. *Nature* 358: 749–750.

Xu, Fei and Spelke, Elizabeth S. (2000). Large number discrimination in 6-month-old infants. *Cognition* 74: B1–B11

Yates, Francis A. (1966). *The Art of Memory.* Chicago: University of Chicago.

Young, Bill (2005). Theory and data in language typologies. February 2005 Center for the Advanced Study of Language presentation.

Young, Mark C. (1997). *The Guinness Book of Records, 1997.* New York: Bantam Books.

Yu, Alan C. L. (2004). Reduplication in English Homeric infixation. In Keir Moulton and Matthew Wolf (eds.), pp. 619–633 *Proceedings of the 34th annual meeting of the North East Linguistic Society.* Amherst: GLSA.

Zaslavsky, Claudia (1999). *Africa Counts: Number and Pattern in African Culture.* 3rd edn. Chicago: Lawrence Hill Books.

Zegura, Stephen L., Tatiana M. Karafet, Lev A. Zhivotovsky, and Michael F. Hammer (2004). High-Resolution SNPs and microsatellite haplotypes point to a single, recent entry of native American Y chromosomes into the Americas. *Molecular Biology and Evolution* 21(1): 164–175.

Zent, Stanford (2001). Acculturation and ethnobotanical knowledge loss among the Piaroa of Venezuala. In Maffi (ed.) (2001), pp. 190–211.

Zeshan, Ulrike (2002). Towards a notion of word in sign languages. In R. M. W. Dixon and Alexandra Y. Aikhenvald (eds.), Word : *A cross-linguistic typology*, pp. 153–179. Cambridge: Cambridge University Press.

——— (2006). Negative and interrogative constructions in sign languages: A case study in sign language typology. In Ulrike Zeshan (ed.), *Interrogative and Negative Constructions in Sign Languages*, pp. 28–69. Nijmegen: Ishara Press.

Zhukova, L. N. (1986). Yukagirskoe piktograficheskoe pis'mo. [Yukaghir pictographic writing]. *Polyarnaya Zvezda* 6: 121–124.

Ziker, John P. (2002). *Peoples of the Tundra: Northern Siberians in the Post-Communist Transition.* Prospect Heights, Ill.: Waveland Press.

# Index